Creative Involution

A novel is never anything but a philosophy
put into images. And in a good novel, the whole of the
philosophy has passed into images.
Albert Camus, review of *Nausea* by Jean-Paul Sartre

Creative Involution

Bergson, Beckett, Deleuze

S. E. Gontarski

EDINBURGH
University Press

© S. E. Gontarski, 2015

Edinburgh University Press Ltd
The Tun – Holyrood Road
12(2f) Jackson's Entry
Edinburgh EH8 8PJ

www.euppublishing.com

Typeset in 11/13 Adobe Sabon by
Servis Filmsetting Ltd, Stockport, Cheshire,
and printed and bound in Great Britain by
CPI Group (UK) Ltd, Croydon CR0 4YY

A CIP record for this book is available from the British Library

ISBN 978 0 7486 9732 8 (hardback)
ISBN 978 0 7486 9733 5 (webready PDF)
ISBN 978 1 4744 0835 6 (epub)

The right of S. E. Gontarski to be identified as the author of this work has been
asserted in accordance with the Copyright, Designs and Patents Act 1988, and
the Copyright and Related Rights Regulations 2003 (SI No. 2498).

Contents

For Marsha,
again and again

Other Becketts:
Series Preface

General Editor: S. E. Gontarski, Florida State University

In 1997 Apple computers launched an advertising campaign (in print and on television) that entreated us to 'Think Different', and Samuel Beckett was one of Apple's icons. Avoiding Apple's solecism, we might modify the appeal to say that *Other Becketts* is a call to think differently as well, in this case about Beckett's work, to question, that is, even the questions we ask about it. *Other Becketts*, then, is a series of monographs focused on alternative, unexplored, or under-explored approaches to the work of Samuel Beckett, not a call for novelty *per se*, but a call to examine afresh those of Beckett's interests that were more arcane than mainstream, interests that might be deemed quirky or strange, and those of his works less thoroughly explored critically and theoretically, the late prose and drama, say, or even the poetry or criticism. Volumes might cover (but are not restricted to) any of the following: unusual illnesses or neurological disorders (the 'duck foot, goose foot' of *First Love*, akathisia or the invented duck's disease or panpygoptosis of Miss Dew in *Murphy*, proprioception, or its disturbance, in *Not I*, perhaps, or other unusual neurological lapses among Beckett's creatures, from Watt to the Listener of *That Time*); mathematical peculiarities (irrational numbers, factorials, Fibonacci numbers or sequences, or non-Euclidian approaches to geometry); linguistic failures (from Nominalism to Mauthner, say); citations of or allusions to contrarian aesthetic philosophers working in a more or less irrationalist tradition (Nietzsche, Bergson, or Deleuze, among others), or in general 'the simple games that time plays with space'. Alternative approaches would be of interest as well, with foci on objects, animals, cognitive or memory issues, and the like.

Abbreviations for Works by Samuel Beckett

Arikha	*Arikha*, Paris: Hermann, 1985.
CDW	*The Complete Dramatic Works*, London: Faber and Faber, 1986.
CSP	*The Complete Short Prose, 1929–1989*, ed. S. E. Gontarski, New York: Grove Press, 1995.
Dream	*Dream of Fair to Middling Women*, ed. Eoin OBrien and Edith Fournier, Dublin: Black Cat Press, 1992; New York: Arcade Publishing, 1993.
Endgame	*Endgame*, New York: Grove, 1958.
Godot	*Waiting for Godot*, New York: Grove Press, 1954.
Letters 1	*The Letters of Samuel Beckett Volume 1, 1929–1940*, ed. Martha Dow Fehsenfeld and Lois More Overbeck, Cambridge: Cambridge University Press, 2009.
Letters 2	*The Letters of Samuel Beckett Volume 2, 1941–1956*, ed. George Craig, Martha Dow Fehsenfeld, Dan Gunn and Lois More Overbeck, Cambridge: Cambridge University Press, 2011.
Murphy	*Murphy*, New York: Grove, 1957.
Proust	*Proust*, New York: Grove, 1957.
Three Novels	*Three Novels: Molloy, Malone Dies, The Unnamable*, New York: Grove Press, 1955.
Watt	*Watt*, New York: Grove, 1959.
Worstward	*Worstward Ho. Nohow On*, New York: Grove Press, 1996.

Acknowledgements

Such extended scholarly meditations inevitably gestate through a protracted process, from postgraduate seminars, through conference presentations and preliminary publications, to, finally, a book, and this study is no exception. My postgraduate students in seminars on Modernism and Bergson, Beckett and Deleuze, in various configurations and at various universities, have not only allowed me to continue my research interest on the intersections of these figures and philo-literary Modernism but have often led it, supporting and enhancing this research through their enthusiasm, initiative, diligence, clear thinking and scholarly dedication. Through my Bergson seminars in particular, two of my students, Paul Ardoin and Laci Mattison, have become collaborators, co-editors of a pair of volumes having grown out of those seminars at Florida State University: *Understanding Bergson / Understanding Modernism* and *Understanding Deleuze / Understanding Modernism*. Those volumes have now developed into a robust book series, *Understanding Philosophy / Understanding Modernism*, and Ardoin and Mattison join me as General Editors of the series with Bloomsbury Academic.

Early versions of many of the chapters herein have been presented at various international conferences and workshops, including two meetings of the ongoing Samuel Beckett Working Group, one in Dublin as part of the Beckett centenary in 2006 and one in Tokyo in 2012, and I am grateful to the organizers of those sessions, Linda Ben-Zvi, the late Julie Campbell, and Mariko Hori Tanaka, for opportunities to work with that group. The indefatigable Tomasz Wisniewski, of the University of Gdansk, Poland, has been more helpful than he knows, first by inviting me to deliver a keynote address at the *Back to the Beckett Text: Beckett na Plazy* conference in Sopot, Poland in 2010 and then to subsequent yearly conferences, even when Beckett was not their focus; these opportunities afforded me a continuous outlet for this material as it was developing (and simultaneously a chance to recover the language of my grandparents and my childhood). Those occasions have included not only lectures but opportunities to lead acting workshops that have been an invaluable testing ground for some of the ideas in this book. Furthermore, Tomasz's sponsorship of performances of my theatre piece, *Breath-Text-Breath*, performed originally at the Calder Bookshop and Theatre in London in 2010 and in Gdansk and Sopot in 2011 (https://www.youtube.com/watch?v=FxnTzeCtdOo), and the development of a Polish version with Beckett scholar, translator, novelist and performer, Antoni Libera (https://www.youtube.com/watch?v=VCjp7Shr2Ow), were crucial to my continued exploration of the possibilities of Beckett's theatre, especially set against the rich tradition of twentieth-century Polish theatre.

A lecture 'Beckett and Bergson: There is no outside the Image' was delivered at 'Samuel Beckett: Debts and Legacies, 2010', a series of seminars sponsored by the University of Oxford and the University of Northampton, held at Regent's Park College, Oxford University on 11 June 2010. The lecture was podcast (as were all the 'Debts and Legacies' lectures) by Backdoor Broadcast Company and is currently available at: http://backdoorbroad-casting.net/2010/07/stan-gontarski-there-is-no-outside-the-image-bergson-on-movement. My gratitude to the organizers of that series, Matthew Feldman and Erik Tonner, for that opportunity. An early version of Chapter 4, '"Thought Thinks in its Own Right": A. A. Luce, Samuel Beckett and Bergson's Doctrine of Failure', was delivered as the opening lecture of the inaugural Samuel Beckett Summer School meeting at Trinity College, Dublin on 11 July 2011. My thanks to the Summer School organizers and directors, Steve Wilmer and Sam Slote, for so useful and collegial an opportunity. Another series of presentations was delivered to the Samuel Beckett Research Group in Brazil between 2005 and 2014 at Universities in São Paulo, Goiania and Brasilia. I am delighted to be able to thank my hosts, who have often also doubled as translators of my work into Portuguese; they have been incalculably helpful in allowing me to develop this material: Marcus Mota of the Federal University of Brasilia, Fábio de Souza Andrade of the University of São Paulo, and the man who generated my ongoing infatuation with Brazil in 2005, Robson

Correa de Camargo of the Federal University of Goiania. In addition, I am delighted to thank one of the most innovative theatrical groups I have ever known and worked with for invitations to work with them in Rio de Janeiro, Brasilia and São Paulo. It has been my honour to be associated with them. Their continuing work with Beckett's texts, both staging them directly and developing artworks, installations and performance pieces based on Beckett's work, is nonpareil: Coletivo Irmãos Guimarães (http://www.coletivoirmaosguimaraes.com). In particular I am grateful for the support of the irmãos themselves, talented, visionary artists in their own right, Adriano and Fernando Guimarães. These colleagues and students cited above, knowingly or not, became collaborators on this volume.

Early versions or portions of this material have appeared as follows:

'"Ruse a by": Watt, the Rupture of the Everyday and Transcendental Empiricism', in *The Edinburgh Companion to Samuel Beckett and the Arts*, ed. with an Introduction by S. E. Gontarski, Edinburgh: Edinburgh University Press, 2014, 345–52.

'Creative Involution: Bergson, Beckett, Deleuze', *Deleuze Studies* 6:4 (2012), 'Beckett Dossier', ed. Steve Wilmer, 601–13, revised, expanded and reprinted under that title in *Deleuze and Beckett*, ed. Stephen Elliot Wilmer and Audrone Žukauskaite, London: Palgrave, 2015, 50–83.

'Trinity College, Dublin', in *Beckett in Context*, ed. Anthony Uhlmann, Cambridge: Cambridge University Press, 2012, 29–41.

'"What it is to have been": Bergson and Beckett on Movement, Multiplicity, and Representation', *Journal of Modern Literature* XXXIV:2 (2011), 65–75.

'Recovering Beckett's Bergsonism', in *Beckett at 100: Revolving It All*, ed. Linda Ben-Zvi and Angela Moorjani, Oxford: Oxford University Press, 2008, 93–106.

I am grateful to the editors of the publications listed above for permission to reprint these earlier versions.

I am especially grateful as well for the continued support of the editors, staff, and the Editorial Board at Edinburgh

University Press, particularly Jackie Jones, Commissioning Editor for Philosophy and Literary Studies, for her commitment to 'Beckett Studies', first by taking on the administration, production and distribution of the *Journal of Beckett Studies* in 2008, thus insuring the *Journal*'s future; for publishing the second series of 'the best' of the *Journal* as *The Beckett Critical Reader: Archives, Theories, and Translations* in 2012, insuring the continued vitality and wider distribution of those excellent essays, many of which focused on primary documents; for commissioning what I consider the best, certainly the most comprehensive of my 'companions', *The Edinburgh Companion to Samuel Beckett and the Arts* in 2014; and for suggesting and guiding the approval of the book series, Other Becketts, for which *Creative Involution: Bergson, Beckett, Deleuze* is the inaugural volume.

I am also grateful to colleagues at Florida State University who read portions of this study, particularly Professors Barry Faulk and John Fenstermaker. I have benefited from their careful reading and sage advice even as the remaining errors and omissions are wholly the responsibility of the author.

Finally, and on a more personal note, I would like to thank again, and again, the person to whom this book is dedicated, my helpmate and inspiration, my safe harbour in times of storm, the centre of my life, Marsha Gontarski, who has shared this crazy journey without compass for over fifty years, forty-seven of those as my wife.

'All the Dead Voices': A Preface

Memory believes before knowing remembers, believes longer than recollects, longer than knowing even wonders. (William Faulkner, *Light in August*, Ch. 6)

The past is never dead. It's not even past. (William Faulkner, *Requiem for a Nun*, Act 1, Scene 3)

That Modernism is a 'Breaking Things Open, Breaking Words Open', as Gilles Deleuze suggests in *Negotiations*, that it is inherently transgressive, amorphous, protean, is one of the tenets of this study (Deleuze 1990: 83–93). Modernism is thus less an historical period than a movement, than movement itself, less a bounded or delimited chronological moment than a flow, a way of thinking or pattern of thought, a mode of investigation which foregrounds the past as memory, not as an inferior or diminished version of the former present, however, but as an organic part of it, as an ontological, accumulating entity in itself. As such we might say that Modernism blurs distinctions between past and present, between interior and exterior, an inward turn that we will call, after Deleuze, 'involution'.

Shakespeare was already on to something in *The Tempest*, Act 2, Scene 1, as Antonio tries to persuade Sebastian to murder his father with the following argument: 'What is past is prologue'; that is, all the past has led to and is thus part of this moment, which must be seized. T. S. Eliot has memorably phrased such accumulation of a living past in 'Tradition and the Individual Talent', wherein his 'historical sense involves a perception, not only of the pastness of the past, but of its presence ... a sense of the timeless as well as of the temporal and of the timeless and the temporal together' (Eliot 2007: 538). Or as William Faulkner phrased it in *Requiem for a*

Nun, 'The past is never dead. It's not even past.' Eliot was focused on the dead voices of the past to justify his own deeply historical mode of Modernism, but he and Faulkner were echoing French metaphysician Henri Bergson, whose lectures at the Sorbonne Eliot attended in 1919. Eliot found it necessary to restrict his inquiry to the practicalities of the poet: 'This essay proposes to halt at the frontier of metaphysics or mysticism' (541). The current essay proposes, on the contrary and like Modernism itself, to cross that frontier into Eliot's abandoned terrain and to confront the past as memory and consciousness. Eliot seems to have extracted from Bergson what he needed for his ahistorical historicism, 'These fragments [of cultural memory] I have shored against my ruins', as the narrator of *The Waste Land* has it. But Bergson's past, his rethinking of time and memory, is active, not a diminished reproduction or reconstruction of past events, not a version of the former present, not 'a heap of broken images', but a creative force, a creative duration, hence in what follows a 'creative involution'.

Ezra Pound, having been arrested by the Partisans in Rapallo, Italy in May of 1945 and being led away to the American DTC (Disciplinary Training Center) in Pisa, broke off a sprig of Eucalyptus. As he recalls in Canto 74, the first of what are called the *Pisan Cantos*, 'and eucalyptus that is for memory', from which the *Pisan Cantos* emerged in a kind of duration, the preservation of the past in co-existence with the present. But Pound had been interested in the presence of the past as he recovered troubadour poet Arnaut Daniel and his Provençal tongue and as he translated the Old English of *The Seafarer*, at least its first ninety-nine (of 124) lines. As he told interviewer Donald Hall for the *Paris Review*, discussing the origins of *The Cantos* in 1904:

> the first thing was this: you had six centuries that hadn't been packaged. It was a question of dealing with material that wasn't in the *Divina Commedia*. Hugo did a *Légende des Siècles* [*The Legend of the Ages*] that wasn't an evaluative affair but just bits of history strung together. The problem was to build up a circle of reference – taking the modern mind to be the medieval mind with wash after wash of classical culture poured over it since the Renaissance. That was the psyche, if you like. One had to deal with one's own subject. (Pound 1962)

Samuel Beckett's rendering of 'the psyche, if you like' may have been put most poetically as early as *Waiting for Godot*:

ESTRAGON: All the dead voices.
VLADIMIR: They make a noise like wings.
ESTRAGON: Like leaves.
VLADIMIR: Like sand.
ESTRAGON: Like leaves.
[Silence.]
VLADIMIR: They all speak together.
ESTRAGON: Each one to itself.
[Silence.]
VLADIMIR: Rather they whisper.
ESTRAGON: They rustle.
VLADIMIR: They murmur.
ESTRAGON: They rustle.
[Silence.]
VLADIMIR: What do they say?
ESTRAGON: They talk about their lives.
VLADIMIR: To have lived is not enough for them.
ESTRAGON: They have to talk about it.
VLADIMIR: To be dead is not enough for them.
ESTRAGON: It is not sufficient.
[Silence.]
VLADIMIR: They make a noise like feathers.
ESTRAGON: Like leaves.
VLADIMIR: Like ashes.
ESTRAGON: Like leaves.
[Long silence.]
(Godot 58)

The current volume explores the presence of the past as memory
and consciousness through Henri Bergson's rethinking of memory
as duration and assesses Samuel Beckett's relationship to that
philosophical process, not only to 'All the dead voices', what in
Watt is called a 'mixed choir', but also, and perhaps most impor-
tantly, the need to talk about them, to render memory, that is,
consciousness leavened with imagination. In the life of the mind
– 'head said seat of all. Germ of all. All?', and so, paradoxically,
even of itself, 'If of all of it too' – the narrator of Worstward Ho
reminds us (Worstward 97), any rendering is mutable, ephemeral, spectral, immaterial, its existence thus doubtful. Its forces
are memory and imagination, each infused with the other, but its
product, diffuse as it appears and something of a controlled chaos,

can comprise a unity created by the power of imagination, itself a regenerative, ineradicable force: 'Long sudden gone. Then sudden back', or 'Sudden go. Sudden back' (*Worstward* 102, 94). Beckett was well aware that the Romantic poet Samuel Taylor Coleridge had divided the activity of mind into two categories, fancy and imagination, the latter superior to the former and in two parts. Of the secondary imagination, then, an 'echo' of the primary, Coleridge would tell us in his *Biographia Literaria* of 1817, 'It dissolves, diffuses, dissipates, in order to recreate; or where this process is rendered impossible, yet still at all events it struggles to idealise and unify. It is essentially vital, even as all objects (as objects) are essentially fixed and dead' (Coleridge 2014: 205–6). Beckett had been exploring the vitality of imagination, in one form or another, for most of his writing career, nowhere more directly than in *Imagination Dead Imagine*, a development not only of preliminary versions called 'Fancy Dying' and rendered in a set of four 'Faux Departs' (*CSP* 271–4), but a re-rendering of a longer work, *All Strange Away* (*CSP* 169–81), published finally in 1976 by the Gotham Book Mart in New York with fifteen illustrations by Edward Gorey. Of the preliminary and related fragments and tales, *Imagination Dead Imagine* is the more controlled, concentrated, coherent, abstracted, accessible and moving as we are asked to entertain the implications of a mental paradox, the death of imagination; its demise, however, is itself an act of imagination, and thus in its death or dying a new beginning emerges and, in a continuing process, its product is, in Coleridge's term, esemplastic.

Beckett's poetic narrative thus explores possibilities of imagination at points of extinction and renewal, images vanishing and absences materialized. That is, the theme of the imagination's dying yet conscious of its own decline, its own demise, is itself regenerative. The fourth section of a preliminary 'Faux Depart' of the 1960s ends thus: 'When it [the light] goes out no matter, start again, another place, someone in it, keep glaring, never see, never find, no end, no matter' (*CSP* 273). That 'no end' became, more often than not, a new beginning as Beckett did 'start again'. Set, if that is the word, in a vault, sepulchre, or rotunda, of sorts, amid the familiar closed space of much of Beckett's later fiction, the spatial climate arbitrary, both as regards temperature and illumination, 'two white bodies', alive, since the mirror mists, male and female, are presented in positions mathematically defined, but their two gazes (the devouring 'eye of prey', so called) rarely meeting, and the identity of each, identified in the 'Faux Depart' and *All Strange Away* with 'women's faces on the walls' or as 'Jolly and Draeger Praeger Draeger', remain barely perceptible in *Imagination Dead Imagine*, a 'white speck lost in whiteness'. In *All Strange Away*, the narrator is imagining or re-imagining images of a former love, Emma. In *Imagination Dead Imagine* the lineaments, the details, the specifics have blurred or vanished, references to a world outside the enclosure disappear. What remains are images without external reference, images in and of themselves. Movement persists, if ever so slight, but where movement exists there is life, a life force, vitality, even at its 'Mere-most minimum', as Beckett reminds us in his late masterwork, *Worstward Ho* (91).

Elliot's 1921 critique of 'all the dead voices' that 'all speak together', or Pound's 'medieval mind with wash after wash of classical culture poured over it', or Vladimir's 'A charnal-house! A charnal-house!' again of *Waiting for Godot* (60), might be deemed something of a prologue to this meditation, this interleaving, after Deleuze, of philosophical thought with literary production, especially as Eliot further posits a depersonalized art, whereby, in Eliot's pointedly anti-Romantic critique, poetry is presumably not the expression of a personality but of a form, what Beckett, after Murphy, might call a controlled chaos or a structured flux, the poet, finally, disappearing, perhaps like Murphy, into the flow of words, the art. The following argument moves towards such disappearances neither as a linearity nor a telos but as part of a continual, self-regenerative creative process, even as the flow is towards 'Lessness'. In *Worstward Ho*, 'On. Somehow on' (102), even when 'leastward on' (107), 'Till nohow on' (89).

References

Coleridge, Samuel Taylor (2014) *Biographia Literaria* (1817), ed. Adam Roberts, Edinburgh: Edinburgh University Press.

Deleuze, Gilles (1990) *Negotiations 1972–1990*, trans. Martin Joughin, New York: Columbia University Press.

Eliot, T. S. (2007) 'Tradition and the Individual Talent', in *The Critical Tradition: Classic Texts and Contemporary Trends*, ed. David H. Richter, New York: Bedford/St. Martin's.

Pound, Ezra (1962) 'Ezra Pound, The Art of Poetry No. 5', interviewed by Donald Hall, *Paris Review* 28 (summer–fall 1962). An excerpt from Samuel Beckett's *How It Is* appears in the same issue.

2

'A Mixed Choir' from
The Ditch of Astonishment:
An Introduction

So he crawled out of the ditch, not forgetting his bags, and resumed his journey [. . .] (*Watt* 36)

But now I shall have to get myself out of this ditch. (*Molloy*, *Three Novels* 27)

VLADIMIR: May one inquire where His Highness spent the night?
ESTRAGON: In a ditch. (*Godot* 7)

Mr Rooney: Are you in condition to lead me? [. . .] We shall fall into the ditch. (*All That Fall*, *CDW* 189)

In 2013–14 Peter Brook and his collaborator, Marie-Hélène Estienne, toured one of the latest projects growing out of their centre for theatre research. *The Valley of Astonishment* was actually the second part of their earlier production, *The Man Who* [i.e., *Mistook His Wife for a Hat*], both pieces designed to explore what they call 'the labyrinth of the brain', or what *New York Times* critic Ben Brantley (2014) dubbed their 'wonder-struck contemplation of the enigma of the human mind'. The *Guardian*'s Michael Billington (2014) pithily summarizes the plot:

Fired as a journalist and investigated by cognitive scientists, she [Sammy Costas] turns into a music-hall performer who is ultimately traumatised by her unusual gift [either eidetic imagery or a highly tuned system of mnemonics]. Her story is interwoven with that of a twenty-eight-year-old man who relates music to colours [synaesthesia] and with a study of a senior citizen whose impaired proprioception, or inability to sense his body, means he has to use his brain to overcome muscular paralysis.

Some uncertainty seems to exist among these major theatre critics about what exactly Brook and Estienne are exploring: the human mind or the human brain. While Billington describes their subject as 'the working of the human brain', Brantley, or his editor, titles his review, 'The Mind is a Terrible Thing to Take for Granted'. The production, however, makes little mention of mind, assuming mind and brain to be coeval, perhaps, but the distinction is crucial for much of the discussion to follow and as a formative issue of what will come to be called Modernism, for which the study of the mind's function is not restricted to but includes that of the brain.

Brook and Estienne consistently keep their focus on neurology and the brain, however, inspired as they are by the British-born, celebrity neurologist Oliver Sacks, almost all of whose works are case studies of people with neurological disorders; they thus make almost no mention of an immaterial entity we call mind or of the central, related issue (or mystery) of consciousness. In *The Man Who*, as Brook and Estienne tell us in their programme notes to *Valley*, they explore or depict (visualize, anyway) 'neurological cases who in the past had been conveniently written off as "mad"'. In *The Valley of Astonishment*, they continue, 'We will take the spectator into new and unknown territories through people whose secret lives are so intense, so drenched in music, color, taste, images and memories that they can pass any instant from paradise to hell and back. [. . .] So as we explore the mountains and valleys of the brain we will reach the valley of astonishment.' But how 'new and unknown' this territory remains in 2015 is certainly at issue, since their sources seem firmly rooted in the 1970s and 1980s. Even more at issue is the relationship between a material bodily organ, the brain, and a more metaphysical entity we call mind (or spirit, or soul), whose functioning William James had memorably described in 1892 as a 'stream of consciousness' and which Brook and Estienne ignore but which continues to be a central issue even in contemporary evolutionary biology and neuroscience. James notes the following 'Fundamental Fact' in Chapter XI of his *Psychology*:

The first and foremost concrete fact which every one will affirm to belong to his inner experience is the fact that *consciousness of some sort goes on. 'States of mind' succeed each other in him.* If we could say in English 'it thinks', as we say 'it rains' or 'it blows', we should be stating the fact most simply and with the minimum of assumption. As we cannot, we must simply say that *thought goes on*. (James 1892)

Bergson's version, as we will explore in Chapter 4, is that 'Thought thinks in its own right'. One characteristic of James's 'personal consciousness' is that 'each personal consciousness is sensibly continuous', hence James's image of a 'stream of thought' or 'stream of consciousness'.

Antonio Damasio, for one, decries the distinction, the separation of mind and body, deeming it a form of dualism associated with Descartes that he critiques in his study straightforwardly entitled *Descartes' Error*:

> The Cartesian idea of disembodied mind may well have been the source, by the middle of the twentieth century, for the metaphor of mind as software program. In fact, if the mind can be separated from the body, perhaps one can try to understand it without any appeal to neurobiology, without any need to be influenced by knowledge of neuroanatomy, neurophysiology, and neurochemistry. (Damasio 1994: 250)

Damasio loads his argument here with his own either/or dualism, with the implication that we can ignore science or 'knowledge', if we wish, offering the word 'perhaps' as something of a safety valve, but at our intellectual peril. On the other hand, at the other extreme, perhaps, are those neuroscientists who avoid or bracket the brain in its context, 'who insist that the mind can be fully explained in terms of brain events, leaving by the wayside the rest of the organism and the surrounding physical and social environment – and also leaving out the fact that part of the environment is itself a product of the organism's preceding actions' (250–1). Damasio here suggests a complex, interactive relationship between inside and outside, the brain in relation to that part of the environment as product of 'the organism's [. . .] actions', even as he finally asserts, 'that mind comes from brain is indisputable' (251). Although Brooke and Estienne are working with Oliver Sacks, Damasio's work is often associated with that of Sacks, who wrote the lead, front-cover blurb to the paperback edition of *Descartes' Error*.

These issues are then keenly central to contemporary neurology and to a strain of contemporary literary theory with a philosophical tradition reaching back before Descartes at least to Plato in the *Phaedo*, which Damasio acknowledges. They gained renewed currency late in the nineteenth century and early into the twentieth with the work of Henri Bergson, and have had a profound effect on the art of the subsequent era, an approach to or mode of art that we call Modernist. That is, much of Damasio's anti-Cartesian critique seems congruent with the work of Bergson, whom Damasio, unfortunately, does not cite. Bergson, too, took serious issue with Cartesian dualism, even as he also insisted on something of a distinction between mind and brain, not as separate systems, however, but as elements, one material, one not, performing separate functions within a single system not restricted to a bodily organ. In other words, much of Bergson's work might also be called *Descartes' Error*, a critique certainly that continues through the work of Samuel Beckett and Gilles Deleuze and his collaborators.

Bergson, however, was not a neurologist, although he studied brain abnormalities or malfunctions, particularly autism, and his early writing responded to the prevailing theories of the emerging neuroscience of his day, particularly the work of Théodule-Armand Ribot (1839–1916), professor of experimental psychology at the Sorbonne, whose *The Maladies of Memory* appeared in 1881. Ribot saw memory as engaged with the neural system *within* the brain. Bergson would object to such a reduction of mind to matter in *Matter and Memory* (1896, English translation 1910), whose subtitle is *Essay on the Relation of Body and Spirit* (i.e., Mind). Most memory is utilitarian, 'habit memory', Bergson reminds us, memory close to if not coeval with habit, the repetition of past actions, say, and as such is inscribed within the body. But pure memory, or 'image remembrance', is free and not internal to the body. Bergson, fully engaged with the subject from its inception, thus breaks with the prevalent neuroscience of his day and, we might add, much of ours. As we will argue, such Bergsonism appealed to the imagination of a broad public (for a time) and many a writer (for all time), Marcel Proust and Samuel Beckett among them.

Bergson had personal connections to Proust. He had married Proust's cousin in 1892, for one. Moreover, Proust attended Bergson's lectures at the Sorbonne from 1891–93, and he read

Matter and Memory in 1909 as he began the composition of *Swann's Way*, even as he expressed a certain anxiety about direct influence. Pete A. Y. Gunter reminds us that Proust, 'While working out the ground plan for *À la recherche du temps perdu* [. . .] twice consulted *Matièr et mémoire* (*Matter and Memory*), the book in which Bergson introduced the thesis of an all-preserving human reminiscence' (Gunter 2013: 157–8). On 12 November 1913, however, writing in the newspaper *Le Temp*, Proust denied that *Swann's Way* was 'a Bergsonian novel', arguing that his work is 'dominated by the distinction between voluntary and involuntary memory, a distinction which not only does not figure in the philosophy of M. Bergson but is even contradicted by it' (cited in Baldwin 2013: 79). Such a distinction if not opposition will form the framework for Beckett in his early monograph called simply *Proust*. Writing to Henri Ghéon the following year, Proust further noted, 'I have enough to do without trying to turn the philosophy of M. Bergson into a novel' (Baldwin 2013: 79). Beckett might have offered something of the same disclaimer, and for essentially the same reasons. Neither was an illustrator of the ideas of another, neither 'a slavish follower or copier of Bergson' (Gunter 2013: 158), even as a not insubstantial dose of Bergsonism infiltrated the work of both, Beckett acutely aware of the issue in Proust and in *Proust*. But as Gunter highlights in a review of the Bergson-Proust relationship: despite the latter's resistance and denials one point 'appears inescapable: that Proust owed to Bergson the belief that all human memories are preserved. [. . .] Proust's entire project is impossible without it. There can be no search for lost time unless one is first convinced that what has been lost can nonetheless still be found. Bergson was the first to make this claim: to make it categorically and without apology' (Gunter 2013: 157). Beckett would be less preoccupied with recovering lost time and would probe memory for reasons different from those of Proust; recovered memory is often unrecognizable in Beckett's world, and is always tainted, at least by imagination. Beckett would, however, spend his creative life exploring the intricacies and intersections, the permeability of memory, consciousness, imagination and their impact, their affect on being and becoming, on the lived experience of existence.

* * *

Were I not sitting in a theatre anticipating a 'new' work by legendary director Peter Brook as I read the director's notes for *The*

Valley of Astonishment, I might have thought that the comments pertained to or provided something of a gloss on Samuel Beckett's work, most particularly from his 1945 novel *Watt* onward, with one major difference. What may be most astonishing about Brook and Estienne's exploration of neurology for and in theatre, and their comments about it, is how unastonishing it all is on both page and stage, while Beckett's piece(s) might indeed still take us to and through 'The Valley of Astonishment', or, modified and deromanticized in Beckett's case, to 'The Ditch of Astonishment'. Such a connection is also, at least implicitly, suggested by Brantley (2014) when he calls Brook's latest 'this essayistic work about extraordinary sensory perceptiveness', since perception is as much at issue in Bergson and Beckett as is sensory retention. Brantley, too, might be offering something of an unintentional gloss on *Watt,* if not on *Matter and Memory* and *Creative Evolution* as well.

Unsurprisingly, then, and in the manner of Brook and Estienne, any number of theatre artists have wanted over the years to 'stage' Beckett's astonishing novel of mental process, perception, cognition, memory, conceptualization, and narration, or the failures of narration; and, finally, Barry McGovern, who has something of an inside track with the Beckett estate and Dublin's Gate Theatre, did. The result was produced by the Gate for the Dublin Theatre Festival in July 2010 as another 'one-man show', which has since toured, to London's high-profile Barbican Theatre in February 2013 and, thereafter, the world, to excellent press. But such stagings, such materializations of a metaphysical process, entertaining as they are, superbly executed as they are, deflect or paper over key textual and so epistemological and ontological issues at the heart of the text. On the narrative level alone we might ask whose voice – or better whose voices, that is, what's called in the narrative something of a 'mixed choir' – do we hear in the text, that is, who is narrating *Watt*? Is it, say, as we will argue subsequently, an extended instance of ventriloquism, as is the case in *Endgame.* Does Watt himself have an independent or distinguishable voice in the narrative at all? On stage the answer is simplified, unavoidably and unambiguously single, the actor before us functions both as narrator and narrated, as an illustrator of textual incidents. On the page the issue is, and should remain, indeterminate, inchoate, mutable and plural, complexified rather than simplified, since what we have traditionally called character in literature undergoes substantial renovation in Beckett's wartime novel – and thereafter we will argue. Such issues may be toyed with in production, according to Matthew Harrison (2012) writing in the *Irish Theatre Magazine*, but they are finally deflected: 'The "difficult" original is purposely disjointed and told in a narrative voice that shifts and changes unpredictably. For this stage version, fortunately, *Watt* is given a bit of linear plot.' One might as easily have said 'unfortunately' since 'a narrative voice that shifts and changes' is much of the point of Beckett's literary exploration, and giving the novel 'a bit of a linear plot' sounds decidedly objectionable.

Dressed nattily in white tie (but lacking the tie itself) as if he were about to attend an event at a 'culture park', a theatre opening, say, here Watt's costume apparently signifies his role as servant in the Big House of one Mr. Knott. On stage Watt is a coherent entity, a unified being or character, and is at least removed, rescued, say, from 'the ditch of astonishment' where some of his most profound insights and so revelations occur. Historian Robert Zaller (2011), writing for the *Broad Street Review*, is at least sensitive to the issues: 'In Barry McGovern's dramatization of *Watt*, presented as part of the Gate Theatre's brief Philadelphia run, a single performer – McGovern himself – carries all the "voices" of the text, including that of the implicit narrator, in the simplest of all styles: that of the story-teller.' What happened, we might ask, to the 'we' of the text: 'He made use, with reference to Watt, of an expression that *we* shall not record' (*Watt* 17, emphasis added)? Who or what we? Sam? A generalized, omniscient narrator? Zaller further notes what may be Watt's neurological motor disorder suggested in the text, illustrated to full advantage in the performance:

> Beckett gives a meticulous account of Watt's peculiar stride, which consists of lurching to the side like a compass needle being drawn askew, and then laboriously righting itself. McGovern illustrates this phenomenon as he describes it – something the reader of course can only do in his imagination. The result seems that of an off-kilter automaton, or someone afflicted with severe motor problems.

Presumably, McGovern's depiction or illustration substitutes for the audience member's imagination. Artist Bruce Naumann devised his own sixty-minute 'off-kilter', Watt-inspired work in 1968, which he called 'Slow Angle Walk (Beckett Walk)', filmed in part with a camera strapped to his leg to capture the peculiar angle of a strange and strained gait, but Naumann, at least, avoids the redundancy of re-narrating what he is simultaneously rendering, resists the impulse to illustrate. Zaller concludes with succinct yet trenchant caveats: 'Of course, that is the limitation of McGovern's adaptation. *Watt* is not a play but, in McGovern's hands, a dramatic text delivered as a direct address to the audience. Nor can the richness or quirkiness of the novel be communicated, even though all the words are Beckett's own.' If we've lost that 'richness and quirkiness of the novel' what have we gained?

Zaller's comment is apposite as well for all such re-renderings of Beckett's prose. McGovern himself admits something of the problem, responding to an interviewer in November 2011 who asked, 'When people see "Watt", do you think they'll feel like they've experienced the novel?' 'Not at all', McGovern responded, 'I hope people will feel inspired to read the novel.' Subsequently, however, McGovern opens up another set of epistemological issues, 'I can only get at the essence of it. There are huge sections I can't incorporate. I wanted to delve into the questions of what is real and what is not, and I hope that question is entertainingly posed' (Jones 2011). But what is real and what not (so to speak) is not only the central pun of the narrative but must remain at issue; which a single performer can probably not sustain.

Barry McGovern as Watt

Similar caveats might be expressed for other such stagings of Beckett's prose texts as 'one-man shows', of course, renditions of Beckett's *Three Novels* or *Quatre Nouvelles* in particular, but these are among the most celebrated, even revered of adaptations, carried often by the sheer force of the actors involved, works that have become part of an international Beckett 'culture park', recorded, televised, filmed, repeated: Jackie MacGowran's celebrated *Beginning to End*,[1] presented in March of 1971 at the Arena Theatre, Washington, DC, as *MacGowran in the Works of Beckett*; Conor Lovett's much praised and toured *First Love*, in which he acknowledges playing 'the narrator'; and Barry McGovern's equally celebrated and toured compilation *I'll Go On*, first staged in 1985 by the Gate Theatre at the Dublin Theatre Festival. On the other side of the pond, Joseph Chaikin prevailed upon Beckett in 1981 to allow him to adapt Beckett's post-*Unnamable* set of thirteen narratives called *Texts for Nothing*, to which he added portions of *How It Is* over Beckett's objections, the adaptation (done with Steven Kent) revived in 1992 after Mr Chaikin's debilitating stroke but nonetheless directed by him with Beckett actor Bill Irwin, who has since toured the work, again to excellent press. Likewise, on 6 January 1984, Gerald Thomas, in consultation with Beckett, staged the short narrative 'All Strange Away' at La Mama ETC in New York City, of which critic Mel Gussow (1984) noted in the *New York Times* that the work 'has been artfully brought to the stage by the director Gerald Thomas and by the solo actor Ryan Cutrona'. When Gussow offers reservations, they focus on Thomas's theatricalizing of the text, particularly with the addition of 'a silent prologue in which Mr. Cutrona acclimatizes himself by practicing simian stances, and a later scene in which he lights a cigar that has appeared from nowhere (no way in, none out, but smoke flowing through the roof of the rotunda)'.

Artful as such adaptations may be, what they seem to ignore, in the very conception of such performances, is, well, thought, thinking, that is, the process of thinking, philosophy, ontology and often epistemology, particularly the dissipation, or deterritorialization, we might say, of being, and, consequently, the dispersal of literary character, which may be Beckett's most stunning creative innovation, on page and stage, the replacement of being by becoming. *Watt*, and other Beckett works, with creatures unnamed and finally unnamable, we might add, is an open system that performance tends to close; that is, *Watt* has no final word, but offers instead replicated images that resonate with various intensities, with repetitions that are rhythms or refrains, and for which the material text, with its lacunae, remains part of the sentient, affective experience. The presence of a material text on stage, read, held, discarded, even destroyed, might have come closer to the mark. The paramount example of such may be David Warrilow's 1973 performance of *The Lost Ones*, directed by Lee Bruer and Tom Cathcart, which began as a reading before developing into an environmental performance in which the text remained central, Warrilow in dialogue with the text even as he illustrated the scenes with toy soldiers.

Despite occasional protestations to the contrary, Beckett periodically encouraged directors eager to stage his prose, and he developed several thematically revealing stage adaptations of his short narratives. When American director Joseph Chaikin wrote for permission to stage *Texts for Nothing*, for example, Beckett proposed in a letter of 26 April 1980 to mount a single *Text*, for which he offered a simple, precise staging: a single figure, 'Seated. Head in hands. Nothing else. Face invisible. Dim spot. Speech hesitant. Mike for audibility.' Beckett was intrigued enough with his own adaptation to offer a fuller version to Chaikin on 1 August 1980. The outline was astonishing as Beckett exteriorized memory and complexified being with a multiplicity of voices, offering something like 'a mixed choir' from the valley of astonishment:

> Curtain up on speechless author (A) still or moving or alternately. Silence broken by recorded voice (V) speaking opening of text. A takes over. Breaks down. V again. A again. So on. Till text completed piecemeal. Then spoken through, more or less hesitantly, by A alone.
>
> Prompt not always successful, i.e., not regular alternation VAVA. Sometimes: Silence, V, silence, V again, A. Or even three prompts before A can speak.
>
> A does not repeat, but takes over where V leaves off.
>
> V: not necessarily A's voice. Nor necessarily the same throughout. Different voices, 3 or 4, male and female, might be used for V. Perhaps coming to A from different quarters.
>
> Length of prompt (V) and take over (A) as irregular as you like.
>
> V may stop, A break down, at any point of sentence. (Cited in *CSP* xvi)

Chaikin ultimately rejected Beckett's staging, not understanding, one might guess, the multiplicities, the interplay of memory and imagination that Beckett was suggesting and so preferring his own vision of a medley of texts with a coherent narrator, and Beckett conceded in a letter of 5 September 1980, 'The method I suggest is only valid for a single text. The idea was to caricature the labour of composition. If you prefer extracts from a number of texts you will need a different approach' (cited in *CSP* xvi). Chaikin finally chose another, more 'theatrical' approach, but Beckett's adaptation of his story remains astonishing, a dramatic foregrounding of the mysterious voices, memory dispersed and external to the perceiving part of self, perspectives which might still be deemed Bergsonian. In *Creative Evolution* Bergson suggests such dispersal of memory thus:

> When I no longer know anything of external objects, it is because I have taken refuge in the consciousness that I have of myself. If I

abolish this inner self, its very abolition becomes an object for an imaginary self which now perceives as an external object the self that is dying away. Be it external or internal, some object there always is that my imagination is always representing. (1944: 303)

What is caricatured in Beckett's adaptation is at least the Romantic notion of creativity, the artist's agonized communion with his own pure, uncorrupted, coherent inner being, consciousness, or imagination. In Beckett's vision the author figure 'A' has at least an unnamed collaborator, an external agent or projected memory, memory at least not restricted to the material bodily organ, the brain. 'A' is as much audience to the emerging artwork as its instigator, as he folds the voices of Others, origins unknown, into his own.

Shivaun O'Casey, daughter of the Irish dramatist Sean O'Casey, worked with Beckett to dramatize *From an Abandoned Work*, and Beckett likewise detailed a possible staging for her. O'Casey's initial impulse was to mount the work on the analogy of *Play* with a light as interrogator, but Beckett resisted, 'I think the spotlight face presentation would be wrong here' (cited in *CSP* xvii). Beckett seems to be resisting suggestions of a coherent inner voice, a coherent subconscious, what he calls a 'monologue technique'. His alternative was to foreground text, a materialized, dramatized document, text as character. He went on to offer an alternative that once again separated speaker from spoken, 'speaker . . . not responsible' for text: 'The face is irrelevant. I feel also that no form of monologue technique will work for this text and that it should somehow be presented as a document for which the speaker is not responsible.' Beckett's outline is as follows:

Moonlight. Ashcan a little left of centre. Enter man left, limping, with stick, shadowing in paint general lighting along [sic]. Advances to can, raises lid, pushes about inside with crook of stick, inspects and rejects (puts back in can) an unidentifiable refuse, fishes out finally tattered ms. or copy of FAAW, reads aloud standing 'Up bright and early that day, I was young then, feeling awful and out–' and a little further in silence, lowers text, stands motionless, finally closes ashcan, sits down on it, hooks stick round neck, and reads text through from beginning, i.e., including what he had read standing. Finishes, sits a moment motionless, gets up, replaces text in ashcan and limps off right. Breathes with maximum authenticity, only effect to be sought in [sic] slight hesitation now and then in places where most effective, due to strangeness of text and imperfect light and state of ms. (Cited in Bair 1978: 578)

In such an adaptation the narrative offered to the audience is, as Beckett says, separated from the stage character who is then only an accidental protagonist in the drama, more messenger, say, than character. It was a form of staging that Beckett preferred for most of his prose, a compromise between an unadorned stage reading and a full, theatrical adaptation where characters and not just the text are re-presented on the stage. When the American theatrical group Mabou Mines requested permission through Jean Reavey to stage *The Lost Ones*, Beckett approved at first only a 'straight reading'. In rehearsals, however, the work developed into a complex, environmental adaptation with a naked actor 'demonstrating' the text with a host of miniature figures. Beckett's comment on the adaptation was finally, 'Sounds like a crooked straight reading to me' (cited in *CSP* xviii).

With O'Casey, Beckett resisted the resurrection of a dramatic structure he himself had by then rejected, the monologue, a form he developed in prose with the four *Nouvelles* in 1947 and adapted to the stage with *Krapp's Last Tape* in 1958 and *Happy Days* in 1961. The monologue form embraced an ideology of concrete presence, a single coherent being (or a unified ego – or, in literary terms, a unified character), an idea with which Beckett was increasingly uncomfortable (witness the tapes themselves in *Krapp's Last Tape*) and all pretence to which was finally abandoned in the *Three Novels* and the subsequent *Texts for Nothing*. In the theatre Beckett gave full voice to that disintegration of character and the fragmentation of monologue in *Not I* and with the incorporeal, ghostly figure of May in *Footfalls*. When consulted about stagings of his prose Beckett invariably rejected, as he did with Shivaun O'Casey, adaptations that posited a unity of character and narrative which the monologue form suggests. When I prepared with him stagings of first his novella *Company* and then the story *First Love*, he offered possibilities almost identical to those for Chaikin and O'Casey respectively.[2] The question central to Beckett's dramatization of *First Love*, for instance, was how to break up an unrelieved reading of the text, again discovered in a rubbish heap:

The reading can be piecemealed by all kinds of business – such as returning it to bin (on which he sits to read) – exiting and returning to read to the end – looking feverishly for a flea or other vermin – chewing a crust – getting up to piss in a corner with back modestly to audience – etc. etc. making the poor best of a hopeless job.[3]

The materiality of theatrical adaptations as cited above, their emphasis on the essential portions of Beckett's texts – as in McGovern's 'the essence of it' (as if Beckett's texts had essences) or 'what is real and what not' – runs counter to what we might call the text's *durée*. What is perhaps more misleading is the implication in McGovern's assessment that what is not selected for illustration is *de facto* somehow inessential, avoiding the issue that the texts' central metaphysical implications are beyond illustration. Such coherent staging, such depiction of the narrator as a single, stable entity, such reading *for* the audience, at very least stays textual dynamics. In his own work for theatre and as a creator of prose adaptations for others, Beckett, as author and director, worked assiduously to realize and to maintain the opposite: textual instability, flow. Stagings of Beckett's prose – which too often amount to textual illustration, no matter how expertly and sympathetically rendered, no matter how authentically raspy the actor's voice, no matter how weathered and deteriorating the actor appears, for after all these have become the clichés of Beckettian performance – too often merely represent incidents, select from the vastness of possibility, from the text's virtuality, and offer readings which pause or arrest immanence. Beckett's own late theatre and his adaptations of his texts for other media seem consistently to separate overt theatricality from the idea of performance, a distinction that too many of the great Beckett actors miss.

Call such theatrical stagings *reterritorializations*, a single reading as opposed to a multiplicity of simultaneous readings, a *deterritorialization*, say, the initial letter or syllable making all the difference. As a case in point we find Watt confronted with the slippage, the instability or impossibility of language as the repeated word 'pot' slips from its mooring, from homey familiarity into the morass of multiplying and alternate possibilities, potness become indeterminate: 'it was not a pot, the more he looked, the more he reflected, the more he felt sure of that, that is [*recte* it] was not a pot at all' (*Watt* 81). Watt's crisis, linguistic slippage, seems obviated in performance with a comforting return to familiarity as the

PBS   "Beginning to End: An Anthology of the Works of Samuel Beckett" returns to
PBS in the CONFLICTS drama series _____ at _____
on Channel _____. The late Jack MacGowran, in a one-man performance
interprets feelings on life and death reflected in Beckett's poetry, prose
and drama. (#104).

actor produces a concrete and stable image of a pot that is indeed a
pot, of sorts, a kind of pot, at least the image of a pot, but an image
with undeniable potness. Slippage arrested. That is, what function
might so specific an illustration serve if not to delimit possibilities?
Or is the image a casserole? A baking dish? A Dutch oven? Such a
critique is not designed to denigrate the performances themselves,
more often than not supremely presented by actors dedicated and
sensitive to Beckett's work, but to outline the ways in which they
are misconceived, in which such reterritorialization runs counter
to Beckett's creative enterprise. In fairness, we might offer something of the same critique of much critical discourse, as Beckett
himself often did, criticism as a replacement for direct, affective
textual encounter, as a *reading for us*, as theatre is often (if not
always) a *reading for us*.

* * *

In an interview in Paris with James Woodall on 30 April 2014
called 'On the Making of *The Valley of Astonishment*', excerpted
in the programme, Brook tells the story of how his interest in this
neurological material dates back at least to 1992: 'This new play

really began with research started years ago, with a certain wish to open up certain areas, in this case how the human brain functions. [. . .] I had been very inspired by Oliver Sacks and his book *The Man Who Mistook His Wife for a Hat* about individuals with strange conditions of the brain.' The work's or works' gestation was even longer, Brook admits, going back to Sacks's book of 1973, *Awakenings*, which Harold Pinter gave him with the advice, 'This is remarkable, you must read it.' The idea percolated thereafter, but, as Brook suggests, 'it was only a year ago [2013 that] we made the decision to do this play'. Harold Pinter had acted much more quickly on the Sacks material and produced his theatre piece based on memory where a now middle-aged woman, Deborah (played originally by Judi Dench), who has been in a coma for thirty years, awakens as the sixteen year old she was before her *encephalitis lethargica*. *A Kind of Alaska* opened in London in 1982; the play was then revived some thirty years on, in April 2012, by the Bristol Old Vic, on a programme with Beckett's *Krapp's Last Tape* as something of a memory double bill.[4] Of the production Lyn Gardner writes on 13 April 2012 (what might have been Samuel Beckett's 106th birthday): 'the real beauty is in the daring pairing of two plays that bounce off each other like reflections in a hall of mirrors. Deborah cannot stop remembering. Krapp can't even recall the things he once cited as memorable; even the meaning of words he once knew eludes him. Alone, each of these plays is small but mighty; together, they are like rolling thunder.' Pinter's play was something of a departure to which he never returned, but Beckett's play is part of a lifelong preoccupation with and exploration of memory and consciousness, and so of the human mind. And therein lies the difference. Brook sees his current work as a staging of new material about the fascinating human brain, but *The 'Valley of Astonishment'* says little of contemporary neuroscience, says little of science at all, even as two brain scientists are involved in the action. Its focus, finally, is memory, but memory as something of a parlour trick, a stageable theatrical entertainment, and a means of economic survival.

Samuel Beckett will make a critique of such issues the centrepiece of his lifelong creative enterprise, a critique of memory and perception not as brain function per se, the workings of a material bodily organ, wondrous, even astonishing as that is, that apparently inscrutable grey accumulation of cholesterol. Beckett will offer critiques, then, not of materialized memory, that is, memory as stored and catalogued in the vault or reservoir of the brain, but of a dispersed, complex, neural system, a constantly accumulating, constantly shifting, ineradicable, unlocatable memory, related but not restricted to the brain. For if memory were locatable or chartable, it might indeed be subject to manipulation, to being altered or erased. That is an issue for Brook's protagonist whose brain is filling up like a computer hard drive that she wishes to clean out. But can memory be freed up by erasing stored data to form something like renewal or to lead to *The Eternal Sunshine of the Spotless Mind*? – a quotation from Alexander Pope's *Eloesa to Abelard* used for a 2004 film that won the Academy Award for 'Best Original Screenplay':

> How happy is the blameless vestal's lot!
> The world forgetting, by the world forgot.
> Eternal sunshine of the spotless mind!
> Each pray'r accepted, and each wish resign'd;

The Eternal Sunshine of the Spotless Mind may be something of a misnomer not only because the film has precious little to do with the life of a cloistered nun or desire 'resign'd', the 'spotless mind' achieved in 2004 not by abstinence or sequestration, as Pope would have it, but through a physical procedure that assumes a materiality, locability, and so eradicability to memory that actually seems to run counter to most contemporary neurological research. The blessed may be the forgetful, apparently, if forgetfulness is possible at all, but in the film the blessed are those who have undergone a 'procedure', those who have had forgetting electrically induced. Nietzsche phrased it thus, however, the allusion noted in the film: 'Blessed are the forgetful, for they get the better even of their blunders' (*Beyond Good and Evil*, Maxim 2017, Chapter 7, 'Our Virtues'). But even such induced forgetfulness may finally backfire on the film's protagonists since they don't seem to 'get the better even of their blunders', or, put another way, memory as habit may be ineradicable and so kicks in even after the 'procedure'. The protagonists through their habits of behaviour are brought together once again in something of a reprise of their previous patterns and errors to experience yet again the ecstasy of new passions followed by the inevitable boredom and separation that the quotidian imposes. It is thus the second (or third) act of *Waiting for Godot*, each act like returning on a subsequent night to see the same theatre event again; we find the characters have learned nothing from the previous night's encounters. If forgetting produces a Nietzschean bliss, such bliss, even temporarily, is denied the Sammy Costases, followers of Bergson, and readers of Beckett.

The feats of unforgetfulness, of memory by those involved in the narrative of *Watt*, are indeed prodigious and haunting, replicated at least in part by stage performance. On his departure from the Knott house, Arsene delivers what (materialized on paper) is a twenty-page monologue, which Watt apparently memorizes, 'Haw! How it all comes back to me, to be sure' (*Watt* 39). Such memory is facilitated, admittedly, by certain set pieces that serve as something of a mnemonic device, which device is apparently passed on to Sam (not Sammy) in the novel. One such set piece is (presumably) Arsene's, which begins, 'Personally of course I regret everything' (46), and is punctuated and thus structured by coprological expletives: 'ordure', 'excrement', and 'turd' (46–7). That is, on his departure from the Knott house, Watt finds himself or takes refuge in a pavilion, where he relates his story to one Sam, which story includes Arsene's as an embedded narrative, and Sam in turn tells it to us as something of a direct quotation from Watt, even portions of the narrative that Watt could not have known and so could not have told him. Watt himself seems to have, or at least admits to, or Sam discerns, deficiencies of perception, at times due to neural static, evident as early as his exchange with Mr Spiro, reported, apparently, by something like an omniscient narrator: 'But Watt heard nothing of this [which matter someone has just reported] because of other voices, singing, crying, stating, murmuring, things unintelligible, in his ear. With these, if he was not familiar, he was not unfamiliar either' (29). Brook and Estienne are apparently concerned with practicalities, with the accuracy of memory, which is what makes it stageable, entertaining, both of which seem not to pertain in *Watt* despite attempts to stage it:

For when Watt at last spoke of this time, it was a time long past, and of which his recollections were, in a sense, perhaps less clear than he would have wished, though too clear for his liking, in another. Add to this the notorious difficulty of recapturing, at will, modes of feeling peculiar to a certain time, and to a certain place, and perhaps also to a certain state of health, when the time is past, and the place left, and the body struggling with quite a new situation. Add to this the obscurity of Watt's communication, the rapidity of his utterance and the eccentricities of his syntax, as elsewhere recorded. Add to this the material conditions in which these communications were made. Add to this the scant aptitude to receive of him to whom they were proposed. Add to this the scant aptitude to give of him to whom they were committed. And some idea will perhaps be obtained of the difficulties experienced in formulating, not only such matters as those here in question, but the entire body of Watt's experience, from the moment of his entering Mr Knott's establishment to the moment of his leaving it. (75)

And shortly thereafter a narrator, to be called 'me', notes, 'one is sometimes tempted to wonder, with reference to two or even three incidents related by Watt as separate and distinct, if they were not in reality the same incident variously interpreted' (78).

That Samuel Beckett's lifelong interest in, if not his preoccupation with, the relationship of mind to body (much generated through his interest in and critique of the work of René Descartes – his focus on, presumably, 'Descartes' errors' as well) is well if often uncritically detailed in the critical discourse. Moreover, Beckett had a decided interest in brain function and neurological disorders as well – witness the akathisia of two servants, Cooper in *Murphy* and Clov in *Endgame*, and Watt's 'tardigrade', 'funambulistic stagger' in *Watt* (31), which suggests an unspecified neurological malfunction. Hamm's paralysis may be the result of a stroke or aneurism that has impaired neural function to his lower limbs. Beckett's interest in such issues was evident at least at his 1980 rehearsals of *Endgame* with the San Quentin Drama Workshop at London's Riverside Studios. The rehearsals were something of a semi-public event, as a steady stream of visitors would come by and observe Beckett at work. One of these was the American author Larry Shainberg, who had sent Beckett a copy of his new book on developments in brain surgery called *Brain Surgeon: An Intimate Look at His World*, which Shainberg calls 'an investigation of the world of neurosurgery' (1987: 54). As he suggests in a piece for the *Paris Review* called 'Exorcising Beckett', 'The intimacy and enthusiasm with which Beckett greeted his friends as well as newcomers like myself – acting for the world as if I'd done him an enormous favor to come – was a great surprise for me' (1987: 53–4). By the time of the May 1980 rehearsals it was clear that Beckett had read the book carefully and was fascinated by it. Strolling along the Thames during a break in rehearsals, Beckett and Shainberg discussed the book in considerable detail. Beckett asked innumerable questions: how close had Shainberg stood watching the craniotomy; how much pain was involved in the procedure; how is the skull removed? Perhaps the most curious detail that emerged from these conversations was that in these new developments in neurosurgery patients experienced almost no side or after effects, except for one: they occasionally felt that something was dripping in their head. If one were to press the matter, furthermore, one might find the compulsively pacing figure of a 'dishevelled' May in *Footfalls* to be suffering from another such neurological disorder, and Mouth in *Not I* shows decided signs of proprioception. But it would be Bergson – with his very different sense of the body from that of Descartes (not as machine, necessarily, but as conductor), with his focus on an independent memory as the intersection of mind and body (an image, not a mysterious pineal gland), or as the relationship of the one to the other – who would have the most profound impact on Beckett's thought and so on his work.

Much of Bergson's breakthrough work came out of the study of aphasia, developed particularly in Chapter 2 of *Matter and Memory*, 'Of the Recognition of Images: Memory and the Brain' (1911). Through such clinical studies Bergson would insist on the distinction between mind and brain, the former associated with the vastness of consciousness and perceptions, the latter as more of a selector of the material useful for immediate problems. As Bergson put the matter in his eloquent way at the opening of Chapter 2:

> We have said that the body, placed between the objects which act upon it and those which it influences, is only a conductor, the office of which is to receive movements, and to transmit them (when it does not arrest them) to certain motor mechanisms, determined if the action is reflex, chosen if the action is voluntary. Everything, then, must happen as if an independent memory gathered images as they successively occur along the course of time; and as if our body, together with its surroundings, was never more than one among these images, the last is that which we obtain at any moment by making an instantaneous section in the general stream of becoming. In this section our body occupies the center. The things which surround it act upon it, and it reacts upon them. (Bergson 1991: 77)

In the following chapter Bergson then makes his case for a physical if dependent process of memory and perception:

> we have distinguished three processes, pure memory, memory-image, and perception, of which none of them in fact, occurs apart from the others. Perception is never a mere contact of the mind with the object present; it is impregnated with memory-images which complete it as they interpret it. The memory-image, in its turn, partakes of the 'pure memory', which it begins to materialize, and of the perception in which it tends to embody itself: regarded from the latter point of view, it might be defined as a nascent perception. Lastly, pure memory, though independent in theory, manifests itself as a rule only in the colored and living image which reveals it. (Bergson 1991: 133)

That the physical organ of the brain is not the repository of memory but an instrument of selection is key to Bergsonism and to memory theory of the first part of the twentieth century, and what humans deal with directly is neither what Bergson calls 'pure memory', nor unmediated sensory perception, but the 'memory image' which completes the circuit with our sense as a link between 'pure memory' and one's body or the external world, both of which are themselves images.

Much of the remapping that follows engages the changes in philosophical process initiated by Bergson and his nearly empirical, semi-mystical intuitive epistemology, the literary revolution that followed his emphasis on and redefinition of the image, the conflict between Bergson's metaphysics and the narrative of humanity offered by Christianity and the Catholic Church in particular, and the relationship between the transcendentally divine and the materiality of existence. The arc of such Bergson-driven change is charted by Keith Ansell Pearson and John Mullarkey in the 'Introduction' to their anthology, *Henri Bergson: Key Writings*:

1. To conceive of time in terms of duration and to insist that time not be confused by space.
2. To forge a distinction between two kinds of multiplicity, the continuous (virtual) and the discrete (actual).
3. To approach the question of metaphysics in terms of diverse planes of experience and different fields of knowledge.
4. To demonstrate the need to situate the theory of knowledge in a

wider context of a theory of life. (Ansell Pearson and Mullarkey
2002: 1)

These points constitute less a blueprint for art or philosophy than
they do a mode of thinking, the creative implication of which will
be explored throughout the following discourse. As Ansell Pearson
and Mullarkey suggest, Bergson makes a profound contribution
'to the staging of philosophical problems, problems concerning the
nature of time, of consciousness, perception, representation and
memory, of life and evolution' (2002: 1).

The following exposition then begins with Anterior views, first
by remapping an early twentieth-century mode of discourse about
the nature of memory, consciousness, dreams and perception,
and their political implications for religion and science as well
as for philosophy and literature. This remapping offers something of an enhancement of and so a symbiotic encounter with
(and not a replacement for) the development of what is loosely
called Modernism, particularly in literature, and Samuel Beckett's
relationship to it. The remapping, furthermore, engages with an
emerging empiricist, materialist science in the early years of the
twentieth century that rejects what might be called speculating
or theorizing about what cannot be measured, consciousness in
particular, even as such theorizing will finally come to lead, if not
dominate, the advances of twentieth-century physical science. The
second Anterior chapter will trace some possibilities of when and
how Beckett's intellectual development might have intersected
these developing lines of cultural thought, or what Deleuze will
call lines of flight or 'nomad' thought, and suggest a much earlier
point of entry for Beckett into such metaphysical issues than has
heretofore been acknowledged. Such intersection will finally find a
profound realization not only in the work of Beckett but in that of
Deleuze and his collaborators as well.

Subsequent chapters, Interior views, will detail the development
of nomadic lines of flight in Beckett's creative and critical output, a
charting that might have been done without reference to Bergson,
induced instead, or rather intuited, from the work itself, seen not
as series of separated and published entities, but as a continuous
flow of thought. Reference to and through Bergson (and finally to
and through Deleuze), however, illuminates, clarifies and contex-
tualizes that developing literary thought and, furthermore, helps
put into perspective what might be deemed un-Modern or pre-

Modern strains in Beckett's art: medievalism and scholasticism, say, or mysticism, romanticism, and an interest in altered psychic states, something like out of body experiences or paranormality, issues too often avoided by critics. Such an approach to Beckett's work also allows a rethinking of what have become bromides of Beckett studies, that Beckett's trajectory was towards less and less, towards a minimalism that does not account for sudden, longish bursts into science fiction with *The Lost Ones* (1971) and a resurgence of longer narratives in the *Nohow On* novels of the 1980s. Moreover, such a perspective puts the lie to the reading of Beckett as a poet of despair, preoccupied with misery, death, suicide and the like, and refocuses the work on the impulse to go on, the paradox stated most directly in the 1949 theoretical work, 'Three Dialogues with Georges Duthuit': 'The expression that there is nothing to express, nothing with which to express, nothing from which to express, no power to express, no desire to express, together with the obligation to express' (Beckett 1984: 139). There is something of a Bergsonian driving force in Beckett's 'obligation', delivered as advice to the painter Tal Coat, some inexplicable yet powerful force of rejuvenation, which Bergson deemed an *élan vital*.

Such a line of flight will lead us, inevitably one might say, to and through Gilles Deleuze, whose commentary on Beckett's work is direct and profound. The ultimate section, a Posterior view, examines a process of textualizing the flesh as the author, in the mode of some of his creations, May in *Footfalls*, for instance, dissolves or disappears, not behind a curtain or into the off stage but into his text, 'as the reader will remember', which dissolution Deleuze holds to be the apex of the literary encounter and which textuality, as Beckett had always contended, is, finally, all that the public need concern itself with. Watt, having left the Knott house and having bought a ticket at the train station 'To the end of the line' (*Watt* 244), does not board the train as 'It did not take up a single passenger' (245), but disappears (into the pavilion of the previous Part III, presumably). We might return at this point to Ben Brantley's characterization of Peter Brook's 2014 theatrical endeavour – 'this essayistic work about extraordinary sensory perceptiveness' – and re-read it as a gloss on Beckett's art, at least from *Watt* onward. Such is the magic, the wonder one might continue to experience from direct encounters with Beckett's ditch of astonishment.

Notes

1. Recorded by RTÉ in 1966 and released as a vinyl LP then re-taped, despite Beckett's reservations, in the Mojave desert in 1971 for PBS. Now readily available at http://www.apieceofmonologue.com/2011/03/jack-macgowran-samuel-beckett-video.html.

2. For further discussion of adaptation of Beckett's prose to the stage see my 'Company for Company: Androgyny and Theatricality in Samuel Beckett's Prose' (Gontarski 1987).

3. Samuel Beckett, letter to the author dated 12 September 1986, cited in *CSP* xviii.

4. Programme details available on the Harold Pinter web page: http://www.haroldpinter.org/plays/plays_otherplaces.shtml, which also reprints a short review by Alan Jenkins, 'The Withering of Love', from *The Times Literary Supplement*, 29 October 1982.

References

Ansell Pearson, Keith and John Mullarkey, eds (2002) *Henri Bergson: Key Writings*, London: Bloomsbury Academic.

Bair, Deirdre (1978) *Samuel Beckett: A Biography*, New York: Vintage.

Baldwin, Thomas (2013) 'Philosophy', in *Marcel Proust in Context*, ed. Adam Watt, Cambridge: Cambridge University Press.

Barnard, G. William (2012) *Living Consciousness: The Metaphysical Vision of Henri Bergson*, Albany, New York: SUNY Press.

Beckett, Samuel (1984) 'Three Dialogues with George Duthuit', in *Disjecta: Miscellaneous Writings and a Dramatic Fragment by Samuel Beckett*, ed. Ruby Cohn, New York: Grove, 138–45.

Benton, Arthur L. (1987) 'Bergson and Freud on Aphasia', in *Bergson and Modern Thought: Towards a Unified Science*, ed. Andrew C. Papanicolaou and Pete A. Y. Gunter, Chur, Switzerland: Harwood Academic Publishers.

Bergson, Henri (1944) *Creative Evolution*, trans. Arthur Mitchell, New York: Modern Library (reprint of Henry Holt and Company, 1911).

Bergson, Henri (1991) *Matter and Memory*, trans. Nancy Margaret Paul and W. Scott Palmer, New York: Zone Books.

Billington, Michael (2014) '*The Valley of Astonishment*: A Sensory Meditation on the Human Brain', *Guardian*, 24 June, http://www.theguardian.com/stage/2014/jun/24/the-valley-of-astonishment-review-young-vic-peter-brook.

Brantley, Ben (2014) 'The Mind is a Terrible Thing to Take for Granted',

New York Times, 18 September, http://www.nytimes.com/2014/09/19/
theater/the-valley-of-astonishment-by-brook-and-estienne.html?_r=0.

Damasio, Antonio (1994) *Descartes' Error: Emotion, Reason and the Human Brain*, New York: Putnam.

Gardner, Lyn (2012) 'A Kind of Alaska/Krapp's Last Tape – Review', *Guardian*, 13 April, http://www.theguardian.com/stage/2012/apr/13-/a-kind-krapps-last-review.

Gontarski, S. E. (1987) '*Company* for Company: Androgyny and Theatricality in Samuel Beckett's Prose', in *Beckett's Later Fiction and Drama: Texts for Company*, ed. James Acheson and Kateryna Arthur, London: Macmillan Press, 1987, 193–202.

Gunter, Pete A. Y. (2013) 'Bergson and Proust: A Question of Influence', in *Understanding Bergson, Understanding Modernism*, ed. Paul Ardoin, S. E. Gontarski and Laci Mattison, New York and London: Bloomsbury Books.

Gussow, Mel (1984) '"Strange Away" by Beckett, at La Mama', *New York Times*, 11 January, https://geraldthomasblog.wordpress.com /2014/01/02/30-years-since-three-decades-since-all-this-strange-away.

Harrison, Matthew (2012) 'Watt', *Irish Theatre Magazine*, 24 July, http://www.irishtheatremagazine.ie/Reviews/Current/Watt.

Hemming, Sarah (2014) 'Interview: Veteran Theatre Director Peter Brook', http://www.ft.com/cms/s/2/7aa89596-efea-11e3-9b4c-00144 feabdco.html#axzz3S7xvdUGl.

James, William (1892) 'The Stream of Consciousness', in *Psychology*, Cleveland & New York: World, http://psychclassics.yorku.ca/James/ jimmy11.htm.

Jones, Chad (2011) Interview with Barry McGovern, http://www.sfgate. com/performance/article/Barry-McGovern-in-Beckett-s-Endgame-and-Watt-2289188.php.

Shainberg, Larry (1987) 'Exorcising Beckett', *Paris Review* 104 (fall 1987). Reprinted in *The Paris Review: Playwrights at Work*, ed. George Plimpton, New York: Modern Library, 2000, 50–86.

Zaller, Robert (2011) 'Play on Words, Beckett's Style, or: Is Language Possible?', *Broad Street Review*, 13 November, http://www.broad streetreview.com/theater/watt_at_annenberg_barry_mcgovern_per forms_beckett.

Anteriors

3

The Invention of the Modern:
A Symbiotic Remapping

I cannot escape the objection that there is no state of mind, however simple, which does not change every moment, since there is no consciousness without memory, and no continuation of a state without the addition, to the present feeling, of the memory of past moments. It is this which constitutes duration. Inner duration is the continuous life of a memory which prolongs the past into the present, the present either containing within it in a distinct form the ceaselessly growing image of the past, or, more profoundly, showing by its continual change of quality the heavier and still heavier load we drag behind us as we grow older. Without this survival of the past into the present there would be no duration, but only instantaneity. (Bergson, *An Introduction to Metaphysics*, 44)

The present contains nothing more than the past, and what is found in the effect was already in the cause. (Bergson, *Creative Evolution*, 14, emphasis in the original)

'The Poisonous Error of Philosophical Modernism'

Not long after Henri Bergson's books began to appear in English translation in 1910, the year in which, presumably, as Virginia Woolf proclaimed, 'human character changed', the attacks on Bergson were as virulent as recognition and praise were widespread and effusive. Eight months before he began his lectures in the United States, the *New York Times* of 26 May 2012 dismissed and ridiculed his philosophy as a passing fad: 'Bergson is the popular philosopher of the day. He is the pet of the Intellectuals. Being the newest philosophic fad – the latest drawing room attraction – we must – every one of us – know something about him. Else, how shall we move in the highest intellectual circles? To be sure, we shall all see through Bergson soon: we shall all read his reading of Time out of court.' Six months after Bergson's American lecture tour, which ran from 2–27 February 1913, a lead note carried on the front page of the *New York Times* of 28 August declaimed: 'Pope Denounces Bergson'; according to Pope Pius X, 'In the presence of these false theories of this new Bergsonian philosophy which seeks *to shatter grand fundamental principles and truths*, it is necessary to unmask the poisonous error of philosophical modernism' (emphasis added). The particular offending text was *Creative Evolution*, but by 1914, ironically the same year that Bergson was elected to the Académie française, all of Bergson's works were placed on the *Index liborum prohibitorum*, the Catholic Index of Prohibited Books. The phrase 'philosophical modernism' seems a curious one for the Holy See to be using in this condemnation, but Pius X was responding again to a reform movement in the Catholic Church as well as to changes in philosophical and literary thinking. He had used the term in his 1907 encyclical, *Pascendi dominici gregis*, to speak out against a movement deemed Modern, which aimed to historicize Catholicism, to move it from transcendent and so eternal truths towards a philosophy of immanence, one that might and ought to adapt to social change, its doctrine not invariant but evolving. Bergson's work was something of a set of principles for the reform movement that came to be called Catholic Modernism, and a principal figure in the movement, Edouard Louis Emmanuel Julien Le Roy, was Bergson's close disciple, a philosopher and mathematician at the École Normale Supérieure (ENS), who would succeed Bergson at the Collège de France (1922) and at the French Academy (Académie française 1945). He was author of, among other works, *A New Philosophy: Henri Bergson* (*Une philosophie nouvelle: Henri Bergson*, 1912) and, after Bergson's death, *Bergson et Bergsonisme* (1947). As Pius X and his advisors understood, much was at stake with 'this new Bergsonian philosophy', which was, at the very least, a political struggle for the story of humanity, the church desperate to maintain its control of that narrative. If the Bible contained merely expressions of faith rather than inerrant, invariant, revealed truths, then the Holy See (*Sancta Sedes*) and much of the Vatican apparatus stood on shaky ground rather than on the rock of Peter (see also Barnard 2011: xix–xx).

The particular charges against Bergson and Bergsonism involved his philosophy of immanence, and so a sort of pantheism, that is, the implication that everything, and so God, too, was immanent in the process of creation, the driving force not a being of some sort outside of time, but a force, a spirit of life, an *élan vital*, which Bergson defines, at least metaphorically, at the opening of *Creative Evolution* to be 'like a current passing from germ to germ through the medium of a developed organism' (1944: 27). By implication, then, He too was not transcendent but subject to that spirit, created by or through that process. God is thus neither outside of nor exempt from process, that is, time and so change.[1]

The day after the 'Pope Denounces Bergson' article, on 29 August, the anonymous author of the *New York Times*' 'Topics of the Times' column took up what he called the 'fulmination from the Vatican' with some puzzlement, understanding neither the history of the Pope's condemnation nor its far-reaching implications. The writer further dismissed Bergson as 'only a parlor philosopher': 'It is a decidedly curious phenomenon that the amiable and eloquent professor should have been as severely criticized by the high lay authorities as he is now by the Pope.' For this *Times* critic, Bergson and Bergsonism represented nothing new, especially if one saw him as a purveyor of pantheism: 'The fact is that M. Bergson passes for a bold and original thinker, a shaker of pillars and a disturber of foundations only among those to whom the language of science and philosophy are entirely unfamiliar and for whom big words, adroitly used are deeply impressive', the Pope apparently among the admonished here.

Almost simultaneous with the Pope's denunciation, Bergson's reconception of evolution was seen both as consistent with religious thinking and as coeval with the 'modern spirit': 'It is now clear why religious thinkers make a mistake when they are halfhearted in their acceptance of the philosophy of evolution, and when they try to prove that the spiritual life of humanity is an exception, a miraculous addition to the world-process rather than its outgrowth' (Dodson 1913: 248). Citing British biologist Alfred Russel Wallace (1823–1913, who developed his theory of evolution and natural selection independent of Darwin's) as among those who 'make a mistake', George Rowland Dodson notes in 1913 that Wallace 'agrees with Darwin that man's body was developed by natural process, but he [Wallace] makes an exception of the intelligence [the 'creative' part of Bergson's evolution] of the higher moral qualities'. Dodson, on the other hand, is in full sympathy with the process, the modernism of Bergson, 'Vain is the effort to find some nook or cranny in the cosmic process for the supernatural.' Wallace, then, breaks from Bergsonism on the issue of the supernatural, allowing instead for non-material origins, his famed 'spiritualism', and so retreats to classic dualism. Separating humanity's higher, creative faculties from 'material existence', he asserts that 'Man's spiritual nature [. . .] is superadded, not evolved' (Wallace cited in Dodson 1913: 248). Dodson offers a strong modernist retort: 'I can hardly imagine anything more disastrous to philosophy and religious faith than for Wallace's ideas to have proved true.' Dodson offers, instead, something of his own, qualified monism: 'It is precisely because man is inside the natural realm, wholly inside and all of him inside the natural realm, that we are not only justified in holding, but logically driven toward, a spiritual interpretation of the universe' (249). Such connection, tenuous as it may sound in Dodson, is the 'modern spirit' of Bergson, which Dodson summarizes thus: 'It is true, as Bergson says, that the more we fix our attention on the continuity of life, and we may say on its achievements, "the more we see that organic evolution resembles the evolution of a consciousness"' (245); to which we might add further the phrase from the beginning of Creative Evolution that precedes Dodson's citation: 'Continuity of change, preservation of the past in the present, real duration – the living being seems, then, to share these attributes with consciousness. Can we go further and say that life, like conscious activity, is invention, is unceasing creation?' (Bergson 1944: 23).[2]

Nonetheless, despite reservations and at times condemnation, Bergson's popularity both in the English and French speaking worlds approached cult status leading our dismissive New York Times critic to compare Bergson's popularity to another apostle of Christianity, that of Eddyism, the Christian Science of Mary Baker Eddy, and forcing him to admit that for Bergson's New York lectures, 'attendance will be large and fashionable'. In his 1910 translation of Bergson's Time and Free Will: An Essay on the Immediate Data of Consciousness, for example, F. L. Pogson punctuates that growing popularity, noting that in France the Essai was already in its seventh edition, and including a 'Selected list of books and articles' dealing with Bergson featuring some 132 items. By 1918, Bergson's French publisher, Alcan, had issued twenty-one editions of Creative Evolution, an average of two editions per year for ten years.[3] In 1913, in anticipation of Bergson's New York lectures, Columbia University librarians compiled a fuller, if still partial, *Contribution to a Bibliography* of works on and by Bergson, with an Introduction, dated 12 December 1912, by the eminent pragmatist and Columbia University Professor of Philosophy (since 1904), John Dewey, the book presented to Professor Bergson as a welcome gift on his arrival in New York City in February 1913:

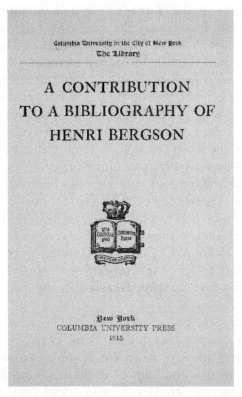

The purpose of the present bibliography is to show the wide-spread and varied interest in Professor Bergson's philosophy, and completeness rather than selection has therefore been the aim of the compilers. No attempt has been made to list the newspaper literature of the subject, and short book reviews have generally been omitted, but all other literature, either book or periodical, which has come to the compilers' attention has been included. Titles which have been included without examination are starred. The bibliography includes 90 books and articles by Professor Bergson (including translations of his works) and 417 books and articles about him. These 417 items represent

11 different languages divided as follows: German 40, Italian 19, Polish 5, Dutch 3, Spanish 2, Roumanian 2, Swedish 2, Russian 2, Hungarian 1. Translations of Professor Bergson's principal works are now available in many languages. So far the one most widely translated is 'Introduction a la Métaphysique', which is now accessible in the English, German, Italian, Swedish, Hungarian, Polish, and Russian languages. (Dewey 1913: vii)

Two translations of the 'Introduction a la Métaphysique' were into English. The first boasts the note, 'As originally issued by Prof. Bergson in the *Revue de Métaphysique et de Morale* and now first translated into English by Sidney Littman' (Bergson 1912a: 1), but it is entitled *Introduction to a New Philosophy*, although the French title is embossed on the book's cover and appears on the title page as well.[4] T. E. Hulme's more influential translation, more influential since it almost immediately provided a foundation for the literary movement that F. S. Flint and Ezra Pound called *Imagisme*, also appeared in 1912 under Bergson's original title, *An Introduction to Metaphysics*, and it carries Bergson imprimatur in a letter dated 18 October 1912: 'I certify that the translation of my volume *An Introduction to Metaphysics*, which has been prepared by Mr. T. E. Hulme, is the only English version to which I have given my authorization. [. . .] I have examined his translation with care and am able to say that it renders with remarkable accuracy the thought and conclusions presented in my volume' (Bergson 1912b: 6).[5]

Dewey's 'Introduction' to the Columbia University bibliography is reserved and circumspect, unsurprising, perhaps, since his own book in (or near) the field, *How We Think* (1910), was published in the same year that the bulk of Bergson's work first appeared in English;[6] subsequently, Dewey would take issue with Bergson directly in an essay called 'Perception and Organic Action', which appeared in the *Journal of Philosophy, Psychology and Scientific Methods* in 1912 and which he sent to Bergson, as something of a fair warning, perhaps, on the eve of Bergson's American lectures. In his 'Introduction', Dewey provides some historical perspective on Bergson's central method of Intuition: 'It happens that in English thought the associations that cluster about the word [intuition] are mainly derived from Platonic transcendentalism, and from the theories of the Scottish School [David Hume, perhaps] and the super-scientific, regarding an organ of knowledge that is independent of experience and superior to science' (1913: ix). While Dewey thus, at least by implication, associates Bergson with Idealism or what he will later call mysticism, he allows Bergson to separate his thought or his process from such traditional conceptions and associations surrounding the term, particularly that of 'knowledge [. . .] independent of experience', as he quotes Bergson's disavowal of transcendentalism and other versions of Idealism, Bergson, conceding some ground to Dewey perhaps, sounding here like an approximation of a Pragmatist: 'my method demands uninterrupted contact with reality. It consists in following reality in all its sinuosities. It demands that our faculties of observation even stretch themselves at times to surpass themselves. [. . .] It aspires to constitute metaphysics as certain and as universally recognized as any of the other sciences.' To effect such certainty, noted Bergson, 'We must break the mathematical framework, take account of biological, psychological and sociological science, and upon this larger base erect a metaphysics capable of going higher and higher by means of the continuous, progressive and organized effort of all philosophers who are associated in the same respect for experience' (Bergson cited in Dewey 1913: ix–x). In his earlier essay, however, which he called to his department chair, Frederick Woodbridge, 'my [. . .] screed on Bergson' (McGath 2013: 613), Dewey is more openly critical as he foregrounds what he sees as tensions if not contradictions in Bergson's thought and methods: a science that rejects scientific method, say, or a critique of perception and so experiential knowledge since it serves purely practical purposes or 'bodily needs'; or statements rejecting a practical philosophy of action as mimicry of science: a rejection of those methods 'with the exigencies of action in view', on the one hand, and a philosophy of total and continuous motion, on the other. With a nod to Bergson's popularity, Dewey succinctly summarizes Bergsonism at the onset of his critique:

EVERY reader of Bergson – and who to-day is not reading Bergson – is aware of a twofold strain in his doctrine. On the one hand, the defining traits of perception, of common sense knowledge and science are explained [that is, criticized and rejected] on the ground of their intimate connection with action. On the other hand, the standing unresolved conflicts of philosophic systems, the chief fallacies that are found in them, and the failure to make definite progress in the solution of specific philosophic problems, are attributed to carrying over into metaphysics the results and methods of the knowledge that has been formed with the exigencies of action in view. Legitimate and necessary for useful action, they are mere prejudices as respects metaphysical knowledge. Prejudices, indeed, is too mild a name. Imported into philosophy, they are completely misleading; they distort hopelessly the reality they are supposed to know. Philosophy must, accordingly, turn its back, resolutely and finally, upon all methods and conceptions which are *infected by implication in action* in order to strike out upon a different path. It must have recourse to intuition which installs us within the very movement of reality itself, unrefracted by the considerations that adopt it to bodily needs, that is, to useful action. As a result Bergson has the unique distinction of being attacked as a pragmatist on one side, and as a mystic on the other. (Dewey 1912: 645, emphasis added)

For Dewey, Bergson remains an unrepentant dualist:

A philosophy which holds that the facts of perception and science are to be explained from the standpoint of their connection with organically useful action, while it also holds that philosophy rests on a radically different basis, is perforce a philosophy of reality that is already afflicted with a dualism so deep as seemingly to be ineradicable. It imports a split into the reality with which philosophy is supposed to deal exclusively and at first hand. We account for perception and science by reference to action, use and need. Very well; but what about action, use and need? Are they [only] useful fictions? If not they must be functions of 'reality', in which case knowledge that is relevant to action, useful in the play of need must penetrate into 'reality' instead of giving it a twist', that is, by being separate from it. (647)

Dewey sees then what appears to be a contradiction in Bergsonism. If we have a philosophy that discounts 'action, use and need' we have a 'split' philosophy, one that seems to reject the immediately material in favour of an abstract and unified reality, but such unity already rejects 'the exigencies of action' as if it were merely a fiction. So, on the one hand, Bergson's emphasis on immediate experience might suggest that he is a pragmatist, but his suggestion of rejecting the 'useful' suggests a certain Idealism or at least a transcendence.

This will finally be the position that Maurice Merleau-Ponty will adopt in his lectures on Bergson as he views with suspicion Bergson's Intuition, which in its insistence on immanence and completeness

deals only with 'the most general structures' of the lived experience and so lacks 'human history which would give a context to
these intuitions' (Merleau-Ponty cited in Cutting 2007: 205). Noted
French critic and Bergson biographer Frédéric Worms, Professeur
de philosophie at the Ecole normale supérieure, approaches such a
division as Dewey and Merleau-Ponty cite, not in direct response to
or even as a summary of Bergsonism but as a general issue in *fin de
siècle* French metaphysics: 'the opposition that Bergson draws is not
an opposition between reality and consciousness, or between the
object and the spirit, but an opposition that takes place *in* reality
(and possibly in each reality) as well as in the *spirit* (including
and before all in our spirit)' (Worms cited in McGath 2013: 606).
Merleau-Ponty will see in Bergson's retention of those oppositions,
however, an 'implicit separation of subject and object, of consciousness and the world' (Merleau-Ponty cited in Cutting 2007: 205).

Bergson began to answer Dewey's critique directly in a letter
of 3 January 1913 by characterizing Dewey's objections to what
Bergson describes as his own 'partial realism', a partiality that
accounts for his being criticized as both an inadequate pragmatist,
Dewey's position, and as a latent Idealist, or, as Dewey phrases it,
'a mystic':

> As I say in the introduction to *Matter and Memory*, I place myself in
> a position *mid-way between realism and idealism* [see, for example,
> Bergson 1991: xi–xii], but in a certain measure I am a realist; and, as
> regards matter, I reckon that the geometry it contains, and which is
> manifest all the more in the measure in which we delve more deeply
> into it, pertains to what is real *in itself*. That is why, here and else-
> where, it would be impossible for me to define *all* reality in terms of
> action, unless one greatly stretches the meaning of this word. I believe
> that this is the essential point that separates us.
>
> According to my position, the action of things on us, be it real or
> virtual, is a part of their reality, but only a part. Besides, I do not see
> any difficulty in confusing [or conflating, say] our virtual action on
> things with the virtual action of things on us. The action by which we
> utilize things is essentially a contact, and in that contact it is irrelevant
> whether one says that we act on the thing or that the thing acts on us.
> (Mullarkey 1999: 86, emphasis added)

Bergson promises Dewey a fuller response, part of which must have
been delivered in his New York lectures since the objection that

Dewey raises and Bergson's succinct summary of a response are at the heart of what has come to be called Bergsonism. As he will say most directly in *The Creative Mind*: 'in order to reach intuition it is not necessary to transport ourselves outside the domain of the senses and of consciousness. Kant's error was to believe that it was' (Bergson 1946: 105). Merleau-Ponty will finally see such a position as one that finds in Bergson *Dasein* as a privileged entity or that privileges an 'absolute observer's viewpoint', which for him suggests something of the transcendental (Merleau-Ponty cited in Cutting 2007: 205).

Recounting summaries of Bergson's lectures at Columbia, lectures offered in full academic regalia and delivered extempore, without notes, critic Larry McGath also suggests that Bergson maintained a theme of dualism throughout his six lectures at Columbia University. Closer to the point, perhaps, is that Bergson was trying to address or deflect Dewey's criticisms, his charge of an unresolved dualism at the heart of Bergsonism. McGath inquires rhetorically, 'Why did Bergson decide to oppose *and then reconcile* dualities in his lectures such as metaphysics and science, understanding and willing, intellect and intuition. Why, in other words, did Bergson frame spirituality in dualist terms? The answer hinges on *the centrality of the dualist method* that Bergson had already employed in his published works' (2013: 603, emphasis added). One might suggest here another 'hinge', an alternate reason for or reading of the apparent 'centrality of the dualist method' to Bergson at Columbia, one which has him moving towards a final reconciliation of the dualist thread in his thought. The emphasis then should be maintained on Bergson's reconciling those dualities both 'in his published works' and in his lectures, particularly, in response to Dewey's critique. That is, Bergson situates himself between dualism and monism, a full advocate of neither even as he is, if partially, of both, what he calls his 'partial realism'. McGath places the emphasis where it should be when he suggests that 'The novelty of Bergson's brand of dualism was to trace what first appear as stark oppositions back to the unities – or composite experiences – from which they diverge' (603). This certainly is the key to a Bergsonian metaphysics, as Merleau-Ponty summarizes it, that 'would be a deliberate exploration of the world prior to the object to which science refers' (cited in Cutting 2007: 205); such, we might add, would be an effective answer to the 'split' that Dewey observes but not to the charge of abstraction levelled by Merleau-Ponty. McGath goes on to suggest that 'The effect [of the Columbia lectures] was to stage a rapprochement between science and aesthetics, analysis and reflection' (2013: 604). Bergson apparently thus worked hard in New York to overcome Dewey's resistance and critique. He even offered an unscheduled series of private seminars at Columbia to that end, these now delivered in English, on 'The Method of Philosophy, Outline of a Theory of Knowledge' which featured discussions of key terms both of Bergsonism itself and as direct answers to Dewey's objections: 'real movement irreducible to space and the indivisibility of real duration' (McGath 2013: 613).

Bergson's reception among academics and in the popular press was, on the whole, warm, most conflicted, not unexpectedly, in departments of philosophy with their established professional territories. Walter Lippmann, writing in the *New York Times* on 17 November of 1912 shortly after the appearance of *An Introduction to Metaphysics*, proclaimed that 'No one interested in the Bergsonian method should fail to read this essay. The central doctrine of intuition is stated and contrasted for the greater work, and if I might offer advice it would be this: Read "Creative Evolution" first, then this essay, then "Creative Evolution" again. They light up each other.' A short, unsigned review in the New York weekly, *The Independent*,[7] on 28 November 1912, compares the competing English translations, if briefly:

> Though this essay is indispensable to the student of Bergson we should hardly recommend it to the layman as an 'Introduction' to Bergson's philosophy, for, being more succinct and abstract, it is hardly so likely to interest as 'Creative Evolution'. Of the rival translations, that by Mr. Hulme is by far the better. It is authorized and revised by Professor Bergson [as Hulme states in his 'Translator's Preface'] and reads well, while the translation by Mr. Littman is very unreliable and in many places quite incomprehensible.

A reviewer for *The Spectator* noted on 26 April 1913: 'The essay is a masterpiece of lucid argument and memorable illustrations, set forth in a style which scarcely ever departs from the language of everyday life.'[8] Eminent Columbia historian J. T. Shotwell,[9] in a longer review essay in *Political Science Quarterly* just after Bergson's American lectures, offers a more reflective summary:

It is a work of genius to have made Metaphysics not only a vogue but the basis of something like a cult. Neither Schopenhauer nor Nietzsche has swung so fully into the focal center of a social movement. [. . . Bergson] challenges the confidence of science. [. . . Bergsonism] has a negative, critical side, and a positive. On the negative it boldly asserts that the rational process of our intellect cannot comprehend reality; on the positive that life itself can produce a kind of intuitive comprehension of just what intellect misses. (Shotwell 1913: 130)

The Independent was a key supporter of Bergson, Bergsonism, and Bergson's American lecture tour chiefly through the efforts of its literary editor, the chemist, biologist, and popularizer of science, Dr. Edwin Emery Slosson (1865–1929),[10] who was a keen follower of Bergson's work and who likely wrote the anonymous Independent review of An Introduction to Metaphysics cited above. Furthermore, he translated and introduced for The Independent two excerpts from Bergson's 1901 analysis of and lecture on dreams, published as 'Such Stuff As Dreams Are Made On: A Study Of The Mechanism of Dreaming'; 'The Birth Of A Dream' appeared a week later.[11] Introducing the former Slossen notes:

Dreams are of interest to everybody and have in all ages been the subject of much speculation. It is only within recent years, however, that successful attempts have been made to bring this nebulous material within the realm of science. The theory here propounded is, like Professor Bergson's other work, distinguished by originality and insight. In the first place he shows that dreaming is not so unlike the ordinary process of perception as had been hitherto supposed. Here, too, is brought forward the idea which he, so far as we know, was the first to formulate, that sleep is a state of disinterestedness, a theory which has since been adopted by several psychologists. In this address [of 1901] also was brought into consideration for the first time the idea that the self may go thru different degrees of tension – a theory referred to in his Matter and Memory. M. Bergson first made public the results of his study of the mechanism of dreaming in a lecture before the Institut Psychologique, March 26, 1901, which was published in the 'Revue Scientifique', June 8, 1901, and has now been revised and adapted by the author expressly for The Independent.

At the onset of his lecture, Bergson lays out the issues of perception, materiality, and the unseen or the absent:

A dream is this. I perceive objects and there is nothing there. I see men; I seem to speak to them and I hear what they answer; there is no one there and I have not spoken. It is all as if real things and real persons were there, then on waking all has disappeared, both persons and things. How does this happen?

But, first, is it true that there is nothing there? I mean, is there not presented a certain sense material to our eyes, to our ears, to our touch, etc., during sleep as well as during waking? (Bergson 1914: 15)

Bergson at least takes issue with the view of dreams put forth by Descartes in his *Meditations on First Philosophy* of 1639, in which the illusory quality of dreams leads him to a sceptical philosophy that discredits or at least urges caution in accepting all perception: 'Whatever I have accepted until now as most true has come to me through my senses. But occasionally I have found that they have deceived me, and it is unwise to trust completely those who have deceived us even once' (First Meditation). Descartes took seriously the propositions of Plato (in *Theaetatus*) and Aristotle (in the *Metaphysics*) that our lives may all be a dream. Beckett alluded to Descartes on dreams in *Murphy*, when, after having told the joke about the 'stout porter', he replays the scene in the theatre of his mind: 'He sank down on the dream of Descartes linoleum, choking and writhing like a chicken with the gapes, seeing the scene' (*Murphy* 140). The proposition is treated more seriously if obliquely as sleep rather than directly as dream in *Waiting for Godot*, where Vladimir entertains the possibility that his perception of the days, and by extension the play we watch, is a dream: 'Was I sleeping while the others suffered? Am I sleeping now? Tomorrow when I wake, or think I do, what shall I say of today? That with Estragon my friend, at this place until the fall of night, I waited for Godot? [. . .] Probably. But in all that what truth will there be?' (*CDW* 84).

Slossen's short preface to the second excerpt from Bergson's 1901 lecture offers a perceptive overview of Bergsonism: 'Professor Bergson believes that memory is imperishable, that all that we have thought, felt and experienced in past life is in some way stored up and may under favorable circumstances be revived. Thus his theory of dreams, as will be observed, forms a consistent part of Bergson's philosophy of life, according to which the totality of the past is involved in the present as a rolling snowball gathers up all that is in its path.'[12] That 'totality of life', for which

Slosson uses a 'snowball' image, is a restatement of Bergson's imagery for *durée* from *Creative Evolution*, where Bergson uses the snowball image for 'the continuous progress of the past which gnaws into the future and which swells as it advances. It is irreversible' (1944: 4–6). Slosson's focus is not on Descartes but on a more clinical application of Bergson's views as he suggests some comparisons between Bergson's study and Sigmund Freud's contemporary, more comprehensive, and clinical work on dreams in *Die Traumdeutung*, of December 1899 (the volume, according to Freud, post-dated to 1900 by the publisher, to mark the new century):[13]

> The cause of this revival of interest [in dreams] is the new point of view brought forward by Professor Bergson in the paper which is here made accessible to the English-reading public. This is the idea that we can explore the unconscious substratum of our mentality, the storehouse of our memories, by means of dreams, for these memories are by no means inert, but have, as it were, a life and purpose of their own, and strive to rise into consciousness whenever they get a chance, even into the semi-consciousness of a dream. To use Professor Bergson's striking metaphor, our memories are packed away under pressure like steam in a boiler and the dream is their escape valve. That this is more than a mere metaphor has been proved by Professor Freud and others of the Vienna school, who cure cases of hysteria by inducing the patient to give expression to the secret anxieties and emotions which, unknown to him, have been preying upon his mind. The clue to these disturbing thoughts is generally obtained in dreams or similar states of relaxed consciousness. According to the Freudians a dream always means something, but never what it appears to mean. It is symbolic and expresses desires or fears which we refuse ordinarily to admit to consciousness, either because they are painful or because they are repugnant to our moral nature. A watchman is stationed at the gate of consciousness to keep them back [Freud's Superego], but sometimes these unwelcome intruders slip past him in disguise. [. . .] Bergson's view seems to us truer as it is certainly more agreeable, that we keep stored away somewhere all our memories, the good as well as the evil, the pleasant together with the unpleasant. (Slosson, 'Introduction' to Bergson 1914: 6)

In April 1914 Bergson's lecture on dreams, called simply *Dreams* in Slosson's translation and with his introductory material reprinted from *The Independent*, was co-published by B. W. Heubsch and *The Independent*. In a footnote to the *Dreams* volume, Bergson added to the second printing, November 1914, the following acknowledgment of Freud's work: 'When the above address was delivered (1901) the work of Freud on dreams (*Die Traumdeutung*) had been already published, but "psycho-analysis" was far from having the development that it has to-day. (H. B.)' (1914: 57). Bergson's acknowledgment may be generous since in *Matter and Memory*, first published in 1896, Bergson draws a distinction between memory and perception and outlines unconscious psychical states that anticipate much of Freud's *Interpretation of Dreams* some four years later. For Slosson, Bergson is finally a pragmatist in the mode of William James and John Dewey, and so he notes, 'The pragmatic character of his philosophy appeals to the genius of the American people as is shown by the influence of the teaching of William James and John Dewey, whose point of view in this respect resembles Bergson's' ('Introduction' to Bergson 1914: 9).

Slosson's analysis, admittedly directed to a popular audience, maintains a certain currency, a duration, say, through the twenty-first century. Susan Guerlac summarizes that duration thus:

> After Deleuze and Guattari's critique of psychoanalysis, we can appreciate in Bergson another way to think unconsciousness, one that does not depend on the structure of repression (or an instance or topography of the unconscious) that psychoanalysis has enmeshed with the story and its normative gender positions. In Bergson, differences between consciousness and unconsciousness become subtle and fluid. A function of fluctuations of tension and attention in relation to action, the two registers become porous to one another. The two extremes of mental life – action and dream – inform one another interactively, as do action and memory. (Guerlac 2013: viii)

* * *

Bergson's popularity on both sides of the Atlantic, in English and French speaking intellectual communities, and indeed across continental Europe, spurred something of a cottage industry in guides and handbooks, expanded versions of J. T. Shotwell's 'Bergson's Philosophy' cited above. A case in point is George Rowland Dodson's *Bergson and the Modern Spirit: An Essay in Constructive Thought* (also cited above) (1913); Darcy B.

Kitchin's *Bergson for Beginners: A Summary of his Philosophy* (1913), revised for a new edition soon after Bergson's New York lectures,[14] Emil Carl Wilm's *Henri Bergson: A Study in Radical Evolution* (1914), and Horace Meyer Kallen's *William James and Henri Bergson: A Study of Contrasting Theories of Life* (1914). Some took a more theological approach, such as E. Hermann's *Eucken and Bergson: Their Significance for Christian Thought* (1913). Such Bergsonism as swept the US between 1911 and 1913 was already well in place in Britain by 1911, when Bergson made his first lecture tour of England. Among the most active of Bergson's early British supporters was Professor of Philosophy at Kings College, London (and head of department in 1914), H. Wildon Carr (1857–1931), who in his little introductory handbook, *Henri Bergson: The Philosophy of Change* (1911), also laid out Bergson's first UK lecture schedule:

> During the present year (1911) Monsieur Bergson has become person-ally known to large circles of philosophical students in England. In May he delivered two lectures before the University of Oxford on 'The Perception of Change' (*La Perception du Changement*. Oxford, The Clarendon Press).[15] He delivered the Huxley Lecture at the University of Birmingham on 'Life and Consciousness', published in the *Hibbert Journal*, October 1911. He also delivered four lectures before the University of London on 'The Nature of the Soul'. (Wildon Carr 1911: viii)

In his 1911 translation of *Creative Evolution*, Arthur Mitchell singled out Carr's work on Bergson thus: 'But above all we must express our acknowledgment to Mr. H. Wildon Carr, Honorary Secretary of the Aristotelian Society of London, and the writer of several studies of 'Evolution Creatrice'.[16] We asked him to be kind enough to revise the proofs of our work. He has done much to revise them: they have come from his hands with his personal mark in many places. We cannot express all that the present work owes to him' (Mitchell in Bergson 1944: vi). Carr would expand his handbook of 1911 into a longer edition, *The Philosophy of Change: A Study of the Fundamental Principle of the Philosophy of Bergson* (1914), the 91 pages of the former developing into the 222 pages of the latter. In his preface to the later work, Carr notes his own academic promotion of Bergson and the fact that his handbooks grew out of them:

This book is the outcome of a course of lectures on *The Philosophy of Bergson* delivered in the University of London. The title *The Philosophy of Change* was suggested to me by M. Bergson himself as a subtitle for the little volume of his philosophy in The People's Books [i.e., 1911]. It emphasizes the fundamental principle of the new philosophy, the principle that change is original. (Carr 1914: i)

The summer of 1911 also saw a new arts magazine, *Rhythm*, appear in London to celebrate something of a new literary spirit generated by Bergson's work, which spirit was beginning to be called 'Modernism' (although T. E. Hulme would insist on calling it 'Classicism'). Writing in the inaugural issue, one of its founders, John Middleton Murray (1889–1957),[17] expressed the Bergsonian spirit in an essay, 'Art and Philosophy', thus:

The philosophy of Bergson has of late come to a tardy recognition in England. In France it is a living artistic force. It is the open avowal of the supremacy of the intuition, of the spiritual vision of the artist in form, in words and meaning. He has shown that the concepts of the reason, while the reason remains untrue to itself, fail before the fact of Life. [. . .] We attain to the truth not by that reason which must deny the fact of continuity and of creative evolution, but by intuition, by the immediate vision of the artist in form.

Murray goes on to detail the impact of this Bergsonian spirit:

[The artist] must return to the moment of pure perception to see the essential forms, the essential harmonies of line and colour, the essential music of the world. Modernism is not the capricious outburst of intellectual dipsomania. It penetrates beneath the outward surface of the world, and disengages the rhythms that lie at the heart of things, rhythms strange to the eye, unaccustomed to the ear, primitive harmonies of the world that is and lives. (Middleton Murray 1911: 9)

His flirtations with Platonism aside, or rather his amalgam of Platonism and Romanticism, that is, this 'exploration of inner self', Murray lays out something of the desiderata of Modernism at a time when 'All human relations have shifted'.

In her 1924 essay 'Mr. Bennett and Mrs. Brown' published by Hogarth Press in October of that year, Virginia Woolf boldly announced that 'On or about December 1910, human character changed.' She offers some qualifications: 'I am not saying that one went out, as one might into a garden, and there saw that a rose had flowered, or that a hen had laid an egg. The change was not sudden and definite like that. But a change there was, nevertheless; and since one must be arbitrary, let us date it about the year 1910.' Her examples are domestic, 'homely':

> In life one can see the change, if I may use a homely illustration, in the character of one's cook. The Victorian cook lived like a levia-than in the lower depths, formidable, silent, obscure, inscrutable; the Georgian cook is a creature of sunshine and fresh air; in and out of the drawing room, now to borrow the *Daily Herald*, now to ask advice about a hat. [. . .] All human relations have shifted – those between masters and servants, husbands and wives, parents and children. And when human relations change there is at the same time a change in religion, conduct, politics, and literature. Let us agree to place one of these changes about the year 1910. (Woolf 1984: 194)

Woolf's comments, delivered first as a talk to the Society of Heretics at Cambridge University in May of 1924 under the title 'Character in Fiction', was provoked by an unfavourable review of *Jacob's Room* (1922) by Arnold Bennett in which, Bennett claimed, Woolf substituted cleverness for what should be the core of fiction, 'character-creating'. The talk, of course, pertained to more than the behaviour of downstairs staff in the new Georgian era. It called for a sweeping away of 'those sleek, smooth novels, those portentous and ridiculous biographies, that milk and watery criticism, those poems melodiously celebrating the innocence of roses and sheep which passes so plausibly for literature at the present time' (Woolf 1924: 23), Mr Bennett's work among them, of course.

A British tradition in the visual arts would also have to be swept away if this new consciousness were to be accounted for. The First Post-Impressionist Exhibition at the Grafton Galleries, organized by Bloomsbury art historian Roger Fry, whose biography Virginia Woolf would write, opened in London in November of 1910. It might be argued that such a show – or shows, since others followed, despite, or rather perhaps because of, the oppo-sition they generated – demarked a shift in human perception, altered our ways of seeing, and hence knowing, taught the public powerful alternatives to photographic realism in the visual and narrative arts. The 1910 Exhibition, which featured the likes of Cézanne, Manet, Van Gogh and Picasso, was important enough to lead to a Second Post-Impressionist Exhibition in 1912. But by 1914 even the impact Roger Fry's Exhibitions generated would be called into question as Wyndham Lewis set out to blast away as much of the old order as he could, the genteel Modernism of Post-Impressionism included, on the eve of the First World War. The pink, typographically audacious magazine Lewis launched was called simply *Blast*. T. S. Eliot, moreover, the year before he began work on his PhD at Harvard University, 'spent the academic year of 1910–11 in Paris, where he attended Henri Bergson's celebrated lectures at the Collège de France' (Menand 2007: 19). Some of Eliot's poems from this period, particularly the four 'Preludes', appeared in July 1915 in the second and final issue of *Blast*.

May of 1910 also saw the death of Edward VII, who, although he gave his name to the first decade of the twentieth century in Britain, is often seen as an extension of his mother's reign, despite the domestic exception that Woolf provided above. His son, George V, however, would rename the family; the House of Saxe-Coburg and Gotha suddenly, overnight, became the House of Windsor, the British royal family freed, at least linguistically, from its Germanic blood lines. May 1910 saw the beginning of a new Georgian era, which Virginia Woolf invokes in her critique of 'Character in Fiction', and our sense of consciousness, memory and perception, our ways of knowing, all changed.

Earlier, in 'Modern Fiction' (1919), Woolf defined the task of artists like herself against the likes of 'Mr. Wells, Mr. Bennett, and Mr. Galsworthy' in decidedly Bergsonian terms:

Examine for a moment an ordinary mind on an ordinary day. The mind receives a myriad impressions – trivial, fantastic, evanescent, or engraved with the sharpest of steel. From all sides they come, an incessant shower of innumerable atoms, and as they fall, as they shape themselves into the life of Monday or Tuesday, the accent falls differently from of old; the moment of importance came not here but there, so that, if a writer were a free man and not a slave, if he could write what he chose, not what he must, if he could base his work upon feeling and not upon conviction, there would be no plot, no comedy, no tragedy, no love interest or catastrophe in the accepted style, and perhaps not a single button sewn on as the Bond Street tailors would have it. [. . .] Life is not a series of gig lamps symmetrically arranged, life is a luminous halo, a semi-transparent envelope surrounding us from the beginning of consciousness to the end. (1984: 154)

William James might have called such a 'luminous halo' the 'fringe of consciousness': 'What must be admitted is that the definite images of traditional psychology [or literature, we might add] form but the very smallest part of our minds as they actually live', and James notes further of this halo, this fringe, the analogy now with music: 'It is just like "overtones" in music: they are not separately heard by the ear; they blend with the fundamental note, and suffuse it, and alter it; and even so do the waxing and waning brain-processes at every moment blend with and suffuse and alter the psychic effect of the processes which are at their culminating point' (James 1982). Amid so Bergsonian and Jamesian an analysis, a depiction of life as it is lived, Woolf takes her stand against materialism, or at least against narratives that focus on the material. Like the Post-Impressionist paintings she championed, Woolf was trying 'to liberate the more substantial reality that lurked behind appearances' as she details a theory, a process, that rejects mimetic representation.

In Search of the Black Cat – or, the X Factor

Such apparent assaults on common sense and 'reason' could not but generate a challenge from another group of moderns, if not 'Modernists'. Almost simultaneous with Bergson's 'tardy recognition' in English, the biologist and psychologist Hugh S. R. Elliot (1881–1930), editor of *The Letters of John Stuart Mill*, launched a counter-attack in his *Modern Science and the Illusions of Professor Bergson*,[18] published with a 'Preface' by the eminent invertebrate biologist, evolutionist and Oxford professor, Sir Ray Lankester (1847–1929), who had met both Darwin and Marx in his youth and had been taught by and worked for a time with Thomas Henry Huxley. Elliot himself would, in fact, go on to write a book called *Human Character* (1922), which deals with the difficulties of creating a 'science of human character', an enterprise at which, as he notes in his 'Preface', both Jean-Jacques Rousseau and, a century later, John Stuart Mill had failed. These are, then, preeminent men of science, of a modern if not Modernist science, of a Royal Academy science, who 'look at the universe through

materialist spectacles' and 'find no necessity therein for postulat-
ing any consciousness whatever' (Elliot 1912: 13). Their treatment
of Bergson's work, then, bordered on the savage, Lankester asserting that Bergson's books were 'worthless and unprofitable matter,
causing waste of time and confusion of thought to many of those
who are induced to read them' (Elliot 1912: vii). For scientists
like Lankester and Elliot, holdovers of a Victorian behaviourism,
consciousness, amid its various meanings, could not be studied
scientifically, was, in a sense, intangible, inconsistent, unpredictable, and so immeasurable, an unknown. Lankester complains,
further, that Bergson is introduced as a French metaphysician but
his work would be of interest only to 'the student of the aberra-
tions and monstrosities of the mind of man' (viii). The analogy
he offers in place of an argument is curious for a scientist: 'a kind
of interest such as a collector might take in a curious species of
beetle', such interest, evidently, Lankester implies, signalling an
immediate disqualification of the investigator's credibility. And
yet, one is impelled to ask why wouldn't a biologist, a psychologist, a scientist, a student if not a scholar of 'human character' (or
a metaphysician, for that matter) take an interest in deviations,
'a curious species of beetle', say, the creature potentially revealing something about at least genus and family, or perhaps all the
way up to phylum, something about beetleness or animalness and
thus something about life? That is, Lankester's off-hand dismissal
appears at the moment that entire fields of Modernist science were
emerging, that of abnormal psychology, dominated at the time by
Freud, on the one hand, and quantum mechanics and, later, the Big
Bang theory that focus on deviations from an inchoate norm, on
the other; as current theorizing has it, the creation of our universe
may, indeed, be just such an inexplicable deviation. Bergson's
most immediate foil was doubtless Théodule Ribot (1839–1916),
one of the founders of French scientific psychology who special-
ized in heredity diseases of memory, and mental illness in general,
and from 1888 onward was professor of experimental psychology
at the Collège de France, to which Bergson would be elected in
1900.[19] Ribot also kept a keen eye on English psychology, translating, with A. Espinas, Herbert Spencer's mechanistic *Principles
of Psychology* as *Principes de Psychologie*[20] (translated from the
second English edition, the first having appeared in 1855, Spencer
a scientist in whom Bergson was interested early in his career) and
writing *English Psychology*,[21] which takes the introductory survey

of the history of psychology back to the Pythagoreans, who 'confounded mathematics with philosophy'.

Lankester goes on to resurrect an old saw about philosophy, the attack in this case on metaphysics, the jibe attributed to an unidentified 'keen thinker and a great lawyer'. The activity of metaphysics in this retelling is that of 'a blind man in a dark room [although if the investigator were blind, the room's light level would hardly matter, but such redundancy may be part of the joke] hunting for a black cat [again, the cat's colour would hardly pertain] which – is not there!' (Elliot 1912: xiv). The problem, evidently, is the preoccupation with and search for the 'not there' as opposed to the ascertainably there, which seems to be defined, at least by implication, as the perceptible, the tangible, the measurable. Lankester gives the immeasurable an algebraic designation: 'The black cat which is not there is the reality represented by x. The search for it surely not a very healthy occupation either for the blind man or for those who solemnly give attention to his accounts of his subtle devices and evergreen self assurance' (xiv–xv).

Reviewing Darcy B. Kitchin's *Bergson for Beginners: A Summary of His Philosophy*, the anonymous reviewer in the 30 October 1913 issue of *The Independent* (doubtless Slossen) calls attention to another Lankester quip: 'The widening influence of Bergson's thought is shown by the increasing number of articles and books year by year which explain or criticize his philosophy. Some few are harshly hostile, as, for instance, Sir Ray Lankester, who borrows Voltaire's witticism about the Holy Roman Empire and says "the great French philosopher" is neither great nor French nor a philosopher.'

The primary objection of these materialist scientists is to Bergson's assertion, and admittedly it is that, of the materiality of time, 'that time is a stuff both "resilient and substantial"' (Lankester in Elliot 1912: xv). On the other hand, Bergson is equally attacked for his disputation of the materiality and localization of memory. If memory is a function of the brain, as Ribot argued in *The Maladies of Memory* in 1881, then it has a materiality. Bergson's position from *Matter and Memory* (1896, 1910 in English) onward, in opposition to Ribot, was to focus on a non-localized view of memory that did not reduce it to a function of the brain, although the brain has a function in a process that selects from memories those useful for particular actions. In his 'Introduction' to *Dreams*, Slossen cites Bergson's acceptance of the presidency of the British Society for Psychical Research, and he quotes liberally from Bergson's Presidential address of 28 May 1913, 'Phantasms of the Living and Psychical Research', as cited in the *Times* of London:[22]

The rôle of the brain is to bring back the remembrance of an action, to prolong the remembrance in movements. If one could see all that takes place in the interior of the brain, one would find that that which takes place there corresponds to a small part only of the life of the mind. The brain simply extracts from the life of the mind that which is capable of representation in movement. The cerebral life is to the mental life what the movements of the baton of a conductor are to the Symphony. The brain, then, is that which allows the mind to adjust itself exactly to circumstances. It is the organ of attention to life. Should it become deranged, however slightly, the mind is no longer fitted to the circumstances; it wanders, dreams. Many forms of mental alienation are nothing else. But from this it results that one of the rôles of the brain is to limit the vision of the mind, to render its action more efficacious. This is what we observe in regard to the memory, where the rôle of the brain is to mask the useless part of our past in order to allow only the useful remembrances to appear. Certain useless recollections, or dream remembrances, manage nevertheless to appear also, and to form a vague fringe around the distinct recollections. It would not be at all surprising if perceptions of the organs of our senses, useful perceptions, were the result of a selection or of a canalization worked by the organs of our senses in the interest of our action, but that there should yet be around those perceptions a fringe of vague perceptions, capable of becoming more distinct in extraordinary, abnormal cases. Those would be precisely the cases with which psychical research would deal. (Bergson cited by Slossen in Bergson 1914: 11–12)

That is, one can find something of a Modernist convergence here among Lankester's immeasurable 'x factor', James's 'fringe of consciousness', Bergson's 'fringe of vague perceptions' and Woolf's 'luminous halo'.

Evolution vs. Involution[23]

Among the destabilizing ideas that Bergson has put forward is his critique of evolution. While sympathetic to much of Darwin's sequentiation of life forms, he objected to Darwin's natural selection since it was based on life's responses and adjustments to external, material forces, evolution shaped by environment. Summarizing Bergson's relationship to Darwin, Mark Hanson notes, that Bergson rejects 'the core principle of Darwinism, which explains evolution in terms of an external principle of differentiation' (Hanson 2000: 7). With his notion of creative evolution, by contrast, Bergson furnishes an alternate understanding of differentiation: 'for him, evolution follows an internal principle that explains genetic change not as the result of selection from purely contingent variations but rather of a "continuity of genetic energy"' (27). Bergson's view would locate the driving force not externally but internally, tracing it to an inner life force, an *élan vital*, or what Deleuze will finally call neo-Darwinism or involution, a term with currency in philosophy, biology and mathematics to suggest an inward turn. The term for Deleuze is thus something of an appropriation since historically involution also carried suggestions of an enfolding, a turning in on itself, and/or a degradation, as in the shrinking of an organ, say, which suggests paradoxical forces of, at once, a new or renewed vitalism and a deterioration or degeneration. Such a paradox remains at the heart of Beckett's most entropic drama, *Fin de partie/Endgame*, for instance, where everything, all systems, seem to be running down as 'something is taking its course', even as that something is a constant reinvention if not a regeneration amid that process, a regeneration not only of creativity, as in Hamm's narrative, but the indestructibility of dramatic renewal itself, in the form, in the art of performance, in the theatre itself. A 'creative involution' both breaks free from a linear model of evolution, as a tree, say, evolution progressing towards or culminating in an end, a telos, usually 'man' or humanity, and from a diminution or contraction, a degeneration, in favour of multiple reinventions and regenerations. Such an interplay or paradox between deterioration and regeneration concludes (if that is the word), or at least brings to a close the narrative process, with its copulative flow, the incessant commas of the dream sequence, the fringe of consciousness that Beckett has called *The Unnamable*:

> I don't know, perhaps it's a dream, all a dream, that would surprise me, I'll wake, in the silence, and never sleep again, it will be I, or dream, dream again, dream of a silence, a dream silence, full of murmurs, I don't know, that's all words, never wake, all words,

there's nothing else, you must go on, that's all I know, they're going to stop, I know that well, I can feel it, they're going to abandon me, it will be the silence, for a moment, a good few moments, or it will be mine, the lasting one, that didn't last, that still lasts, it will be I, you must go on, I can't go on, you must go on, I'll go on, you must say words, as long as there are any, until they find me, until they say me, strange pain, strange sin, you must go on. Perhaps it's done already. Perhaps they have said me already. Perhaps they have carried me to the threshold of my story, before the door that opens on my story, that would surprise me, if it opens, it will be I, it will be the silence, where I am, I don't know, I'll never know, in the silence you don't know, you must go on, I can't go on, I'll go on. (*Three Novels* 414)

Much of this involutionary turn is outlined by Deleuze and Guattari in one of the *Thousand Plateaus* called 'Memories of a Bergsonian' (Deleuze and Guattari 1987: 237–9), where involution suggests a 'very special becoming-animal traversing human beings and sweeping them away, affecting the animal no less than the human'. These are myths, 'fragments of tales', the *Three novels* something of a 'becoming animal' without deterioration, a multidirectional becoming, a becoming other, not 'a playing animal or imitating an animal. [. . .] Becoming produces nothing other than itself':

If there is originality in neoevolutionism, it is attributable in part to phenomena of this kind in which evolution does not go from something less differentiated to something more differentiated [. . .] Accordingly, the term we would prefer for this form of evolution between hetero-geneous terms is 'involution' on the condition that involution is in no way confused with regression. Becoming is involutionary, involution is creative. (Deleuze and Guattari 1987: 238)

As early as 1917, in his collection of essays and reviews called *Unicorns*, the American art, music and book critic James Huneker (1857–1921) took up the issue of 'Creative Involution', particu-larly through a book of that title by Cora L. Williams, 'an unusual book by a woman', notes Huneker, one which explores 'the fourth dimension' of space from a solidly mathematical perspec-tive and focuses on 'the conduct of certain molecules and crystals' (Huneker 1917: 195). As Williams noted in the unpaginated Preface to the second, slightly augmented edition of her book: 'The physical sciences are using time as the fourth dimension of space'

(1925). This essentially is the position that Albert Einstein will take in his debates with Bergson on simultaneity.

Huneker himself offers what appears to be a refutation of a mechanistic materialism: 'Man can't live on machinery alone, and the underfed soul of the past period of positivism craves more spiritual nourishment to-day. [. . .] It is a pluralistic world now, and lordly Intuition – a dangerous vocable – rules over mere mental process' (1917: 196–7). He goes on to note Williams's comment that 'Creative Involution is to supersede the Darwinian evolution' (198), and praises this fourth dimension or spiritual world, time as the fourth dimension of space, the world of the black cat, say, thus: 'Time may be in two dimensions. Heraclites before Bergson compared Time to a river always flowing, yet a permanent river' (197). Reviewing John Mullarkey's collection of essays, *The New Bergson*, for the *Times Higher Education Supplement*, Ray Scott Percival observes that

> For Einstein, time forms the fourth dimension of a so-called Parmenidean 'block universe'. [. . .] a block universe because the whole of reality – past, present and future – is thought of as fixed. Any subjective feeling of duration is merely an illusion. For Parmenides there was nothing new under the sun. [. . .] At the other extreme, Heraclitus taught that everything is in flux: one cannot step into the same river twice, as new waters continually flow in upon one. Bergson's philosophy of time is somewhere between these two extremes. He argues that the universe shows a real succession of events, and grows by the emergence of radically unforeseeable new things that cannot be reduced to what went before. The emergence of life and the self-conscious mind are examples. The world itself is creative in as fundamental a way as is possible. (Percival 2000: n.p.)

In a lecture before the British academy on 20 March 1918, H. Wilden Carr points out that

> In Bergson's doctrine a certain static view of external reality is absolutely essential to the *practical form of our internal activity*, and this prejudices and handicaps the mind in its efforts to attain a theoretical concept of the reality itself. An intellectual effort is called for from all who would obtain true philosophical insight, an effort to overcome a bias, which bias is very part [*sic*] of human nature itself. Such an effort would be impossible, even inconceivable, and therefore in an absolute

sense absurd, were the intellect the whole of our cognitive nature, were there not also in that nature another cognitive mode. This is Bergson's doctrine of intuition. (Carr 1918: 4, emphasis added)

Carr too returns us to the Ancient Greek dispute, the paradox of motion, with an argument from common sense: 'Let any one compare the two great paradoxes of Greek philosophy, the "nothing moves" of Zeno and the "all things flow" of Hericleitus [*sic*], and test for himself which to his own mind is the most contrary to his natural inclination' (1918: 5). Carr goes on to argue, prefiguring the famous contretemps between Bergson and Einstein, 'time [. . .] is really space. It is a dimension, but it is not even a special non-spatial kind of dimension; it is itself spatial, and without spatial category absolutely incomprehensible.' As Carr summarizes Bergson's position: 'This, however, is not true time', what Bergson will call 'true duration' (1918: 6).

Huneker then seems to reject 'positivism' and mechanism and goes on to praise 'Intuition' (1917: 197). He is careful to separate himself from Bergsonism, however, and to insist that 'Miss Williams is not a Bergsonian', although she opens *Creative Involution* with something of an ode to, if not Bergson, then at least to Bergsonism: 'Creative Evolution (After Bergson)': 'No prestablished harmony this', she writes. Huneker's argument, however, is finally and essentially *ad hominem*:

Henri Bergson is a mystagogue, and all mystagogues are mytho-maniacs. He has yet to answer Professor Hugh S. R. Elliot's three questions: 1. Bergson says that 'Time is a stuff both resistant and sub-stantial.' Where is the specimen on which this allegation is founded? 2. Consciousness [and he might have added memory here as well] is to some extent independent of cerebral structure. [. . .] 3. Instinct [or more to the point, perhaps, intuition, although Bergson uses the terms interchangeably at times] leads us to comprehension of life that intel-lect can never give. Will Professor Bergson furnish instances of the success of instinct [read intuition] in biological inquiries where intel-lect has failed? (Huneker 1917: 201)

Huneker here quotes Elliot's very short conclusion (1912: 245), each point of which corresponds to one of the three books Bergson then had in print, 1. *Matter and Memory*, 2. *Time and Free Will*, and 3. *Creative Evolution*, and he goes on to praise both Elliot's 'solidly reasoned confutation' and Lankester's overarching thesis expressed in his preface to the Elliot volume that Bergsonism offers little more than 'metaphysical curiosities' in what should be seen as a materially driven world.

Nevertheless, as Huneker suggests, Lankester's absolute empiricism or positivism is itself at least under stress in this period, in face of what we might call the move from an absolute sense of space and time (and so eternal, as Aristotle suggested, a universe with neither starting nor end points), to a sense of their relativity, which we will suggest is a (if not the) major concern or driving force of Beckett's wartime novel *Watt*. Such theories of relativity are developed over and dominate the twentieth century and continue through into the twenty-first: in Max Plank's theory of relativity of 1906, Einstein's space-time curvature of special relativity in the four published papers of 1905, his General Theory of Relativity of 1915 and his quest for a classical unification theory, the emergence of the 'Copenhagen interpretation', Niels Bohr's wave function collapse of 1924–27,[24] through to Steven Hawking's theorizing of time, string theory or its refinement M-theory, the experimental confirmation in 2012 of the previously theorized 'God particle', the Higgs boson (still in some doubt, however), and Stephen P. Martin's theory of supersymmetry. What becomes quantum mechanics, particle physics, particle theory, or quantum field theory, which themselves might be dubbed something of a philosophy of change, has dominated physical science for over a century, producing theory often, but not always, confirmed by experiment; this despite such challenges as those posed by Lankester and thought experiments such as that of Schrödinger's cat (the counterpart, perhaps to Lankester's black cat).[25]

Clov's dream in *Endgame*, we may recall, is a return to an inchoate world, to a state anterior to deviations: 'I love order. It's my dream. A world where all would be silent and still and each thing in its last place, under the last dust' (*CDW* 120). Such a connection to a new science and its links to philosophy, in this case metaphysics, is emphasized early on by H. Wildon Carr in *The Philosophy of Change: A Study of the Fundamental Principle of the Philosophy of Bergson*, where he suggests that Bergsonism is at the heart of such change:

> It seems to me that the present generation is witnessing a wide extension of science in directions unimagined by, and inconceivable to, the

last generation. In two directions especially experiment is opening up realms of reality the existence of which has until now been unsuspected, and the discovery of which is probably destined to widen immeasurably the horizon of human knowledge and thereby increase indefinitely human power. One of these new realms of reality may be fitly described as the world beyond the atom, the other is the spiritual (or mental, if that word is preferred) reality revealed in the new method and science of psychoanalysis. (Carr 1914: i)

Carr would continue this line of connecting contemporary science with philosophy by translating Bergson's *Mind Energy: Lectures and Essays* (1920; in preparation when the war of 1914 broke out, the publication was delayed some years), which included essays and lectures from the period 1901–13, particularly the lecture on dreams from 1901 translated by Slossen, the lecture on psychical research excerpted by Slossen for his 'Introduction' to the *Dream* lecture and book, and 'The Soul and the Body' from 28 April 1912.[26] As Carr notes in his 'Translator's Preface': 'The separate articles here collected and selected are, partly lectures in the exposition of philosophical theory, partly detailed psychological investigations and metaphysical research. [. . .] They are chosen by M. Bergson with the view of illustrating his concept that reality is fundamentally a spiritual activity' (Bergson 1920: v).[27]

Neutral Monism

Unlike his successor, John Dewey, William James (1842–1910) would become an early and consistent defender, commenting on Bergson's complexity in the sixth of his Hibbert lectures delivered at Manchester College in 1908, 'On the Present Situation in Philosophy'. Lecture six was entitled 'Bergson and His Critique of Intellectualism':

> I have to confess that Bergson's originality is so profuse that many of his ideas baffle me entirely. I doubt whether any one understands him all over, so to speak; and I am sure that he would himself be the first to see that this must be, and to confess that things which he himself has not yet thought out clearly had yet to be mentioned and have a tentative place assigned to them in his philosophy. (James 1909: 59)

In this lecture, first published in the *Hibbert Journal* in April 1909, then reprinted in *A Pluralistic Universe*, James goes on to establish Bergson as a critical starting point for a revolution in human thought and analysis of consciousness: 'Originality in men dates from nothing previous, other things date from it, rather. [. . .] Old fashioned professors, whom his ideas quite fail to satisfy, nevertheless speak of his talent almost with bated breath, while the youngsters flock to him as to a master' (1909: 59–60). In his 'Translators Note' to *Creative Evolution*, Arthur Mitchell opens with praise for James:

> In the writing of this English translation of Professor Bergson's most important work, I was helped by the friendly interest of Professor William James, to whom I owe the illumination of much that was dark to me as well as the happy rendering of certain words and phrases for which an English equivalent was difficult to find. His sympathetic appreciation of Professor Bergson's thought is well known, and he has expressed his admiration for it in one of the chapters of *A Pluralistic Universe*. It was his intention, had he lived to see the completion of this translation, himself to introduce it to the English readers in a prefatory note. (Bergson 1944: v)

Bergson would find his strongest resistance, however, among contemporary positivist philosophers in the UK. Bertrand Russell, for one, had thoroughly engaged and assessed Bergson's work for a lecture called 'The Philosophy of Bergson' delivered before 'The Heretics' at Trinity College, Cambridge, on 11 March 1912 (erroneously cited as 1913 in the published volume[28]), and so just two years after the bulk of Bergson was published in English in 1910–11 and almost a year before Bergson's American lectures. Russell had met Bergson in Paris the year before, in March, and he would see him again at the meeting of the Aristotelian Society on Monday, 30 October 1911, where Russell would present a lecture on 'universals and particulars' for which he prepared by reading 'a great deal of Bergson', which ideas form one theme running through Russell's anti-Bergson critique (Griffin 1992: 394). He had dinner with Bergson and George Bernard Shaw two nights earlier, on 28 October, on which he reported, 'all England has gone mad about him for some reason. It was an amusing dinner' (Griffin 1992: 399). But Russell's take on Bergsonism was severe from the first:

Bergson's philosophy, though it shows constructive imagination, seems to me wholly devoid of argument and quite gratuitous; he never thinks about fundamentals but just invents pretty fairy tales. Personally, he is urbane, gentle, rather feeble physically, with an extraordinarily clever mouth, suggesting the adjective 'fin' [that is, delicate, perhaps . . .]. He is too set to be able to understand or answer objections to his views. (Griffin 1992: 400)

Russell's talk to the Heretics was first published in *The Monist* on 22 July 1912, then as a monograph, *The Philosophy of Bergson*, in 1914,[29] revised and collected in his *A History of Western Philosophy* in 1945,[30] and, finally, shortened, as Bergson's philosophical reputation declined and so he became less formidable an adversary, for the edition of 1961. Between 1912 and 1961, however, Russell's position on key issues of Bergsonism had changed, yet he kept repeating his earlier objections: 'Russell had changed his mind on this question [separation of subject and object] when adopting neutral monism, but his criticism was repeated verbatim in the *History of Western Philosophy*', even as 'in the next chapter he praised William James for denying a fundamental distinction between subject and object' (Wood 1963: 198). Much of Russell's support for the metaphysics called 'neutral monism' is laid out in *The Analysis of Mind* (1921), *An Outline of Philosophy* (1927, 1951), and *The Analysis of Matter* (1927). The idea that reality is a 'neutral' unity, neither wholly material nor immaterial, neither wholly mental nor physical, is decidedly Bergsonian; rather, it is the very core of Bergsonism.

Russell's talk was designed, at least in part, to counter the enthusiastic championing of Bergson by T. E. Hulme, who himself delivered a talk before the Heretics on 'Anti-Romanticism and Original Sin' on 25 February 1912, which 'anti-Romanticism' formed much of the core of what would become imagism, or *Imagisme*, if not modern poetry, or Modernism itself. Shortly thereafter he delivered a lecture specifically on Bergson – 'Bergson's Theory of Art', which he found, curiously, 'exactly the same as Schopenhauer's' (Hulme 1924: 149) – to the students at Girton College (the residential college for women at Cambridge), and four subsequent lectures in London in 1913, with a decidedly Deleuzian title, 'The Philosophy of Intensive Manifolds', these as Hulme was translating Bergson's *An Introduction to Metaphysics*.[31]

Russell's attack on Bergsonian 'intuition' was countered in part by his niece, Karin Costelloe, whom he had tutored as she was preparing for her Tripos (on which she received a First). She wrote a paper on Bergson at Newnham in 1910 (Griffin 1992: 336) and published a pointed response to her tutor four years later, 'An Answer to Mr. Bertrand Russell's Article on the Philosophy of Bergson', published in *The Monist* (Costelloe 1914: 145–55), where two years earlier Russell's lecture had appeared. Costelloe notes straightforwardly, 'Mr. Russell is therefore wrong' and that he 'caricatures this theory'. Russell's summary of the issues, however, is often pithily accurate, up to a point: 'Intellect is the power of seeing things as separate one from another, and matter is that which is separated into distinct things. In reality there are no separate solid things, only the endless stream of becoming, in which nothing becomes and there is nothing that this nothing Becomes' (Russell 1912: 324). Costelloe defends this basic Bergsonian principle of the interpenetration or comingling of matter and spirit, of subject and object, joined in the process of perception through 'pure intuition':

> Thought about, knowledge by, concepts [what Russell calls 'intellect' above], involves the distinction between subject and object. It is only in *pure intuition* that Bergson ever claims that this distinction is transcended. It may fairly be questioned whether such a claim can be justified [the position of Elliot and Lankester, say], but in any case criticisms levelled against Bergson's theory and perception as though it applied to conceptual thought will always be wide of the mark. (Costelloe 1914: 146, emphasis added)[32]

The Russell/Hulme conflict at Cambridge played out before the Heretics Club was one between amateur and professional philosopher at a university dominated by ordinary language philosophy, and the Vienna school in general, even as Hulme's strong opposition to and Russell's strong advocacy of pacifism fuelled their animosity.[33] For Russell and his band and brand of New Philosophers at Cambridge, Bergson's new philosophy simply lacked method,[34] although Russell began to move away from his strict empirical stance and move closer to a Humean idea of the neutrality of basic entities,[35] what William James called 'the primal stuff or material in the world', of which there exists a plurality, as early as 1918, but certainly by 1921. The neutrality of basic entities suggests that percepts or objects can be either, depending on particular contexts, that is, mental and physical are two ways of organizing the same monist entities.[36]

* * *

In the early years of the twentieth century, it appeared that Bergson would lead the revolution in human consciousness and rewrite the narrative of the human that would dominate Modernism. In *A New Philosophy: Henri Bergson*, Edouard Le Roy, Bergson's chief French disciple, would mark the shift in human consciousness, or 'human character', with the emergence of Bergsonism:

> Beyond any doubt, and by common consent, Mr. Henri Bergson's work will appear to future eyes among the most characteristic, fertile, and glorious of our era. It marks a never-to-be-forgotten date in history; it opens up a phase of metaphysical thought; it lays down a principle of development the limits of which are indeterminable; and it is after cool consideration, with full consciousness of the exact value of words, that we are able to pronounce the revolution which it effects equal in importance to that effected by Kant, or even by Socrates. [. . .] The curtain drawn between ourselves and reality, enveloping everything including ourselves in its illusive folds, seems of a sudden to fall, dissipated by enchantment, and display to the mind depths of light till then undreamt, in which reality itself, contemplated face to face for the first time, stands fully revealed. The revelation is overpowering, and once vouchsafed will never afterwards be forgotten. (Le Roy 1912: 1)

Le Roy argues that with the advent of Bergson, 'the revolution [. . .] on a never-to-be-forgotten date in history', *has occurred* and that, in Woolf's famous phrase, 'human character changed'. Karin Costelloe reviewed Le Roy's book enthusiastically for the *International Journal of Ethics*, suggesting that 'M. Le Roy rightly claims that the most original and essential thing in Bergson's philosophy is his new method of thought. Critics completely misunderstanding him sometimes accuse him of discrediting all use of reason and preaching a return to effortless immediacy' (Costelloe 1913: 103). The comment seems again pointedly directed at her uncle. Such a poetic revelation as Le Roy details will be echoed by the sublime image of Beckett's Krapp standing on the Kingstown pier in a howling storm. Krapp seems to have made little of this epiphany.

'Say a Body. Where None.'

Bergson's conception of memory and/or dreams, his focus on perception, and its inadequacies, the ill-seen, the ill-heard, and, consequently and inevitably, the ill-said, his sense of action and betweenness, his critique of movement and stillness, his analysis of the will, that is, free will as the faculty of creativity, all serve as a useful structure for much of Samuel Beckett's thought and creative output. In particular, for the spectral in the late dramatic, narrative and televisual work, where hazy, often fragmented or not fully-formed images of a persistent and ineluctable past comingle with, impinge on, cross-pollinate with and insinuate themselves into, or more fully and incessantly become, some form of the present, as if the present were only an accumulated recurrence and reconstituted past in a waking or sleeping, or in some mode, a moment, say, or state in between, images that suggest not so much a debilitating haunting as a regenerative desire, but desire as a creative force, as reinvention or creation. These are, in many respects, images of duration, particularly of what Bergson calls 'inner duration', which 'is the continuous life of a memory which prolongs the past into the present, the present either containing within it in a distinct form the ceaselessly growing image of the past, or, more profoundly, showing by its continual change of quality the heavier and still heavier load we drag behind us as we grow older' (Bergson 1912b: 44). At times such a heavy load of the past is painful or assailing, tinged, as it is, with regret, as in *Krapp's Last Tape*, where it is mechanically stored and where this 'ceaselessly growing' is rendered as a warehouse of 'spools' complete with library catalogue, or in *Eh, Joe*, where the past might be strangled, or in the late masterwork *Footfalls* where time, being and memory become interlaced and comingled in an inseparable flow, a flux, if a controlled flux, but such flow, such images, are or can be more benign as well, agents of creative reflection and reinvention as in *That Time*, '. . . but the clouds . . .', and 'Ghost Trio', say. Such a state of in betweenness opens and dominates Beckett's late extended narratives, excessively punctuated and so emphatically segmented, the almost stuttering *Worstward Ho* in particular:

On. Say on. Be said on. Somehow on. Till nohow on. Said nohow on.

Say for be said. Missaid. From now say for missaid.

Say a body [i.e., missay a body]. Where none. No mind. Where none. That at least. A Place. Where none. For the body. To be in. Move in. Out of. Back into. No. No out. Only in. Stay in. On in. Still.

All of old. Nothing else ever. Ever tried. Ever failed. No matter. Try again. Fail again. Fail better. All of old. Nothing else ever. Ever tried. Ever failed. No matter. Try again. Fail again. Fail better. (*Worstward Ho* 89)

Such failures of language are punctuated by intense narrative segmentation and isolation in paragraph blocks, a stuttering of failure and renewal towards a possibility of a language yet to be born. Moreover, since memory, for Bergson, was independent of brain function and so not materialized as or warehoused in a bodily organ, it could, theoretically at least, escape, roam, persist as consciousness, say, beyond biological brain or bodily function or exist in some form detached from brain and body. Bergson's study of aphasia in *Matter and Memory* suggested that memory and so mind (or spirit, or soul) is or can be separate from the body, which disconnection might have suggested a certain congruence for Beckett between Bergson and Descartes, the creative possibility of which would be the externalization of memory manifest through voices. Bergson was most revolutionary when he challenged the traditions of western philosophy and offered us a new way of thinking, and hence a new way of reading, one that 'neither depends on a point of view nor relies on any symbol'. Instead it requires of the reader a 'kind of *intellectual sympathy* by which one places oneself within an object in order to coincide with what is unique in it and consequently inexpressible' (Bergson 1912b: 6). Such a method of thinking and, subsequently, of reading 'is an extended act of intuition. The method and the concepts are thus inseparable; they are one and the same', as Mary Anne Gillies describes it (2013: 11). Such a method will be most helpful for Samuel Beckett as a thinker, reader and writer, and will likewise help Beckett's readers enter his texts, for they are best read from the inside, the reader part of the process rather than apart from it. Beckett's life, his thought, his work will repeatedly explore, entertain and intersect the arc of such philosophical strains, these lines of flight, this new narrative of the human with its emphasis on consciousness and perpetual process, and featuring intuition as a method. He will create an art, a poetics, a literature not of interiors per se, nor of discrete characters or beings, not even of pre- or sub-human creatures, but of the interior of thought itself. At what points and to what degrees such intersections occur, how Beckett's 'modernity' reflects an immanent spirit some might see as religious or mystical, as sympathetic with strains of the Romantic spirit, even as he is decidedly, remains committedly, avant-garde, will constitute the commerce of the subsequent essays.

Notes

1. On this issue in particular see J. Alexander Gunn, *Bergson and His Philosophy*, New York: E. P. Dutton and Co., 1920. Reviewed by E. C. Wilm in *The Philosophical Review* XXX:5 (September 1921), 534–5. For an assessment of such Catholic Modernism and Irish literature see Geert Lernout, *Help My Unbelief: James Joyce and Religion*, London: Bloomsbury Academic, 2010.

2. Paul-Antoine Miquel critiques this passage thus: 'Of course, we can conclude that this analogy is nothing but a pure anthropomorphism. How can we compare the continuity of genetic energy with the human stream of consciousness? Are we not fantasizing, in the strict Bergsonian meaning of the word? Are we not instinctively putting some human attributes in Nature in order to explain its properties? But in *The Origin of Species* Darwin deals with a very similar analogy. As a man selects profitable variations for his own good, Nature also selects favorable variations "for and through the good of each being." Are we not attributing to it some active or "divine power"? Are we not putting a will in Nature, like in human consciousness? Darwin examines the question in the sixth edition of the book. The insightful answer that he gives is that "Nature" personifies the action of a very great number of natural laws, then, the action of complexity. It is, therefore, an objective complexity such as "universal attraction", for instance, and not a subjective property' (Miquel 2005: 1156).

3. According to http://en.wikipedia.org/wiki/Henri_Bergson.

4. Given the title, some potential confusion might be generated with Edouard Le Roy's *A New Philosophy: Henri Bergson* (1912).

5. The 'Introduction' was retranslated into English in 1946, collected and printed along with the two lectures Bergson delivered at Oxford University in 1911, just after his work began to appear in English. These were gathered with other unpublished essays and lectures in *The Creative Mind: An Introduction to Metaphysics*, published

by the Philosophical Library, the new translations by Mabelle L. Andison.

6. Dewey's book is fundamentally inductive and pragmatic not intuitive, and grew out of his work at his 'Laboratory School' at the University of Chicago. It focuses particularly on reforming and so modernizing educational practice, as he details in his 'Preface': 'Our schools are troubled with a multiplication of studies, each in turn having its own multiplication of materials and principles. Our teachers find their tasks made heavier in that they have come to deal with pupils individually and not merely in mass. Unless these steps in advance are to end in distraction, some clew of unity, some principle that makes for simplification, must be found. This book represents the conviction that the needed steadying and centralizing factor is found in adopting as the end of endeavor that attitude of mind, that habit of thought, which we call scientific. This scientific attitude of mind might, conceivably, be quite irrelevant to teaching children and youth. But this book also represents the conviction that such is not the case; that the native and unspoiled attitude of childhood, marked by ardent curiosity, fertile imagination, and love of experimental inquiry, is near, very near, to the attitude of the scientific mind. If these pages assist any to appreciate this kinship and to consider seriously how its recognition in educational practice would make for individual happiness and the reduction of social waste, the book will amply have served its purpose' (1910: Preface). Much of Bergson's work, of course, will not only take serious issue with 'that habit of thought, which we call scientific' but will offer intuitive alternatives.

7. Owned and published by *The Independent Weekly*.

8. These reviews are summarized in *Book Review Digest*, 1913, archived online at: https://archive.org/stream/bookreviewdigest19139hwwi/bookreviewdigest19139hwwi_djvu.txt. Other reviews of Bergson's work can be found at http://www.ibiblio.org/HTMLTexts/John_Alexander_Gunn/Bergson_And_His_Philosophy/bibliography-part 2-3.html.

9. Shotwell, who became Professor of International Relations at Columbia University, was nominated for the Nobel Peace Prize in 1952, a year in which no award was made however.

10. Slosson himself was quite an interesting figure of his time. While working for *The Independent* he travelled to Europe to interview leading philosophers and writers, Henri Bergson and H. G. Wells among them. For more background on Slosson see http://en.wikipedia.org/wiki/Edwin_Emery_Slosson.

11. *The Independent* 76, 23 October 1913, 160–3, and 30 October 2013, 200–3.

12. *The Independent* 76, 30 October, 200.

13. Freud's *The Interpretation of Dreams* appeared in English a year earlier than Bergson's *Dreams*, in 1913, translated by A. A. Brill, New York: The Macmillan Co.; London: George Allen and Co.

14. The second edition of 1914 adds a summary of 'three of Professor Bergson's more recent addresses and a note entitled "Bergson and Science"'.

15. Available at http://fr.wikisource.org/wiki/La_Perception_du_change ment/Texte_entier. Both of these Oxford lectures were finally collected in *The Creative Mind*.

16. *Proceedings of the Aristotelian Society*, vols ix. and x., and *Hibbert Journal* for July 1910 [note as in the original].

17. Murray would take over the editorship of the very influential *Athenaeum* in 1919.

18. Number 403 in the Columbia bibliography, with reviews at nos. 388, 417 and 453, no. 388 by H. Wildon Carr.

19. For the politics of such appointments and the emergence of scientific psychology and sociology in late nineteenth-century France, see John I. Brooks, *The Eclectic Legacy: Academic Philosophy and the Human Sciences in Nineteenth-century France*, Newark, Delaware: University of Delaware Press, 1998.

20. Published in Paris by Librairie Germer Baillière et Co., 1875, and Félix Alcan, 1892, available online at https://archive.org/details/ principesdepsyco2spengoog.

21. Théodule Ribot, *English Psychology*, London: Henry S. King, 1873; New York: D. Appleton and Company, 1874. Includes Ribot's essays on and analyses of David Hartley, James Mill, Herbert Spencer, Alexander Bain, George Henry Lewes, Samuel Bailey, John Stuart Mill.

22. A very useful annotated chronology can be found in *Henri Bergson: Key Writings*, ed. Keith Ansell Pearson and John Mullarkey, London: Bloomsbury, 2002, pp. viii–xi.

23. For an excellent overview of contemporary evolutionary theory, Neo-Darwinism, and complexity theory see Keith Ansell Pearson, 'Bergson and Creative Evolution / Involution: Exposing the Transcendental Illusion of Organismic Life', in Mullarkey 1999: 146–67.

24. For a detailed portrayal of the consequences of such a theory during the Second World War, just before Bohr escaped Denmark for the

United States and worked on the Manhattan Project, see Michael Frayn's excellent play, *Copenhagen* (1998), about this Heisenberg / Bohr meeting in 1941; see also the follow-up (with Davis Burke), *The Copenhagen Papers: An Intrigue* (2000). For the issues of quantum mechanics during the Cold War rendered as theatre see Tom Stoppard's *Hapgood* (1988).

25. For a good overview see Timothy S. Murphy, 'Beneath Relativity: Bergson and Bohm on Absolute Time', in Mullarkey 1999: 66–81.

26. *Mind Energy* includes the following lectures and essays: 'Life and Consciousness', 'The Soul and Body', '"Phantasms of the Living" and "Psychical Research",' 'Dreams', 'Memory of the Present and False Recognition', 'Intellectual Effort', 'Brain and Thought: A Philosophical Illusion'.

27. This in contrast, we might note, to the materialist and so pragmatist assurances that Bergson offered Dewey before and during his New York lectures of 1913.

28. Bertrand Russell, *The Philosophy of Bergson*, Cambridge: Bowes and Bowes, 1914. The book's front matter notes: 'Mr. Russell's criticism of Bergson was read before "The Heretics", in Trinity College, on March 11th, 1913, and was *afterwards* published in *The Monist*, July 1912' (emphasis added).

29. The volume included a reply by H. Wildon Carr, Secretary of the Aristotelian Society, and a short rejoinder by Russell in which he acknowledges some of his excesses.

30. Bertrand Russell, *A History of Western Philosophy*, London: George Allen and Unwin, 1945.

31. Both of these lectures, along with notes for four subsequent London lectures on Bergson, were published after Hulme's death at the front in 1917 as *Speculations*, edited by Hulme's friend Herbert Read and published under the auspices of the International Library of Psychology, Philosophy, and Scientific Method, C. K. Ogden, General Editor, by Keegan Paul, Trench, Trubner & Co., Ltd. in London and Harcourt, Brace & Co., Inc. in New York in 1924.

32. Costelloe also published 'What Bergson Means by "Interpenetration"', *Proceedings of the Aristotelian Society*, New Series, 13 (1912–13), 131–55. This is doubtless the lecture that Virginia Woolf attended on 4 February 1913 (see Banfield 2000: 34). Almost a decade later and under her married name, Karin Stephen, Costelloe published *The Misuse of Mind: A Study of Bergson's Attack on Intellectualism*, which includes a Prefatory letter by Bergson (London: Kegan Paul, Trench, Trubner & Co., Ltd., 1922). Leonard Woolf famously

claimed that his wife, Virginia, never read Bergson (see Banfield 2000: n. 393).

33. They would also be at odds over the ideology of the First World War: Russell the pacifist and Hulme the militarist who would lose his life in that war.

34. See Edward P. Comentale and Andrzej Gasiorek, eds, *T. E. Hulme and the Question of Modernism*, London: Ashgate Publishing, 2006.

35. See David Hume, *Treatise on Human Nature*, London: John Noon, 1739: 'I shall at first suppose; that there is only a single existence, which I shall call indifferently *object* or *perception*, according as it shall seem best to suit my purpose, understanding by both of them what any common man means by hat, or shoe, or any other impression, convey'd to him by his senses . . .' (366). Also: 'What we call a *mind*, is nothing but a heap or collection of different perceptions, united together by certain relations [. . .] Now as every perception is distinguishable from another, and may be consider'd separately existent; it evidently follows, that there is no absurdity in separating any particular perception from the mind; that is, in breaking off all its relations, with that connected mass of perceptions, which constitute a thinking being [. . .] If the name of *perception* renders not this separation from a mind absurd and contradictory, the name of *object*, standing for the very same thing, can never render their conjunction impossible. External objects are seen, and felt, and become present to the mind; that is, they acquire such a relation to a connected heap of perceptions, as to influence them very considerably in augmenting their number by present reflexions and passions, and in storing the memory with ideas. The same continu'd and uninterrupted Being may, therefore, be sometimes present to the mind, and sometimes absent from it, without any real or essential change in the Being itself. An interrupted appearance to the sense implies not necessarily an interruption in the existence. The supposition of the continu'd existence of sensible objects or perceptions involves no contradiction' (207–8).

36. Comentale and Gasiorek, eds, *T. E. Hulme and the Question of Modernism*.

References

Ardoin, Paul, S. E. Gontarski, and Laci Mattison, eds (2013) *Understanding Bergson, Understanding Modernism*, New York: Bloomsbury Academic.

Banfield, Ann (2000) *The Phantom Table: Woolf, Fry, Russell and the Epistemology of Modernism*, Cambridge: Cambridge University Press.

Barnard, G. William (2011) *The Living Consciousness: The Metaphysical Vision of Henri Bergson*, Albany, New York: SUNY Press.

Bergson, Henri (1912a) *The Introduction to a New Philosophy*, trans. Sidney Littman, Boston: John W. Luce & Co.

Bergson, Henri (1912b) *An Introduction to Metaphysics*, trans. T. E. Hulme, New York: G. P. Putnam's Sons.

Bergson, Henri (1914) *Dreams*, trans. with an Introduction by Edwin E. Slosson, New York: B. W. Huebsch, http://www.gutenberg.org/files /20842/20842-h/20842-h.htm.

Bergson, Henri (1920) *Mind Energy: Lectures and Essays*, trans. H. Wildon Carr, London: Macmillan and Co.

Bergson, Henri (1944) *Creative Evolution*, trans. Arthur Mitchell, New York: Modern Library (reprint of Henry Holt and Company, 1911).

Bergson, Henri (1946) *The Creative Mind*, trans. Mabelle L. Andison, New York: The Philosophical Library.

Bergson, Henri (1991) *Matter and Memory*, trans. Nancy Margaret Paul and W. Scott Palmer, New York: Zone Books.

Bergson, Henri (2001) *Time and Free Will: An Essay on the Immediate Data of Consciousness*, trans. Frank Lubecki Pogson, New York: Dover Publications.

Carr, H. Wildon (1911) *Henri Bergson: The Philosophy of Change*, New York: Dodge Publishing Co.

Carr, H. Wildon (1914) *The Philosophy of Change: A Study of the Fundamental Principle of the Philosophy of Bergson*, London Macmillan and Co.

Carr, H. Wildon (1918) '"Time" and "History" in Contemporary Philosophy; with Special Reference to Bergson and Croce', Published for the British Academy by H. Milford, Oxford University Press.

Costelloe, Karin (1913) 'Review of *A New Philosophy: Henri Bergson* by Edouard Le Roy', *International Journal of Ethics* 24:1, 102–4.

Costelloe, Karin (1914) 'An Answer to Mr. Bertrand Russell's Article on the Philosophy of Bergson', *The Monist* 24:1, 145–55.

Cutting, Gary (2007) 'Recent French Philosophy of Science', in *The Oxford Handbook of Continental Philosophy*, ed. Brian Leiter and Michael Ross, Oxford: Oxford University Press.

Deleuze, Gilles and Guattari, Félix (1987) *A Thousand Plateaus: Capitalism and Schizophrenia*, trans. Brian Massumi, Minneapolis: University of Minnesota Press.

Dewey, John (1910) *How We Think*, Boston: D. C. Heath & Co.

Dewey, John (1912) 'Perception and Organic Action', *The Journal of Philosophy, Psychology and Scientific Methods* IX:24 (November 21), 645–68, http://archive.org/stream/jstor-2012697/2012697_djvu.txt.

Dewey, John (1913) 'Introduction' to *A Contribution to a Bibliography of Henri Bergson*, ed. by Isadore Gilbert Mudge, New York: Columbia University Press, ix–xiii. Reprinted in *The Middle Works of John Dewey, Volume 7, 1899–1924: Essays, Book Reviews, Encyclopedia Articles in the 1912–1914 Period, and Interest and Effort in Education* (*Collected Works of John Dewey 1912–1914*), ed. by Jo Ann Boydston, Carbondale: Southern Illinois University Press, 2008, 201–4.

Dodson, George Rowland (1913) *Bergson and the Modern Spirit: An Essay in Constructive Thought*, Boston: The Beacon Press.

Elliot, Hugh S. R. (1912) *Modern Science and the Illusions of Professor Bergson*, Harlow: Longmans, Green and Co.

Elliot, Hugh S. R. (1922) *Human Character*, Harlow: Longmans, Green and Co.

Ferguson, Kennan (2006) 'La Philosophie Americaine: James, Bergson, and the Century of Intercontinental Pluralism', *Theory and Event* IX:1, https://www.press.jhu.edu/journals/theory_and_event/sample2.html.

Gillies, Mary Ann (2013) '(Re)Reading *Time and Free Will*: (Re)Discovering Bergson for the Twenty-First Century', in *Understanding Bergson, Understanding Modernism*, ed. Paul Ardoin, S. E. Gontarski and Laci Mattison, New York and London: Bloomsbury Books.

Griffin, Nicholas, ed. (1992) *The Selected Letters of Bertrand Russell: Volume I, The Private Years, 1884–1914*, New York: Houghton Mifflin Company.

Guerlac, Susan (2013) 'Foreword' to *Understanding Bergson, Understanding Modernism*, ed. Paul Ardoin, S. E. Gontarski and Laci Mattison, New York and London: Bloomsbury Books.

Hanson, Mark (2000) 'Becoming as Creative Involution?: Contextualizing Deleuze and Guattari's Biophilosophy', *Postmodern Culture* XI:1 (September 2000): http://muse.jhu.edu/journals/postmodern_culture/vo11/11.1hansen.html.

Hermann, E. (1913) *Eucken and Bergson: Their Significance for Christian Thought*, Boston: The Pilgrim Press.

Hulme, T. E. (1924) *Speculations: Essays on Humanism and The Philosophy of Art*, ed. Herbert Read, London: Kegan Paul, Trench, Trubner & C., Ltd.

Huneker, James (1917) *Unicorns*, New York: Charles Scribner's Sons.

James, William (1892) 'The Stream of Consciousness' in *Psychology*, Cleveland & New York: World, http://psychclassics.yorku.ca/James/jimmy11.htm.

James, William (1909) *A Pluralistic Universe: Hibbert Lectures at Manchester College*, Harlow: Longmans, Green & Co.

Kallen, Horace Meyer (1914) *William James and Henri Bergson: A Study of Contrasting Theories of Life*, Chicago: University of Chicago Press.

Kitchin, Darcy B. (1913) *Bergson for Beginners: A Summary of his Philosophy*, New York: Geo. Allen and Unwin.

Le Roy, Edouard (1912) *A New Philosophy: Henri Bergson*, trans. Vincent Benson, New York: Henry Holt and Company.

McGath, Larry (2013) 'Bergson Comes to America', *Journal of the History of Ideas* 74:4 (October), 599–620.

Miquel, Paul-Antoine (2005) 'Evolution of Consciousness and Evolution of Life', *MLN* CXX.5 (December, Comparative Literature Issue), 1156–67.

Menand, Louis (2007) *Discovering Modernism: T. S. Eliot and His Context*, Oxford: Oxford University Press, second edition.

Middleton Murray, John (1911), 'Art and Philosophy', *Rhythm* 1 (summer).

Mullarkey, John, ed. (1999) *The New Bergson*, Manchester: Manchester University Press.

Percival, Ray Scott (2000) 'Challenger to Einstein's Theory of Time', *Times Higher Education*, 6 October, http://www.timeshigheredu cation.co.uk/books/challenger-to-einsteins-theory-of-time/155599.article.

Russell, Bertrand (1912) 'The Philosophy of Bergson', *The Monist* XXII:3 (July), 321–47, http://www.jstor.org/stable/27900381?seq=1#page_scan_tab_contents.

Shotwell, J. T. (1913) 'Bergson's Philosophy', *Political Science Quarterly* 28:130 (March), 130–5.

Slosson, Edwin E. (1911) 'Major Prophets of To-day', *Independent* (June).

Slosson, Edwin E. (1913) 'Recent Developments of Bergson's Philosophy', *Independent* (June), http://archive.org/stream/independent76newy/independent76newy_djvu.txt

Williams, Cora L. (1925) *Creative Involution*, Berkeley: The Williams Institute, second edition.

Wilm, Emil Carl (1914) *Henri Bergson: A Study in Radical Evolution*, New York: Sturgis & Walton Company.

Wood, Alan (1963) *Bertrand Russell: The Passionate Sceptic*, London: Allen & Unwin.

Woolf, Virginia (1924) *Mr Bennett and Mrs Brown*, London: Hogarth Press.

Woolf, Virginia (1966) *Collected Essays*, Vol. 3, London: Hogarth Press.

Woolf, Virginia (1984) *The Virginia Woolf Reader*, ed. Mitchelle Leaska, New York: Harcourt Brace.

4

'Thought Thinks in its Own Right': A. A. Luce, Samuel Beckett and Bergson's Doctrine of Failure

Religion is to mysticism what popularization is to science. (Bergson, *The Two Sources of Morality and Religion*, Chapter III, 239)

Perhaps there is no whole, before you're dead. (*Molloy*, *Three Novels* 35)

In the autumn of 1923, a seventeen-year-old Samuel Beckett took up his third level education and enrolled as a Junior Freshman in Trinity College, Dublin. He would thus become part of the second full class at Trinity under the Saorstát Éireann, the Dáil Éireann having ratified the Anglo-Irish Treaty the previous January, 1922. The young Samuel was assigned Trinity Fellow Arthur Aston, that is, A. A. Luce (1882–1977) as his advisor and tutor. It would be a fortuitous conjunction, this middle class, athletic student from the south Dublin suburb of Foxrock and the Doctor of Divinity, former Captain of the Late 12th Royal Irish Rifles, recipient of the Military Cross in 1917, and adept fly-fisherman, a relationship, in some respects at least, as formative to the young Beckett's future as that of his acknowledged university mentor, Ruddy, Thomas Rudmose-Brown, whom Beckett would finally travesty as the Polar Bear in his first attempt at a novel, *Dream of Fair to Middling Women*. Luce would go on to become an international authority on the Idealist philosopher George Berkeley, Bishop of Cloyne, writing Berkeley's biography, several critical books on his work, including one called *Berkeley's Immaterialism* (1945), editing, with Thomas Edmund Jessop, the complete works in nine volumes (1948–57), and compiling, again with Jessop, a bibliography of Berkeley's work. Charles J. McCraken in 'Berkeley's Realism' called the pair 'two of the twentieth Century's foremost

Berkeley scholars' (McCraken 2008: 25). Almost every time the connection between Luce and Beckett is cited in the critical discourse, the emphasis falls on Luce's introducing Beckett to the Idealist, immaterialist philosophy of George Berkeley. But in 1921, Luce was preoccupied with another metaphysician, the French philosopher Henri Bergson, Luce having delivered the prestigious Donnellan lectures[1] that year, published, with the support of the Board of Trinity College, by the Society for Promoting Christian Knowledge in March of the following year as *Bergson's Doctrine of Intuition*. The Donnellan lectures, originally conceived as sermons 'for the encouragement of religion, sound learning, and good manners', were endowed by Anne Donnellan and have been a fixture at Trinity continuously, if irregularly, since their endowment in 1794, sponsored at first by the School of Hebrew, Biblical and Theological Studies. The topic of the lectures, at least until 1919, was invariably religious. Luce was the first layman to be invited to deliver the lectures.

From our contemporary perspective, Luce's assessment of Bergson is misconceived, his analysis overly selective, his book too often oversimplified and wrongheaded, not only reading Bergson's intuition, for example, as a doctrine rather than as a scientific method, as Bergson himself insisted it was, but aligning the 'doctrine' almost exclusively with mysticism, particularly, but not exclusively, Christian mysticism, and too often confusing intuition with impulse and other like extra-rational methods. It is this emphasis on the extra-rational that the great pacifist and analytic philosopher Bertrand Russell would take up in his review of *Bergson's Doctrine of Intuition*, and in which Russell manages to misrepresent Bergson almost as completely as Luce misapprehends him. Thinking of Bergsonism as 'mystic intuition, which sees deeper than the mere analytic intellect', Russell remains faithful, but he further notes that 'Bergson's "intuition", in the opinion of the present reviewer, is nothing but an invitation to abandon self-control in certain cases in which it is painful' (Russell 2000: 378). Bertie Russell, no friend of Bergsonism in general, goes on in his review to call Luce, whom he nicknames 'Reverend Rifleman', a 'gallant divine', putting the emphasis on Luce as 'The Christian Warrior', the title he gave his review of Luce published in *The Nation and the Anthanaeum* (9 September 1922) (379). Russell further saw that, amid the peaceful aftermath of the Great War, *Bergson's Doctrine of Intuition* was a continuation 'of promoting Christian Knowledge' (378), and, in his opening paragraph, notes that Luce's work captures 'the spirit of Irish Protestantism', adding the caveat 'not mentioned by name but implicit throughout the book' (378), and, further, that Luce's interpretation of Bergson supports the tenets of the Church of Ireland. In his attack on Luce (and Bergson), and on the eve of the establishment of the Irish Free State, Russell takes up the Irish question as well, suggesting economic motives for the British defeat in the 'Anglo-Irish war' and scurrilously, if indirectly, blaming the loss of Ireland on Bergson: 'We had an "intuition" that Sinn Fein ought to be put down', notes Russell, 'until we found that doing so would add a shilling to the income tax' (379), and so the spirit of intuition, which Russell admits is in 'closest touch with the spirit of the Western world of to-day', finally 'has led to the appalling outrages by all parties in Ireland' (379).

Luce's book, then, might have placed him amidst the very foundations of Modernist discourse, the strand at least leading from Bergson through Hulme to Pound, Eliot, Woolf, Joyce and, finally, Beckett, whom Anthony Cronin calls *The Last Modernist*. Knowingly or not, then, Luce, despite his Christian, Church of Ireland emphasis, stepped into one of Modernism's great early conflicts, between metaphysicians and analytic philosophers, the early battles played out before the Heretics Society at Cambridge University, much of whose emphasis was the questioning of religious dogma, a conflict which Russell's sometime student Karin Costelloe Stephen and Luce's student Samuel Beckett would take up more directly.

It is this thread of contemporary philosophy and potentially Modernist literature that Luce, even inadvertently, picks up, for a time, after the Great War. With Luce's assessment, or rather précis, of Bergson in 1921, he joins the Modernist discourse in philosophy and literature, placing a strong emphasis on evolution, particularly the evolution of mind or consciousness as outlined by Bergson, while omitting all mention of Bergson's powerful critique of nothingness. Luce does, however, make a strong argument for what we might call Bergson's Doctrine of Failure.

Very little of Luce's argument would have struck a sympathetic chord with the callow Beckett of 1923, fresh from his mother's religiosity, but the denigration of the rational process and the description of a universe in perpetual flux, without fixity, matter and memory inseparable if not indistinguishable, a point to which

Russell vehemently objected, may have struck a chord in Beckett's growing rebellious spirit. At least it did at some point; that is, something triggered a rebellious spirit in the university student, and Luce's book, in its own timid way, can be read as a call to overthrow the old order. But Luce, who was at least nominally Beckett's tutor for his first two years at Trinity, found the young Beckett an indifferent, unreceptive student at best, according to Beckett's first biographer, Deirdre Bair, showing none of the promise that would blossom in his third year under the tutelage of Professor of Romance Languages, Thomas Rudmose-Brown, and Walter Starkie. Much has been written about those latter relationships (see, e.g., Little 1984). Some also has been written about A. A. Luce's direct influence on Samuel Beckett, particularly Luce's work on George Berkeley (see, e.g., Berman 1984). But the possibility of this shy, lacklustre student's paying any attention to the work and publication that was very much on Luce's mind when Beckett entered university in the autumn of 1923, which Luce had recently completed editing and revising for publication, his second book, is almost wholly ignored. Deidre Bair suggests that Beckett's relationship with Luce was distant since Beckett lived at home for his first two years at Trinity, and Luce himself has admitted that Beckett had 'very little need for a college tutor'; in his first two years, Luce notes, 'he hadn't found his métier [. . .] his first two years were actually quite dismal' (Bair 1990: 37–8). Anthony Cronin reminds us that Beckett's 'main interests, amounting almost to passions into which all other passions were sublimated, were golf, cricket and motor-bikes' (1999: 53). What is clear, however, is that Luce would outline to this lacklustre student, through his assessment of Bergson, what would become the central preoccupations of Beckett's life work.

The book Luce published as *Bergson's Doctrine of Intuition* is divided into four parts, the format following that of the lectures delivered in the Trinity College Exam Halls off the Parliament Square (the venue alluded to on page 87): 'The Method of Intuition' essentially focuses on *Creative Evolution*; 'Free Will' takes as its starting point Bergson's *Time and Free Will*; 'Mind and Body', perhaps the most important chapter in both the book and for Beckett's future, explores *Matter and Memory*, and finally 'Theory of Evolution' returns to Bergson's *magnum opus*, *Creative Evolution* by way of summary. Despite the overriding Christian framework to which Russell objected, the added aegis of the Christian publishing house, and the Christian emphasis of the Donnellan Lectures in general, the book's themes are flux, failure, and inadequacy, 'The inability of the conceptual mode of thinking to express duration' (Luce 1922: 4), that is, the process, the continual evolution of life itself, and hence the ineluctable process of movement and change, becoming. In terms of classical philosophy, Luce tells us, we find 'In Bergson Heraclitus asserting his primary conviction and tracing to its source the error of Parmenides' (4), a comparison Luce returns to regularly. Russell picks up Bergson's critique of Zeno in favour of Heraclitus on this essential Bergsonian point: 'The Eleatics said that there were things but no changes; Heraclitus and Bergson said that there were changes but no things. The Eleatics said there was an arrow, but no flight; Heraclitus and Bergson said there was a flight but no arrow' (Russell 1914: 18). Bergson, Luce tells us, thus requires of us a new way of thinking: 'the stock in trade of intellect will serve our purposes only as long as we are dealing with a universe that is [static]; a universe that becomes, a universe in the making, demands more [. . .]. It requires the growth of new powers of apprehension' (Luce 1922: 4), what Luce calls, 'a binocularity of inner vision' (6). The function of intelligence, then, 'is to enable the organism to act upon its environment' (11). The objection is to 'structure', 'the abiding structure under which man [humanity] thinks', structure that 'we call categories' (12), which fix and make manageable 'the flux of things' (13; cf. Bergson 1944: CE, 174), which is the 'multiplicity of heterogeneous elements' (16). The focus then is on the collapse of cause and effect, which suggests linear thinking as opposed to the rhizomatic approach that Luce, after Bergson, is here advocating, as Luce develops in his analogy of attempting to eradicate the single dandelion only to 'find it a hydra containing the possibilities of an unlimited number of similar hydras' (13). Luce in his 1921 lecture, summarizing Bergson, is thus already anticipating Gilles Deleuze. By 1931, in his post-graduate essay on Marcel Proust, Beckett will chastise the French author for remaining tied to cause and effect. Beckett's Proust cannot ignore *causality*; he must accept 'the sacred ruler and compass of literary geometry' (*Proust* 12).

It is Arsene who lectures Watt, in the novel that bears his name, on the slippage of causality, on the failures of the step by step approach of percepts to concepts, the slippage that is life off the ladder, say. The change of kind that Arsene tries to explain is the slippage from an incremental change of degree to a change of kind, or at least 'a change, other than a change of degree had taken place'. It is now life off the metaphorical sequence of the ladder: 'Do not come down the ladder, Ifor, I haf taken it away' (*Watt* 44). Happiness, however, in Beckett's version of the myth of Sisyphus, resides in the continued longing for the impossible ladder: 'The glutton castaway, the drunkard in the desert, the lecher in prison, they are the happy ones. To hunger, thirst, lust, every day afresh and every day in vain, after the old prog, the old booze, the old whores, that's the nearest we'll ever get to felicity [. . .]' (*Watt* 44). But that is Arsene, presumably. The quest drives Watt mad, and it may bring the enigmatic May to the brink as well as she ponders, or revolves, the paradox of her footfalls, her life segmented into seven or nine successive sounds, footsteps, footfalls. Russell picks up Bergson's image of succession from *Time and Free Will* (Bergson 2001: 86) and notes: 'When we hear the steps of a passer-by in the street, he [Bergson] says, we visualize his successive positions' (Russell 1914: 15). For Bergson such succession is a segmentation, a spatialization, and so a falsification of motion, becoming, life. What is puzzling to the central character of *Footfalls*, or to some consciousness projected as a pacing figure, is the disjunction between a life reduced to the repetition of nine segments, repeated in an infinity of motion, and the lived experience of life, *durée*, time as lived, the enigmatic, ineffable 'it all' of the play. At some point such paradoxes as Bergson expresses will appeal to the young Beckett.

Much of the oral quality of Luce's original lectures remains in the printed record. Luce may be overly fond of clichés and of sports metaphors, particularly involving golf and tennis, but he includes some salient anecdotes as well. In one, Luce speaks of discussing Bergson with Trinity's Provost and leading Kantian, John Mahaffy, whom, he says, 'was too good a Kantian to approve the substance of this new doctrine. But he was unstinting in praise of its literary form. He spoke in the highest terms of the charm of Bergson's pen' (1922: 17). Summarizing that eloquence, Luce, presumably, dubs Bergson 'Chrysostom' (17), a compliment that evidently could not be returned. The term would appear in February that same year, the year before Beckett entered Trinity, in James Joyce's landmark novel *Ulysses* when Buck Mulligan's oratory and gold-tipped teeth earn him the title, which St John Chrysostom's preaching earned him, 'golden-mouthed', 'Chrysostomos'. As

Stephen, Joyce's independent, exiled genius notes of Mulligan: 'He peered sideways up and gave a long low whistle of call, then paused awhile in rapt attention, his even white teeth glistening here and there with gold points. Chrysostomos.' The reader need not labour too deeply into *Ulysses* to come across the allusion since it appears on the novel's first page so that even those reading it for the wrong reason might come across it. The web of allusions here is to Mahaffy, whose book not on Kant but on Descartes Beckett studied closely enough to plunder for his own Bergso-Cartesian poem about time, *Whoroscope*,[2] and Beckett would certainly have come across at some point Stephen Dedalus's praise of the oratory of Buck Mulligan in terms of St John Chrysostom, Archbishop of Constantinople, images of whose legendary living like a beast for his sins of sexuality and, finally, murder, were painted or engraved by any number of artists including Albrecht Durer, a favourite of Beckett. It is difficult not to conclude that the young Beckett's introduction to Bergson and Bergsonism would come through his first tutor. The difficulty is to gauge the depth and timing of that early influence.

In his second chapter Luce turns to an earlier book, Bergson's *Time and Free Will*, where he takes up the issue of 'intensity', which 'gives us the picture of a multiplicity of interpenetrating psychic states' (Luce 1922: 37), which is decidedly different from quantity, the multiplicity of number. Much of the focus, however, is on time, but 'Time thought *in abstracto* is nothing; time lived is for Bergson the stuff of reality. Real time is the time whose lapse we feel. He calls it duration' (39), that is, time undifferentiated, instant inseparable from instant. Freedom, then, is the release from mechanism, necessity, the release from the linearity of cause and effect, which is spatial: 'There is no room for freedom in space or in spatial time. In space each part determines the position of each other part. In linear time each instant determines the next instant' (42); it is thus time on the ladder, the time and motion that traps May in *Footfalls*. Such succession is mechanism, which, as Russell summarizes it, 'regards the future as implicit in the past' (1914: 3). Beckett will dub such life on the ladder as the operation of 'clockwork cabbages' in *Dream of Fair to Middling Women*. Freedom, on the other hand, and so creativity, constitutes the frustration and deniability of prediction, at least in the psychic field; a free act is an uncaused act, not simply a matter of alternate choices or possibilities not pursued. Beckett will finally find such a breakdown across the Modernist landscape, in the 'acte gratuit' from Gide to Camus, from Lofcadio to the *Pied-noir* Meursault, and among the emergent surrealists, but its nearest iterations were in Bergson, perhaps through, at first, Luce's summaries.

Luce begins his third lecture with an apology since despite its title, 'Mind and Body', his focus will be on perception, our primary connection to the world, or to matter, or to the real, and through which Luce explains away the mind- body conflict of Descartes, 'We see with the eye and hear with the ear, because in the sensory cerebral process mind and body meet. Perception then is a union of mind and body, a solution of the problem of perception is our quest' (Luce 1922: 64). 'Both idealist and realist methods', Luce continues, 'set up a barrier between thought and thing. Both make a clean cut between percipient and percipienda, and thus they never touch the concrete perception. [. . .] Every sense action is an interaction' (65). The resolution of the mind- body split and the interpenetration of perceiver and perceived are thus resolved in the Bergsonian image, as Luce summarizes almost verbatim from the opening pages of *Matter and Memory*: '"Image" is an exist-ence, more than a representation and less than a thing', that is, 'surrounding objects act on the brain and the brain [acts] on those objects' (67). This is a philosophical and aesthetic position that Beckett will explore for the whole of his creative life, stated most discursively at the opening of his 1934 essay 'Recent Irish Poetry'. In fact, Beckett will go further to adopt the Bergsonian position, here expressed by T. E. Hulme in his Bergson essays, whereby the process of perception as a habit of mind is inherently distortive: 'The habit of mind which [Bergson] thinks distorts instead of revealing is simply the ordinary use of the logical intellect' (Hulme 1924: 123). The entire process of perception is thus inevitably ill seen, ill heard, and so, of necessity, ill represented. Representation itself is, by definition, distortion.

The brain, rather the mind, or particularly 'The cerebrum is not an information bureau, nor a storehouse of memory, but a distri-bution centre of action. [. . .] The body is the centre of perceptions not its source' (Luce 1922: 71). This is Bergson's alternative both to realist and idealist philosophers, and Luce uses phrasing that both he and Beckett will later associate with Berkeley: 'This theory rules out the subjective origin of things; it shows that there is more in their *esse* than their *percipi*' (73). The conclusion: 'perception [is] a purely material process. [. . .] the stimulus from without and the nervous process within the body form one homogeneous movement', 'concrete perception', that effected by memory (75); that is, the body is 'grafted' onto 'pure perception'. It is difficult to resist reading such observations through Beckett's own study of immaterialism, *The Unnamable*, as Luce discusses the possibilities of 'disembodied mind': 'The first effort of intuition gave us a picture of mindless perception: the second will offer a picture of disembodied mind' (76). All 'Vision is [thus] re-vision' (77), or the interplay of 'concrete memory', that is, voluntary memory, a bodily mechanism, on the one hand, and what Luce here calls 'spontaneous memory' (83) and Beckett will call in *Proust* and after Proust, 'involuntary memory'. As he concludes the chapter, Luce returns to his, and Bergson's, central points: pure and concrete perceptions, spontaneous and voluntary memory, and a central observation for Bergson and Beckett that our 'perception forms part of the things, the things participate in the nature of our perception' (93). Again, the issues are those that dominate *The Unnamable*: 'Mind is not brain', Luce reminds us; 'nor is memory stored in protoplasm or in brain cells. [. . .] Mind then depends on the body for its power of acting into space, but not for its being. Thought thinks in its own right' (96–7). Such revelation is the result of 'intuition' and, as Karin Costelloe puts it, 'The theory that in pure intuition the subject which knows becomes its object, is certainly of very fundamental importance for Bergson' (1914: 145), and for Beckett, we might add.

After such startling observations most of which run counter to received wisdom or common sense, especially for their time, Chapter IV (or lecture 4) could only be anticlimactic, but Luce rises to the occasion of a classical peroration. It is his most passionate, elegant and aphoristic chapter, where he even seems to predict the young Beckett's transformation at university: 'The student knows that his Senior Freshman self is not the same as his Junior Freshman self'; this is 'the truth of personal existence' (101). The emphasis on such personal existence is the subject of Luce's final chapter, as he tells us, 'Bergson intuits the essence of personal existence as an incessant tendency to self creation' (103). In his critique of 'nothing' in *Creative Evolution* Bergson put such radical regeneration thus:

> When I no longer know anything of external objects, it is because I have taken refuge in the consciousness that I have of myself. If I

abolish this inner self, its very abolition becomes an object for an imaginary self which now perceives as an external object the self that is dying away. Be it external or internal, some object there always is that my imagination is always representing. My imagination, it is true, can go from one to the other, I can by turns imagine a nought of external perception or a nought of internal perception, but not both at once, for the absence of the one consists, at bottom, in the exclusive presence of the other. (1944: CE 303)

In 1931 Beckett put the matter more sharply: we are not simply more weary because we are further on the way, but we are other, 'no longer what we were before the calamity of yesterday' (*Proust* 13). Samuel Beckett will adopt such a position for his life's work, yet as a process that his characters, his creatures, from *Watt* onward, resist. The rendering of that process, however, is inevitably doomed to failure. In Luce's understatement, 'It is hard to put into words what personal existence feels like' (1922: 101), yet this will be the task that Samuel Beckett will set for himself, and it is feeling or affect not philosophy that Beckett will emphasize. The *élan* is neither aimless nor predictable, and so, as Luce notes, 'A biography cannot be written in advance' (102). That is, for the biography to be written or completed, change must have ceased. In her retort to Russell, Karin Costelloe put the issue thus: 'if we try to describe change we have always to regard it as change completed and not in the process of changing' (1914: 148). Beckett put the matter concisely in his novel *Molloy*: 'Perhaps there is no whole, before you're dead' (*Three Novels* 35), and it is why *Endgame*, replete with threats of ending, cannot end.

This feature of incompleteness, the inability to capture the whole of a life, in biography, autobiography, or narrative, the inability of characters or narrators to tell their full and complete stories, will pervade Beckett's art, but what dominates in kind is the need, the persistent desire, desire as a Deleuzian creative force rather than a response to a lack, to do so. All we can capture, perhaps, is how it feels to try. In the outline for a book on 'Modern Theories of Art', Hulme, in notes to an unwritten Chapter 4, 'French – Bergson', says of Bergson: 'least apriori of all theories – springs from actual and intimate acquaintance with emotions involved' (1924: 263). Russell will call such emphasis on emotions a lack of system.

Luce deals with the great Bergsonian subjects, evolution and endurance, but evolution not of the species, not physical, biological evolution, but that of the individual organism, the individual psyche. The 'ego', Freudian or otherwise, however, is what Luce calls 'an arrest of a current of being', and, as Luce grows more eloquent he calls it, 'the hanging wave of a flowing tide' (1922: 102); being, thus, cannot be described or represented without distortion or contradiction since it entails arresting the *élan vital*, stopping time, ending the process of *durée*. All attempts at representation, of the *élan*, of *dureé*, of time and being, that is, all attempts to make a life-like copy, a simulacrum, must end in failure. Being, what Luce calls 'the living body', 'is a closed system, not an artificially closed system like those postulated by science or made by human perception, but closed by nature' (103). Beckett will take up the issue in the novel *Murphy*, and thereafter. The feel of life, the organism that endures, impossible to capture on Krapp's tapes, or in the photographs of *Film* or 'A Piece of Monologue', impossible to represent as a pacing figure in *Footfalls*, impossible to capture completely in language, is the great subject of Beckett's work and the core of Bergson's mystical, intuitive metaphysics: 'Duration is [. . .] the ultimate reality', Luce tells us; 'Duration is not spatialized time; it is not passive continuance while something else continues [. . .] it is the interpenetration of past and present events, a cumulative carrying forward of past into the future' (104–5).

All this Beckett will study and, finally, embrace, not as a doctrine but as a creative method. We know that by 1931, Beckett participated in an evening of French theatre organized by the Modern Language Society of Trinity College. In addition to the short melodrama Beckett selected, *La souriante Madame Beudet*, he acted in his own adaptation of Corneille's tragedy *Le Cid*, which was re-titled *Le Kid*, in homage, apparently, to the Chaplin film. What resulted on the boards in Beckett's first theatrical venture was a travesty, in all senses of that term, which Beckett found necessary to defend in a polemical essay called 'The Possessed'. The performance was generally regarded by both defenders and detractors alike – the latter far outnumbering the former – as an all out assault on theatrical tradition and conventions of the stage, which pastiche Beckett described to his confidant Thomas MacGreevy as a combination Corneillian parody and the philosophy of Bergson (*Letters 1* 68). When and how Beckett acquired enough Bergsonism to stage it, as it were, is not yet possible to ascertain with any certainty. We know neither what or how much

Bergson Beckett read directly, nor how much he picked up from secondary sources, but we do know that he was almost simultaneously teaching him at Trinity as he was writing, playing and defending *Le Kid*. What we can discern is that Beckett was often curious enough or showed enough initiative as a student to read the works of his tutors and dons. That fact has been thoroughly documented by critics and biographers. We know how thoroughly he read Mahaffey's little introduction to Descartes, for instance. Moreover, Dirk Van Hulle and Mark Nixon suggest how early Beckett was beginning seriously to engage the work of his teachers as they report in *Samuel Beckett's Library* that 'Apart from being Beckett's Professor of Romance Languages at TCD, Rudmose-Brown was an editor of Corneille. Beckett purchased Rudmose-Brown's edition *La Galerie du Palais* (1920) [along with two other works by Corneille] for the Michaelmas term 1923' (Van Hulle and Nixon 2013: 47), the same year he began his study at Trinity and only a year after Luce's book on *Bergson's Doctrine of Intuition* was published. And Van Hulle and Nixon demonstrate that Beckett was already a serious reader of French and a collector of odd vocabulary, a lifelong habit, by 1923. At very least we know when the young Beckett would have had the opportunity to engage Bergson, on his own or at the suggestion of his tutor. If we cannot determine when Beckett read Luce on Bergson, we can say that Luce's little book on Bergson would have been Beckett's first opportunity to study the evolution of the individual psyche and engage the discourse of human freedom and creativity.

Notes

1. It is difficult to ascertain the degree of interest Samuel Beckett may have had in the Donnellan lectures at Trinity, but it is worth noting here that the series of three lectures for 1924, in June of that year so at the end of Samuel Beckett's first year at Trinity, were delivered by F. C. Burkitt. Their subject was 'The Religion of the Manichees', and they were published by Cambridge University Press under that title in 1925. Surely, Dr Luce attended those lectures, but whether or not he persuaded his young student to attend as well we can only conjecture. If he did, one might guess that something of at least Burkitt's conclusion may have been retained: 'this view of human life taught that Man went and still goes wrong because he had always lived in a Dualistic world, a world where the Light and Dark existed in opposi-

tion before Man was, and where though the Light is stronger than the Dark it will never quite illuminate it altogether' (Burkitt 1924: 104). See particularly James Knowlson's analysis of Manicheanism in *Light and Darkness in the Theatre of Samuel Beckett*, delivered as a public lecture at Trinity College Dublin on 17 February 1972 and published in an edition of 1,000 copies by Turret Books that same year. See also Knowlson's collaboration with John Pilling, *Frescos of the Skull: The Later Prose and Drama of Samuel Beckett* (London: John Calder, 1979), particularly pages 86–7: 'Krapp is clearly following here in a Gnostic, even specifically Manichean tradition.' Knowlson also references Beckett's theatrical notebook for his production of *Krapp's Last Tape* in 1977: 'Krapp decrees physical (ethical) incompatibility of light (spiritual) and dark (sensual) only when he *intuits* [emphasis added!] the possibility of their reconciliation as rational-irrational', what is finally a most Bergsonian statement. Further, Knowlson notes, 'Krapp created a prison for himself by choosing at the age of thirty-nine to plumb the darkness of his own being in an attempt to create an *opus magnum* in which light and darkness would be reconciled' (93). Knowlson also references Kenneth and Alice Hamilton, *Condemned to Life: The World of Samuel Beckett* (Grand Rapids, MI: W. B. Eerdmans, 1976), 51–8. Of late the Donnellan lectures have been offered, roughly, triennially by the Department of Philosophy and have been delivered by the likes of Martha Nussbaum (1992), Richard Rorty (on Pragmatism in 1998) and Stanley Cavell (on 'The Wittgensteinian Event' in 2002).

2. See Francis Docherty, 'Mahaffy's *Whoroscope*', *Journal of Beckett Studies* 2:1 (1992), 27–46; reprinted in *The Beckett Critical Reader: Archives, Theories, and Translations*, ed. and with an Introduction by S. E. Gontarski, Edinburgh: Edinburgh University Press, 2012.

References

Bair, Deidre (1990) *Samuel Beckett: A Biography*, New York: Summit Books (a slightly revised and corrected reprint of the 1978 biography).

Bergson, Henri (1944) *Creative Evolution*, trans. Arthur Mitchell, New York: Modern Library (reprint of Henry Holt and Company, 1911).

Bergson, Henri (1954) *The Two Sources of Morality and Religion*, New York: Doubleday Anchor Books.

Bergson, Henri (2001) *Time and Free Will: An Essay on the Immediate Data of Consciousness*, trans. Frank Lubecki Pogson, New York: Dover Publications.

Berman, David (1984) 'Beckett and Berkeley', *Irish University* Review XIV:1, 42–5.

Burkitt, F. C. (1924) *The Religion of the Manichees: The Donnellan Lectures for 1924*, Cambridge: Cambridge University Press.

Costelloe, Karin (1914) 'An Answer to Mr. Bertrand Russell's Article on the Philosophy of Bergson', *The Monist* 24:1, 145–55.

Cronin, Anthony (1999) *Samuel Beckett: The Last Modernist*, New York: Da Capo Press.

Hulme, T. E. (1924) *Speculations: Essays on Humanism and The Philosophy of Art*, ed. Herbert Read, London: Kegan Paul, Trench, Trubner & Co., Ltd.

Little, Roger (1984) 'Beckett's Mentor, Rudmore-Brown: Sketch for a Portrait', *Irish University Review* XIV:1 (1984), 34–41.

Luce, A. A. (1922) *Bergson's Doctrine of Intuition: The Donnellan Lectures for 1921*, London: Society for Promoting Christian Knowledge. Available at http://ia351405.us.archive.org/2/items/bergsonsdoctrine00lucerich/bergsonsdoctrine00lucerich.pdf.

McCracken, Charles J. (2008) 'Berkeley's Realism', in *New Interpretations of Berkeley's Thought*, ed. S. H. Daniel, New York: Humanity Books.

Mahaffy, J. P. (1901) *Descartes*, London: William Blackwood.

Russell, Bertrand (1914) *The Philosophy of Bergson* (with a Reply by Mr H. Wildon Carr, Secretary of The Aristotelian Society, and a Rejoinder by Mr Russell), London: Macmillan and Co., Ltd; Glasgow: Jas. MacLehose and Sons.

Russell, Bertrand (2000) *Uncertain Paths to Freedom: Russia and China 1919–1922. The Collected Papers of Bertrand Russell*, Vol. 15, ed. Richard A. Rempel and Beryl Haslam, with the assistance of Andrew Bone and Albert C. Lewis, London: Routledge.

Van Hulle, Dirk and Nixon, Mark (2013) *Samuel Beckett's Library*, Cambridge: Cambridge University Press.

Interiors

5

Towards a Creative Involution

That's not moving, that's *moving*. (*Whoroscope* 40)

But if he could say, when the knock came, the knock become a knock, or the door become a door, in his mind, presumably in his mind, whatever that may mean. (*Watt* 77)

To elicit something from nothing requires a certain skill. (*Watt* 77)

In their critique of Sigmund Freud's (psycho)analysis of the Wolf-Man in *A Thousand Plateaus*, philosopher Gilles Deleuze and psychoanalyst Félix Guattari take on the methodology and ideology of psychoanalysis, which they deem 'a mixed semiotic: a despotic regime of significance and interpretation' (Deleuze and Guattari 1987: 125), and so they take on much of the regime of Modernism itself. For Deleuze and Guattari, Freud misreads the Wolf-Man's narrative, imposing nominalist, patriarchal presuppositions on the narrative's multiplicity, reducing an assemblage to the name of the Father, or the name of the Wolf-Man, in the crafting of a coherent, unified subconscious. Deleuze and Guattari replace the constrictive unity of psychoanalysis with its emphasis on the subconscious with the multiplicity of schizoanalysis and its emphasis on the unconscious. Freud's misreading confuses the two, the unified subconscious with an unconscious as assemblage that is 'fundamentally a crowd' (29), an analysis of Freud that parallels Deleuze's critique of Heidegger's *Sein*. In their analysis Deleuze and Guattari are careful to distinguish between, in its Bergsonian echo, the simple multiplicity of space, 'numerical or extended multiplicities', and that of the assemblage with its 'qualitative' multiplicities (33). They will use a variety of terms to distinguish between a multiplicity which is a sequence or series, to which one can always add another entity, an N+1, say, and 'rhizomatic multiplicities' or 'molecular, intensive [as opposed to extensive] multiplicities' which are non-totalizable. Within that assemblage, that crowd, the Wolf-Man, as pack, as qualitative multiplicity and molecular process rather than molar entity, is apprehensible as it 'approaches or moves away from zero':

> Zero is the body without organs of the Wolf-Man. If the unconscious knows nothing of negation, it is because there is nothing negative in the unconscious, only indefinite moves toward and away from zero, which does not at all express lack but rather the positivity of the full body as support and prop ('for an afflux is necessary simply to signify the absence of intensity') (Deleuze and Guattari 1987: 31)

Quoting Nietzsche on 'Eternal Return' thus (see Klossowski 1997: 48), Deleuze and Guattari sound decidedly Bergsonian in this critique of Freud, as they echo not only Bergson on multiplicities but his critique of nothingness as well. Both of these elements find their elaborations in the perpetually unfolding narratives of Samuel Beckett, who, situated between these French metaphysicians, is neither scion of the one nor progenitor of the other, that is, is not one in a series but one of a multiple, simultaneously a one and a pack. One might thus read not only Beckett through Bergson, but Bergson through Beckett; Bergson through Deleuze, and also Deleuze back through Bergson, or, as one of the narrating voices in Beckett's *Company* notes, 'vice-versa'. Speaking of the painter Bram van Velde, Beckett notes of him that he feels 'himself to be plural (at least) while all the time remaining (of course) one single being' (cited in Gontarski and Uhlmann 2006: 18). Deleuze reminds us, as a case in point, that he has created an entity with and through Bergson as he essentially makes Bergson say what he, Deleuze, wants him to say. It is thus something of Deleuze's buggering of Bergson:

> I saw myself as taking an author from behind and giving him a child that would be his own offspring, yet monstrous. It was really important for it to be his own child, because the author had to actually say all I had him saying. But the child was bound to be monstrous too, because it resulted from all sorts of shifting, slipping, dislocations, and hidden emissions that I really enjoyed. I think my book on Bergson's

a good example. And there are people these days who laugh at me simply for having written about Bergson at all. It simply shows that they don't know enough history. They've no idea how much hatred he managed to stir up in the French university system at the outset and how he became the focus for all sorts of crazy and unconventional people right across the social spectrum. And it's irrelevant whether that's what he actually intended. (Deleuze 1995a: 6)

Beckett's images for the generation of art, in this case speaking of Bram van Velde's paintings, are as aggressive, as sexually charged, as ejaculatory as those of Deleuze, as Beckett tries to explain the creative process to Georges Duthuit in 1949: 'If you ask me why the canvas doesn't remain blank, I can only invoke this clear need, forever innocent, to fuck it with color, if need be through vomiting one's being' (cited in Gontarski and Uhlmann 2006: 20).[1] Beckett seems, however, self-conscious about forcing van Velde to speak thus, from behind, of his ventriloquizing van Velde, and buggering him in this way: 'I had always thought that he [van Velde] hadn't the faintest idea of what he was doing and neither do I' (cited in Gontarski and Uhlmann 2006: 20). Beckett too may thus have created a monster.

One of the most compelling discourses in *Creative Evolution* is Bergson's thinking through the issues of nothing,[2] in which any negation, any inclusion of a 'not' in a statement announces 'that some other affirmation, whose content I do not specify, will have to be substituted for the one I find before me' (Bergson 1944: 315). Such is the 'zero' of Deleuze and Guattari's critique, and centre stage in Beckett's first two published, eponymous, English novels, *Murphy* and *Watt*, the former in its pursuit of not annihilation but fulfilment, the latter plagued by self-generated apparitions in the house of Mr Knott. It is the nothingness of routine, of the quotidian, in the latter that gives way or mounts up to the nothing of existence and the waste of being: 'on the waste, beneath the sky, distinguished by Watt as being, the one above, the other beneath, Watt', as Addendum 22 has it (*Watt* 249). Beckett's negations, then, produce or result in neither absence nor void. Like Deleuze, Beckett has nothing to admit, or rather he has 'no need to prove anything' (*Letters* 2 140). Contrary to its title, in his letter to Michel Cressole, Deleuze will admit a 'secret link' to those orphan philosophers against a rationalist tradition: 'I see a secret link between Lucretius, Hume, Spinoza and Nietzsche, constituted by their critique of negativity' (Deleuze 1995a: 6). For Bergson, who might, even should, have been included in Deleuze's list (as he is in Brian Massumi's 'Translator's Foreword' to *A Thousand Plateaus* [Deleuze and Guattari 1987: x]), the statement 'There is nothing', although a contingent, negative fact, would have to be grounded on some positive entity, an '*All*', say, 'to which it is very closely akin' (Bergson 1944: 322). Such an entity would ensure that something, rather than nothing, remained. As a demonstrative, Bergson's discourse suggests that 'Nothing is [over] there'. The perpetual philosophical conundrum that began Martin Heidegger's list of questions central to philosophy, 'Why is there something rather than nothing', was thus always a false problem for Bergson, and for Deleuze, and such expressions of exclusionary binary become not unlike the Cartesian mind-body duality.[3] *The Stanford Encyclopedia of Philosophy* (2003, revised 2012) begins its entry on Nothingness with such a duality: 'ever since Parmenides in the fifth century BCE, there has been rich commentary on whether an empty world is possible, whether there are vacuums, and about the nature of privations and negation'. The binary of something and nothing is thus finally a minor variation on the principle of the One and its degraded parts. Negative theology, however, posits as axiomatic that what can be said of God, say, or of the One, is only that she has no qualities known to human intelligence: 'The original ground of all things, the deity, must [. . .] lie beyond Being and knowledge; it is above reason, above Being; it has no determination or quality, it is "Nothing"' (Windelband 1914: 335). The deity, finally, exhibits the '*complete absence of all qualities* [. . .] no name names him' (237), and 'we can predicate of God only what he is not' (290). Windelband was the source of much of Samuel Beckett's understanding of ancient philosophy, and residua can be found in Beckett's first two English novels of exile, *Murphy* and *Watt*, whose protagonists (or whose subjects) vainly attempt to name, that is, to ground, their being in the world by exhausting the possibilities of unknowing. Such negation by serial exhaustion in order to know Mr Knott, for example, encounters at best only residual effects or after effects, Knott's attributes, and Watt finally knows nothing of his essence:

> For the only way one can speak of nothing is to speak of it as though it were something, just as the only way one can speak of God [a weightless entity, immaterial, apparently nothing, a cipher, nought, zero] is

to speak of him as though he were a man, which to be sure he was, in a sense, for a time . . . (*Watt* 77)

Watt's mistake may have been in trying to see Mr Knott as a knowable singularity, even as he or Sam asks 'But what do I know of Mr Knott? Nothing' (119), or again, third person singular, 'What did he know of Mr Knott? Nothing' (148). Knott's abode, at least in Watt's orbit, moreover, is perpetual change in its changelessness: 'Yes, nothing changed, in Mr Knott's establishment, because nothing remained, and nothing came or went, because all was a coming and a going' (131–2). Watt's demise seems to stem from an inability to accept such ceaseless process, such incessant becoming and from the fact that:

> [N]othing had happened, that a thing that was nothing had happened, with the utmost formal distinctness, and that it continued to happen, in his mind [. . .] Yes, Watt could not accept, as no doubt Erskine could not accept, as no doubt Arsene and Walter and Vincent and the others [in the pack] had been unable to accept, that nothing had happened, with all the clarity and solidity of something . . . (*Watt* 76)

Such 'coming and a going', such materializations of nothingness, permeate Beckett's *oeuvre* and are central to at least Bergson's defence of motion, a world in motion, and so subject to change. Preoccupation with bodies in motion, or motion itself, has more traditionally fallen within the province of physics than metaphysics, even for Aristotle. Bergson, however, situates himself on the bridge between those disciplines, as he does between matter and spirit, and so his emphasis on motion undergirds and so coincides, overlaps, or intersects with the spirit of change, of evolution, of constant becoming, of time's flow, of *durée*; it is an embrace of natural law, life's vital force, an *élan vital*, the implications of which have all too often been ignored in philosophy, Bergson reminds us. Aristotle himself acknowledged such a vital force in his punning coinage, 'entelechy', but Aristotle's vision too was finally binary, entelechy opposed to stasis, which may contain the potential of such motion, or kinesis, or entelechy but is in opposition to it. Of such fixity or stasis, Bergson will say that it is 'only an ephemeral arrangement between mobilities' (1946: 177).

The opening to the first of two 'Introductions' that Bergson wrote specifically for his second collection of lectures and essays, those delivered or published between 1903 and 1923, *The Creative Mind*, is: 'What philosophy has lacked most of all is precision' (1946: 9); that is, philosophy has tended to ignore natural laws. In this autobiographical opening, Bergson recalls his youthful infatuation with the Victorian theorist Herbert Spencer, who embraced an all-encompassing system of evolution, a philosophy that took account of the physical, biological world. It was Spencer not Darwin who in *Principles of Biology* (1864), and after reading *On the Origin of Species*, coined the phrase 'survival of the fittest', and hence natural selection, an evolutionary principle which Bergson will finally oppose with his involutionary *élan vital*. Spencer was a synthetic philosopher and psychologist who saw congruence not threat in what others deemed the polar opposites of scientific method and traditional, historical belief systems. Synthetic philosophy saw the unity of natural laws, human and nonhuman alike.[4] As influenced as he was by the capacity of Spencerian synthesis to overcome more traditional dualities, Bergson was determined to remedy much of what he saw as Spencer's tendency to dwell on 'vague generalities' (1946: 10). Evolution thus led Bergson to what he calls 'real time' and how it eludes mathematics because it flows: 'not one of its parts is still there when another part comes along' (10). If this time that flows were measurable, it would 'have the essence of non-duration' (11). Measurement, then, is 'not carried out on an aspect or an effect representative of what one wishes to measure [in this case 'Time'], but on something which excludes it' (11).

One of Beckett's most profound literary encounters with such Bergso-Deleuzism is developed throughout his 1936 novel *Murphy*, particularly the presentation of 'Murphy's mind' in Chapter 6. Murphy, bound to his chair but in motion, slips past the mind's first zone, that of 'forms with parallel' (*Murphy* 111), to the second, the contemplation of 'forms without parallel' (111), but stable forms, nonetheless, thence to the third, the dark, 'a flux of forms, a perpetual coming together and falling asunder of forms' (112). Such 'dark [contains] neither elements nor states, nothing but forms becoming and crumbling into the fragments of a new becoming, without love or hate or any intelligible principle of change. Here there was *nothing* but commotion and the pure forms of commotion. Here he was not free, but a mote in the dark of absolute freedom' (112, emphasis added). This then was not only the nothing that Murphy so ardently desired, in constant movement but within a stationary skull, a stasis achieved through the ferocious rocking of his chair. But Murphy's goal is less stasis than nothingness, which he achieves in a sense: 'Murphy began to see nothing, that colourlessness which is such a rare postnatal treat, being the absence (to abuse a nice distinction) not of *percipere* [to perceive] but of *percipi* [to be perceived]' (246). Such nothing offers, 'the positive peace that comes when the somethings give way, or perhaps simply add up, to the Nothing, than which in the guffaw of the Abderite [Democritus] naught is more real' (246). One might accuse Murphy of a certain dualism himself if the 'somethings' simply 'give way' to but not if they 'add up to the Nothing', that plenitude which Deleuze calls Zero, as Murphy in motion continues 'to suck in [. . .] the accidentless One-and-Only, conveniently called Nothing' (246). Celia finally takes a similar route in the absence of Murphy, out of her clothes and into the rocker for the 'silence not of vacuum but of plenum' (148). This is a Bergso-Deleuzian world of perpetual motion and becoming, not 'states', the still moments of movement to which Bergson and Deleuze object, but constant movement, 'nothing but forms becoming and crumbling, without love or hate or any intelligible principle of change' (112). Such issues remain a preoccupation for Beckett into the postwar years, in the midst of his most creative period, as he notes to art critic Georges Duthuit in August of 1948:

> I shall never know clearly enough how far space and time are unutterable, and me caught up somewhere in there [. . .] One may as well dare to be plain and say that not knowing is not only not knowing what one is, but also where one is, and what change to wait for, and how to get out of wherever one is, and how to know, when it seems as if something is moving, which apparently was not moving before, what it is that is moving, that was not moving before, and so on. (*Letters* 2 98)

And so Murphy is not territorially Murphy, we learn, as Watt is not territorially Watt but some sort of blend, a multiplicity, Sam's Watt, or Watt's Sam, part of a cluster, a band at Knott's abode that includes Arsene, whose narrative Watt absorbs, Vincent, Walter and Erskine, among others. Murphy too then is a pack, one in what looks like a quantitative series but is revealed as a molecular multiplicity in the *Three Novels*, a one and a many, part of a pattern of regenerative transformations: 'Then it will be all over with the Murphys, Merciers, Molloys, Morans and Malones, unless it goes on beyond the grave' (*Three Novels* 236). Or at the opening of *The Unnamable*: 'Malone is there. [. . .] Sometimes I wonder if it is not Molloy. Perhaps it is Molloy wearing Malone's hat. [. . .] To tell the truth I believe they are all here, at least from Murphy on' (*Three Novels* 292–3). These manifestations, accompanied by other entities in the pack, are in something of perpetual motion, or perpetual becoming, where the observer is either centre, circumference, both, or something in between: 'It is equally possible [. . .] that I too am in perpetual motion, accompanied by Malone, as the earth by its moon' (295). And this line of flight, a phrase Beckett uses in his seminal letter to Georges Duthuit of 9 March 1949, 'lignes de fuite' (cited in Gontarski and Uhlmann 2006: 15), has neither origin nor goal: 'Going nowhere, coming from nowhere, Malone passes' (294). It is the motion of nothing in *Murphy* as well, 'a missile without provenance or target, caught up in a tumult of non-Newtonian motion' (*Murphy* 112–13). 'That's not moving, that's *moving*', the Boatswain will tell us in *Whoroscope*. And of two, dim, colliding shapes in *The Unnamable*, the narrative voice notes, 'I naturally thought of the pseudocouple Mercier-Camier' (*Three Novels* 297). What, we might ask, is the relationship among such avatars, or of each 'atavistic embryon' (*Proust* 25), as Beckett suggests of Proust's characters in his monograph on the French author? For they continue, and diverge, and disappear, and reappear as the Basils and Mahoods, Morans, or even Mollose, Molotte, or Molloc, of *Molloy*, Malone even added to the English iteration, or those who might be 'others', Saposcat and Macmann of *Malone Dies*, who evidently have much in common with their counterparts, Molloy and Malone, enlisted all, evidently, as 'sufferers of my pains' (*Three Novels* 303). 'All these Murphys, Molloys and Malones do not fool me' (303), as they have fooled many a reader, we might add. Such becoming is not, however, 'a resemblance, an imitation, or, at the limit, an identification' (Deleuze and Guattari 1987: 237), and does not, again to reference Beckett's letter to Duthuit (cited in Gontarski and Uhlmann 2006: 14), create any sort of relation. These are not discrete characters who inhabit discrete territories, but 'fundamentally a crowd' (Deleuze and Guattari 1987: 29) in a zero degree of motion, the reader struggling to re-territorialize through memories what the narrative flight has deterritorialized. When Deleuze and Guattari turn to specific examples it is to H. P. Lovecraft's *The Statement of Randolph Carter* (1920), whose title character is also a multiplicity: 'moving outrageously amidst back-grounds of other planets and systems and galaxies and cosmic continua [. . .] Merging with nothingness is peaceful oblivion' (cited in Deleuze and Guattari 1987: 240). Amid the multiplicities of *Watt*, Arsene utters the warning that characterizes the un-representable: to speak the unspeakable, to 'eff' the ineffable, 'is doomed to fail, doomed, doomed to fail' (*Watt* 62). At the end of his 'short statement' (39) Arsene 'became two men' (63). Some sorcery seems to be at work here, and in the 'Memories of a Bergsonian' section of *A Thousand Plateaus*, Deleuze and Guattari note that such 'very special becoming-animal' is not a 'degradation representing deviation from the true order' (1987: 237), nor is it a 'playing animal or imitating an animal [. . .] Becoming produces nothing other than itself' (238); attempts to represent it 'doomed, doomed to fail' (*Watt* 62).

We can thus characterize something of a philosophical gene-alogy, a line of flight that has neither need for nor interest in the periodization of Modernism, a line of which Beckett (even reluctantly) is part. Murphy et al. are deterritorialized as much as Beckett's landscapes are, and so he/they become a 'complexifica-tion' of being that manifests itself in Beckett not as represented, representative, or a representation, since so much of Beckett deals with that which cannot be uttered, known, or represented, but whose image the works (and its figures) have become, a thinking through of negativity, becoming and multiplicity through non-Newtonian motion, of being as becoming, where every movement brings something new into the world, but in something of a reverse Darwinism that moves from complex to simple organism, from Murphy to Worm, or Watt to Pim, or among the nameless figures in the short prose, a 'becoming-animal', in something not so much of a creative devolution but rather of a 'neoevolution', or to adopt another term from Deleuze and Guattari, an 'involution', which 'is in no way confused with regression' (1987: 238), becomings creating nothing less than new worlds. Writing casually to his postwar confidant Georges Duthuit in July 1951, Beckett noted in the midst of gardening chores, 'Never seen so many butterflies in such worm-state, this little central cylinder, the only flesh, is the worm' (*Letters* 2 271). The observation comes after the writing but before the premiere performance of *Waiting for Godot* in which Gogo tells Didi, 'You and your landscapes! Tell me about the worms!' (*Godot* 39). Such 'becoming-animal always involves

a pack, a band, a population, a peopling, in short a multiplicity'
Deleuze and Guattari tell us (1987: 239).[5] For Beckett it defines
creativity as well, only possible through such untethered selves
or beings, amid the generation of varieties and differences, accessible through moments of deterritorialization, characterized by
a 'fearsome involution calling us toward unheard-of becomings'
(Deleuze and Guattari 1987: 240).

Towards a Transcendental Empiricism

Watt's engagement with the quotidian 'under Mr Knott's roof'
(*Watt* 82, n. 1), then, proves a formative encounter, to the point
that his appearance in his subsequent abode, an asylum called
a pavilion,[6] suggests: 1) that the latent schizoid voice, which
announced (rather celebrated since it is encountered as music)
the irrationality inherent in the everyday, in one case as the ratio
of weeks to days in the year, both in the normal year (52.14285
...) and every fourth year in what Arsene (presumably) calls the
'February débâcle' (52.285714 ...) (*Watt* 47), begins to dominate. Its origin, however, whether internal or external, self or
other, remains indeterminate, so that an external, transcendent
world, too, remains indeterminate, the movement between the
two a series of border crossings. Watt, we are told, 'never knew
quite what to make of this particular little voice, whether it was
joking, or whether it was serious' (91). Arsene, on the eve of his
departure, anticipates, better, already embodies 2) Watt's linguistic crisis, what are called 'the eccentricities of his syntax' (75), in
his poem, 'We shall be here all night': 'Night here, here we, we
night' (47), the 'we' already subsuming Watt and night, Watt's
appearance already a serial repetition or multiplicity, a crossing
between fixed representations of phenomena or being, and as such
Arsene presumably suggests an ontological dispersal, the plurality
or multiplicity of being and the mirroring of effects that Watt will
encounter, or confront afresh, during his stay at or on his departure from the Knott house and his transition to the pavilion. The
detailed engagement with the everyday, joking or serious, forced
upon him or exacerbated by his position, serial servant in the big
house of Mr Knott, features 3) the 'incident of note' in the music
room with the Galls, father and son, 'come [. . .], all the way from
town, to 'choon the piano' (70), the incident suggesting something
of the failure of the empirical, a breakdown both of percept and

concept, that is, a bleeding between or among percepts and the failure to conceptualize and so stabilize them, such experience of slippage part of what Deleuze might finally call 'pure difference'. The Galls themselves (presumably) announce a failure of correspondence, or what Beckett will call in his 'Three Dialogues with Georges Duthuit', written in the wake of *Watt*, 'an absence of relation', in this local case among the piano's hammers, dampers (which control vibrato), and strings, the decay of which apparently dooms not only piano but tuners and players alike:

> Nine dampers remain, said the younger [Gall], and an equal number of hammers.
> Not corresponding, I hope, said the elder.
> In one case, said the younger [. . .].
> The strings are [also] in flitters, said the younger. (*Watt* 72)

The piano may, then, function enough to emit, at best, a single note or sound, but it too remains indistinct since its resonance or vibration cannot be controlled, so that ancillary strings (if any there be) also respond to the diffusion of energy, depending on which strings, even those in 'flitters', have dampers. Other sensory stimuli, the corresponding interrelation of 'lights and shadows', say, and the passing from sound to silence or silence to sound that Watt apprehends or perceives, remain indistinct and thus unpredictable, inexpressible, which phenomena 'gradually lost [. . .] all meaning, even the most literal' (*Watt* 72–3). This experience 'of note' in the music room offers something of a narrative model as well, as incidents and characters lose singularity and distinction. Such phenomenal slippage generates in Watt not only images of his father but 'a voice urging him, in terms of unusual coarseness, to do away with himself' (73). Such episodes – images of his father excepted since they appear contained, or at least 'no tendency appeared, on the part of his father's trousers, for example, to break up into an arrangement of appearances, grey, flaccid and probably fistular, or of his father's legs to vanish in the farce of their properties' (74) – tend towards the inchoate, and to which Watt's response is finally affective rather than intellectual since most perceptions or apperceptions have tended 'to break up into an arrangement of appearances' (74).

This phenomenon of the Galls, then, is very soon dispersed into undifferentiated stimuli and seems to 'belong to some story heard long before, an instant in the life of another, ill told, ill heard, and more than half forgotten' (74). Such perception or experience of both material phenomena and finally of self suggests both phenomenological and ontological disjunctions and crossings, and hence epistemological multiplicity, and is of a piece with nothing, the fullness of nothing, the nothing that Watt encounters in the abode of Mr Knott and which recurs to him long after the ebb of initial stimulus and perception, however ill they were perceived, and which he 'could not accept', as multiplicity, apparently, as other entities in the pack, other parts of the ontological multiplicity, that is, 'Arsene and Walter and Vincent and the others[,] had been unable to accept' (76). What Watt is on the cusp of accepting, and from which he finally withdraws, is molecular life, life as a series of border crossings that Deleuze calls 'worlding', the fullness of pure potentiality: 'Watt learned towards the end of his stay in Mr Knott's house to accept that nothing had happened, that a nothing had happened, [. . .] and even, in a shy way, to like it' (80).

Entities in the group, the pack, the multiplicity are each inchoate, susceptible to the dispersal of being as well. As Arsene is discussing the necessity of body shapes in perpetual orbit around Mr Knott, he notes the pattern: 'two men for ever about Mr Knott in tireless assiduity turning' (61). '[T]he case with you and Arsene', he continues, then corrects the misattribution, 'forgive me, with you and Erskine' (61), is less a simple slip, although slip it is, than a perpetual and perceptual indistinction, an overlap or comingling. This flow of undifferentiated stimuli, perceived now as one incident, now as another, so that 'the Galls and the piano were long *posterior* to the phenomena destined to become them' (79, emphasis added), suggests Watt's own defective perception, after Arsene, of spatiotemporal slippage ('glissant' not only in language but including same), or, in summary, 'the simple games that time plays with space' (75), which games suggest, finally, the triumph of the temporal over the more static spatial, and so another sort of slippage, rather than their unity.

Another case in point is Arsene's narrating what was perhaps Watt's confusion about his initial and inexplicable entry into Mr Knott's house. After plagiarizing one of Beckett's poems, 'Dieppe', Arsene notes on first meeting Watt (presumably) and of Watt, and perhaps even speaking as Watt, as Sam will speak not only for Watt but as Watt: 'he is not as yet familiar with the premises. Indeed it is a wonder to him, and will remain so, how having found the neighbourhood he found the gate, and how having found the gate he found the door, and how having found the door he passed beyond it' (40). The episode mirrors what appears to be Watt's earlier rumination, mediated by Sam, offered to the reader before Arsene's short statement:

> Watt never knew how he got into Mr Knott's house. He knew that he got in by the back door, but he was never to know, never, never to know, how the backdoor came to be opened. And if the backdoor had never opened, but remained shut, then who knows Watt had never got into Mr Knott's house at all, but turned away, and returned to the station, and caught the first train back to town. Unless he had got in through a window. (*Watt* 37)

Such a sense of pure flow of phenomena or of pure movement soon infects Watt's language as the word 'pot' slips free of signification or is complexified from abstract to plural, to innumerable and proliferating possibilities (81) as Watt's language grows increasingly 'foreign' or 'minor', that is, slips, Beckett thus working at the limits of language. This release from linguistic circumspection, from relation or correspondence, we might say, offers, or might have offered, the possibility of a transcendent experience that Watt may have 'almost liked', that of the sublime, say, or of something beyond habit or the quotidian, the experience of the unlimited, unfettered, and unformed that Murphy so assiduously sought in the third zone of his mind, an undifferentiated, incommunicable, ineffable fullness of phenomenological potential in all its movement and change, what might thus be called 'negative' representation,[7] negative, that is, attempts to represent noumena or the unknowable, 'things in themselves'. Watt's entire encounter with Arsene, and the latter's twenty-four pages of 'short statement', for example, happened, apparently, 'long before my [that is, Watt's, or rather Sam's, or perhaps Sam's as Watt since Sam only emerges, as such, at the pavilion] time', as Watt reports it, and so it was with all the servants who preceded Watt in Mr Knott's house: 'they all vanished, long before my [Watt's or Sam's, Sam never having spent 'time' at Knott's house] time' (126). Not only is the noumenal world inaccessible to Watt, but the phenomenal, perceptions, being and language, will not stand still for him either, as they did not for Arsene. They will stand still for no one, for that matter, but Watt needs them to stand still to turn perception into understanding; that is, he needs beings and phenomena to remain stable and discrete. Watt seems frustrated by the potentiality of variation and difference, which set of possibilities he might have embraced – if he were someone other than Watt, that is. Such 'becoming' produces new possibilities continually, simulations without end, a creative rather than a negative power. Watt thus approaches a line of flight, a concrete, material, transcendent insight of the phenomenal or virtual world, even as he remains in something of his own closed system, and hemmed in by assumed terms and received ideology. He is thus a political animal whose possible worlds are constrained, whose power to produce images is limited by his need for grounding. But the world of pure flow, of phenomenal and ontological multiplicity, and its narratological mirror, is the only way to understand, rather to experience the phenomenal feats of memory that we are asked to accept, Watt's memorizing Arsene's speech, relaying it long after to Sam who then retells or recreates it, from memory, in language, including episodes that took place in Watt's absence and so those Watt could not have known about to tell.

'Mr Knott's establishment' may, however, be a closed system to which 'nothing could be added [. . .] and from it nothing taken away, but that as it was now, so it had been in the beginning, and so it would remain to the end, in all essential respects, any significant presence, at any time' (*Watt* 131), presuming, of course, there were beginnings and ends. Such a closed system suggests neither stasis, nor lack of movement, nor change, however, but the opposite. So monadic an image may be seen as a virtual world, one definition of 'Nothing' in the sense of Bergson and Deleuze, nothing which might contain all potential becomings, and so the system is one less closed to change than the opposite, one open to all possibility, to all change and movement, one already including possibilities yet undreamt. In other words, Knott's establishment was all 'a coming and a going', already a virtual multiplicity. The *harmonia praestablita* or pre-established harmony associated with Leibniz and his monads (and skewered by Voltaire[8]) is inverted here to the 'pre-established arbitrary' (*Watt* 131) of *Watt*, a randomness that nonetheless suggests infinite possibility.

Such inversion of what might be expectation, of the categories of common sense or the everyday, say, as Watt experiences in the house of Mr Knott – and doubtless elsewhere and apparently since 'the age of fourteen or fifteen' (73) – and which challenges Watt's categories and concepts, leads to a rupture of those expectations that Deleuze, reversing Kant's 'transcendental idealism', has called 'transcendental empiricism', particularly 'the simple games that time plays with space' (75), or the subject's (Watt's) inability to unify those categories into a totalized and so stable experience, or to treat them as an idea.[9] Other possibilities may be available in other rooms in the Knott house: Erskine's room, for instance, where Watt confronts another 'object of note' (128), the painting of a circle, which appeared to be moving, receding, perhaps, and a point or dot, which might (or might not) be its centre, time, thus, apparently playing with space. Watt is drawn to the room to investigate the ringing bell used to summon Erskine in the dead of night to some task or other, but Erskine's room is kept locked and the key secreted on his person in a specially sewn pouch, which Watt knows about, Sam informs us, through the intervention of Lachesis, one of the daughters of necessity, at least according to Plato in Book 10 of *The Republic* (Richards 2003: 192; *Watt* 127). Watt apparently got into Erskine's room, as he got beyond Mr Knott's gate, as he got into Mr Knott's house, 'Ruse a by' (128), which recalls his linguistic encounter with Arsene's tale, exacerbated by his own slippage, the experience with the Galls and the pot which have had their effect since Watt is already reversing received syntax.

In the room he discovers no functioning bell. He does, however, encounter the painting, which he immediately tries to understand by enumerating its representational possibilities: 'By what means the illusion of movement in space, and it almost seemed time, was given, Watt could not say. But it was given' (128). For one, movement in space would inevitably suggest time, change. That is, he does perceive it moving, and its affect affects him. For Watt, then, the painting seems to simulate or represent something beyond itself, to be tied to an actual, recognizable, quotidian world, and he tries (again) to circumscribe the experience by enumerating its possibilities of representation. In his summary of the manuscript changes Beckett made to the *Watt* material, Chris Ackerley outlines the 'swelter of previous inchoate detail [shaped] as significant themes: the break-down of figure and ground; the move into the virtual world of the mirror, anticipating the breakdown of Watt [. . .]; the serial theme; and the deterioration of Watt as he fails increasingly to respond to his world' (2006: 328). The first of these, 'the breakdown of figure and ground', is something of a perceptual issue and consequently an aesthetic and ontological issue, as is the second, 'the move into the virtual world of the mirror'. Two others focus on Watt's 'breakdown' and 'deterioration', which from one perspective is precipitated by insights into the richness of the virtual world, the world of nothing, which in fact is the world of everything.[10] Much of Ackerley's conclusion, then, focuses on the painting in Erskine's room, or more pointedly on Watt's response to it, than on the larger issue of representation, but he does note of the encounter with the abstract painting, circle and point, that 'Watt's attempts to "explain" the picture illustrate a representational fallacy, the belief that art can somehow be made to mean, rather than to express' (2006: 329). And that is exactly the point, as far as it goes,[11] but Ackerley's generalized emphasis on expression is what Deleuze might call 'affect', the power of art to generate or elicit emotional response.

The seriality of exhaustive enumeration, which Beckett reminds us in *Proust* is vaudevillian (*Proust* 71), such as that surrounding Watt's feeding of Mr Knott and the redistribution of the leftovers on occasion to dogs kept explicitly for this purpose (*Watt*, 86–100), is already initiated in Arsene's story as a catalogue of Mr Knott's preferred body shapes among his servants, for instance, 'small fat shabby seedy juicy bandylegged potbellied potbottomed men' (59), or his enumeration of the earth in relation to his familial possibilities, 'my earth and my father's and my mother's and my father's father's [etc.]' (46). This strategy is pursued by Watt in terms of conceptual or spatial circumspection. Of Mr Knott's eating habits, a narrator tells us: 'Twelve possibilities occurred to Watt, in this connexion' (89). 'Other possibilities occurred to Watt' (90), of course, but he decides not to pursue them, to exhaustion, perhaps, the experience always exceeding the confines of his categories, the experience always unfettered, the experiencer thus unhinged, untethered. And Sam, the mirror image of Watt, as they walked 'breast to breast' on the pavilion grounds (165), who himself may be a mirror image of Arsene, who may be a . . ., characterizes the eccentricities of Watt's speech in direct quotation (presumably), the one time when we may hear Watt's voice directly, although narrative mediation is inescapable, as the narrator enumerates the possibilities of Watt's speech as a series of relative clauses: 'that the inversion affected, not the order of the sentences, but that of the words only', etc. (164). Such is Watt's struggle, as it is Sam's, as it was Arsene's, to describe but also to contain, to limit, to circumscribe, to spatialize, as Bergson might say, to exhaust, as Deleuze might say, what cannot be contained without its cessation or without a halting of differentiation or a congealing of desire, a movement to generalize and develop concepts rather than embrace difference, a process in which the reader is often implicated. Beckett may have characterized or pre-viewed the Watts of the world in a letter to Thomas McGreevy of 31 January 1938: 'the kind of people who in the phrase of Bergson can't be happy till they have "solidified the flowing"' (*Letters 1* 599). He was, as well, engaging Bergsonism directly in his discussions with Georges Duthuit, who, writing to Beckett on 5 March 1949 noted that André Masson and Tal Coat were struggling to move away from the limitations of space to some-thing Duthuit calls a moving space, 'human space' (*Letters 2* 143, n. 5), not unlike, we might add, Watt's perception of the painting in Erskine's room. Duthuit explains their failures in their focus on 'concepts which they go on and on presenting to me as being the very core of reality. They do not stop time, because they place themselves in a time which is no more than a succession of stops, which is nothing other than immobility' (*Letters 2* 143, n. 5). Beckett responds to Duthuit by separating Bram van Velde's work from such failure of Masson and Tal Coat:

> to say that the painter, by spreading colour on a canvas, is necessarily setting out along a road of spatial and temporal references, seems to me true only for someone who has never stopped bringing them in in the form of relations [which may be the case for Watt, but], which is not the case for Bram, if I have misexpressed myself aright. (*Letters 2* 141)

Deleuze's most direct treatment of Beckett's work is an essay entitled '*L'épuisé*' ('The Exhausted'), written as an afterword to the French publication of Beckett's four teleplays, *Quad et Trio du Fantôme, . . . que nuages . . ., Nacht und Träume* (Beckett and Deleuze 1992). The essay appears surprisingly taxonomic and progressive, or regressive, or even teleological. Deleuze categorizes all of Beckett's work in terms of three uses of language: Language I is what Deleuze calls the 'atomic language' where 'enumeration replaces propositions' (Deleuze 1995b: 7), or what we might call, after Beckett, the language of vaudeville, and Deleuze's central example here is *Watt*. Language II is a language not of names but of voices: 'The voices are waves or flows that direct and distribute linguistic corpuscles' (7). Here the central examples are the *Three Novels* and *How It Is*. And finally, Language III is that of the teleplays, a language of 'immanent limits that never cease to move about' (8). Language III drives towards the creation of the image, 'pure image, unsullied, that is nothing but image, arriving at the point where it suddenly appears in all its singularity, retaining nothing of the personal, nor of the rational' (8–9). But, of course, Deleuze's categories are already interconnected and multidirectional as *Watt* is already a collection of voices, Watt himself having no discrete, identifiable voice other than his participation in a flow of intermingled voices that includes the multiplicity or pack but has no discrete origin or master. Such absorption in a literary voice is announced repeatedly in the novel as something of a metalanguage, which Deleuze links to the combinatorial exhaustion of words, the relation of objects identical to the relations of words. Watt's attempts to own words then, his need for 'semantic succor' (*Watt* 85), are as futile as his attempts to own objects or possess concepts.

Such exhaustive enumeration as Watt attempts, his (or their) struggle to exhaust the possibilities of the real, say, always comes up short, and is thus always less than the actual; the virtual, by contrast, is always more. The virtual thus is not just, rather just not an unreal copy. The nothingness that Watt confronts, and from which he recoils, finally, suggests the full potentiality of the virtual. Watt's failure, a characteristic of all of Beckett's creations, then, is the failure to embrace that potentiality of the virtual or a failure to respond to or rather to embrace a world of incessant becoming, what Beckett calls 'flow'. Such enumeration, Deleuze tells us, 'does not happen without intermingling with nothing and abolishing the real to which it lays claim. There is only possible existence' (Deleuze 1995b: 4). Such an insight is devastating to the Watts of the world. Such 'nothing', then, the confrontation with nothing, being as only a possibility, potentially exhausts Watt since it leads to a series of disjunctions, which continue to become inclusive since everything divides, not necessarily in a series of multiplications, 'but within itself' (4). One can exhaust the possible through inclusive disjunction only by abandoning preference and signification (5), that is, to embrace the possibility of possibility, or, simply, becoming. This is the case with language, with material objects, with concepts and percepts, and finally with being itself, as Arsene, Watt, Sam, among others of the pack, are intermingled amid the possibilities and potentiality of being, and as such, this cluster already anticipates the ontological fluidity, the possibilities of being inherent in Beckett's work to come. That is, Watt, or by another name of the multiplicity or seriality, Sam, or Arsene, suggests a multiplicity or seriality that anticipates the ontology of the *Three Novels*. Watt, however, still struggles to explain experience, his perceptions, from a single privileged position, confounded repeatedly by its free flow, experience inchoate. What might become transcendental empiricism in the *Three Novels*, remains nascent in *Watt, inachevé*. As Beckett wrote to his friend and sometime literary agent, George Reavey, on 14 May 1947, 'it [*Watt*] has its place in the series, as will become clear in time' (cited in Ackerley and Gontarski 2004: 627), 'in time' itself suggesting a substantial linguistic slippage, slippage as clarity of time itself, say.

The emphasis in the analysis above is focused on a philosophical process, a line of flight, say, favoured by Henri Bergson and Gilles Deleuze, but is intended neither to demonstrate influence nor clear or progressive lines of philosophical transmission or development. More than likely Beckett never read Deleuze, who began publishing when Beckett was disinclined to foreground philosophy, but they shared interests in philosophical and narrative traditions that included Hume, Bergson, Spinoza, Nietzsche and Proust, among others. The issue here is whether or not Deleuze's way of doing philosophy allows us to understand certain perplexing, narratological and ontological questions about what many consider Beckett's most philosophical work, written in a time of unprecedented cultural upheaval. Such an approach to *Watt*, while not exhaustive, which could not, in fact, be exhaustive, places Watt's experiences of becoming untethered and his attempts at control or circumspection via exhaustive enumeration into conversation with Deleuze's rethinking of exhaustion in terms other than fatigue and towards inexhaustible possibility.

Notes

1. Letter to Georges Duthuit, 9–10 March 1949, translated by Walter Redfern, cited in Gontarski and Uhlmann 2006: 15–21. The official translation of Beckett's letter to Duthuit in *The Letters of Samuel Beckett, 1941–1956* sanitizes Beckett's French where 'cet

inintelligible besoin [...] d'y foutre de la couleur' becomes 'this unintelligible, unchangeable need to splash colour on it' (*Letters* 2 141).

2. The opening to Chapter 4 of *Creative Evolution*, say (Bergson 1944: 296–324), although Bergson is occasionally accused of simply dismissing the term, 'le néant', often translated, if somewhat misleadingly, as 'the nought'.

3. In 'A Note on Heidegger's Philosophy of Difference', Deleuze makes clear that: 'The *not* expresses not the negative but the difference between Being and being' (Deleuze 1994: 64).

4. See Herbert Spencer's *A System of Synthetic Philosophy, 1862–93*, for example.

5. Interestingly, Deleuze and Guattari cite Jorge Louis Borges as one who has 'botched at least two books' by his failure of sorcery: 'Borges is interested only in characteristics, even the most fantastic ones, whereas sorcerers know that werewolves are bands, and vampires too, and that bands transform themselves into one another' (1987: 241).

6. This designation for a mental health facility goes back at least to architect and city planner Otto Wagner's redesigned 'Am Steinhof' in Vienna of 1907, a facility which contained sixty separate buildings called Pavilions. Beckett may have known of Wagner's work since Wagner was closely associated with Gustav Klimt. The catalogue for the exhibition *Madness and Modernity: Mental Illness and the Visual Arts in Vienna 1900* at the Wellcome Collection, 1 April to 28 June 2009, describes the 'Am Steinhof' thus under the rubric 'The Modernist Mental Hospital': 'In 1907 the Am Steinhof psychiatric hospital opened on the edge of Vienna. A publicity campaign emphasized its immense size (60 separate buildings [pavilions], room for 2,500 patients and 500 staff), state of the art facilities and physical beauty. Otto Wagner, a groundbreaking Viennese architect, designed the urban plan for the complex. He also designed the hospital church, an icon of modern architecture. Wagner helped to transform a mental hospital into what a critic described as "a white city, shimmering in the bright summer sun". Patients were assigned to a pavilion and daily regime according to gender, the amount of security and supervision they were deemed to need, and ability to pay. Some had the freedom of the grounds, others were confined to cells. Images of patients in this section focus not on their lives but on their physiognomies. They reflect psychiatry's preoccupation with the bodies of the insane' (see http://www.wellcomecollection.org/

whats-on/exhibitions/madness--modernity.aspx). In 1938, the facility also became a site of the Nazi pogroms and medical experiments
when sixty of its psychiatric patients were deemed 'unworthy' of life
(see the BBC News report by Bethany Bell, 9 May 2012: http://www.
bbc.co.uk/news/world-middle-east-18014848).

7. See, for example, *The Critique of Pure Reason*: 'Objects are *given*
to us by means of sensibility', Kant writes, 'and it alone yields
intuitions; they are thought through the understanding and from the
understanding arise *concepts*' (Kant 1965: A19, B33).

8. See *Candide* (passim).

9. Kant dubbed his method of intuiting objects as 'transcendental
idealism', not then like Leibniz, say, where the relation of time and
space exists in the mind of God, and not, furthermore, as the realists
contend, that objects, physical entities, have their being in the physical world, but something in between. Kant somehow tries to position
himself between these realists and idealists, space and time as aspects
of human intuition, the objects as appearances and not things in
themselves, but the process remains grounded or has a foundation in
a human subject for Kant. Deleuze constantly seeks to free thought,
especially the process of becoming, from any single form of grounding,
so while we are thinking through experience (and Deleuze is committed to experience, hence the empiricism), we do so without benefit
of, or rather freed from a stable ground outside the process itself and
certainly not situated or grounded in a human subject, which itself is
an event within the process of experience. See further Colebrook 2002.

10. Again, see Bergson on this issue.

11. Ackerley's useful textual analysis focuses more on Beckett's textual
revisions and less on their philosophical import. The implications of
Beckett's resisting representation appear as almost an afterthought
here and thus remain underexplored for our purposes.

References

Ackerley, Chris (2006) 'An "Other Object of Note": Circle and Point
in Samuel Beckett's *Watt*', *Samuel Beckett Today/Aujourd'hui* 16,
319–32.

Ackerley, C. J. and Gontarski, S. E. (2004) *The Grove Companion to
Samuel Beckett: A Reader's Guide to his Works, Life, and Thought*,
New York: Grove Press.

Beckett, Samuel (2012) *The Collected Poems of Samuel Beckett*, ed. Seán
Lawlor and John Pilling, New York: Grove Press.

Beckett, Samuel and Deleuze, Gilles (1992) *Quad et autres pièces pour la television* [*Trio du Fantôme, . . . que nuages . . ., Nacht und Träume*] (trans. from English by Edith Fournier), *Suivi de 'L'épuisé'*, Paris: Editions de Minuit.

Bergson, Henri (1944) *Creative Evolution*, trans. Arthur Mitchell, New York: Modern Library (reprint of Henry Holt and Company, 1911).

Bergson, Henri (1946) *The Creative Mind: An Introduction to Metaphysics*, trans. Mabelle L. Andison, New York: Philosophical Library.

Colebrook, Claire (2002) 'Transcendental Empiricism', in *Gilles Deleuze*, London: Routledge, 69–78.

Deleuze, Gilles (1994) *Difference and Repetition*, trans. Paul Patton, New York: Columbia University Press.

Deleuze, Gilles (1995a) *Negotiations: 1972–1990*, trans. Martin Joughin, New York: Columbia University Press.

Deleuze, Gilles (1995b) 'The Exhausted', trans. Anthony Uhlmann, *SubStance* 24:3, 3–28.

Deleuze, Gilles and Guattari, Félix (1987) *A Thousand Plateaus: Capitalism and Schizophrenia*, trans. Brian Massumi, Minneapolis: University of Minnesota Press.

Gontarski, S. E. and Uhlmann, A. (eds) (2006) *Beckett After Beckett*, Gainesville: University Press of Florida.

Kant, Immanuel (1965) *The Critique of Pure Reason*, trans. Norman Kemp Smith, New York: St. Martin's Press.

Klossowski, Pierre (1997) *Nietzsche and the Vicious Circle*, trans. Daniel W. Smith, Chicago: University of Chicago Press.

Stanford Encyclopedia of Philosophy (2003) *Nothingness*, available at http://plato.stanford.edu/entries/nothingness.

Richards, I. A. (ed.) (2003) *Plato's Republic, Vol. 3*, Cambridge: Cambridge Archive.

Windelband, Wilhelm (1914) *A History of Philosophy with Special Reference to the Formation and Development of its Problems and Conceptions*, trans. James H. Tufts, New York: Macmillan, second edition.

6

'What it is to Have Been': Movement, Multiplicity and Representation

I can at turns imagine a nought of external perception or a nought of internal perception, but not both at once, for the absence of one consists, at bottom, in the exclusive presence of the other. (Bergson, *Creative Evolution*, 303)

I have nothing to say, and I'm saying it. (John Cage 'Lecture on Nothing' [1949])

... the kind of people who in the phrase of Bergson can't be happy till they have 'solidified the flowing' ... (Beckett to Thomas McGreevy, 31 January 1938)

Bergson's early focus on motion, on change, on evolution, on the flow of time led him to take on those classical philosophers who have seen motion and so change as illusory, most notably Parmenides and Zeno, both Eleatics, whose paradoxes were powerful statements against motion and hence against change. The debate extended into a sense of discontinuous being and the lack of fixity of any sort evident in Heraclitus, a position central to his contretemps with Parmenides. Heraclitus, a process philosopher himself, perhaps the first of that tradition, that is, those who suggest that there are no stable substances per se, emphasized a world of becoming, and such a liminal world in perpetual transition was more consonant with Bergson's sense of *durée* than the monism of Parmenides and his principal disciple Zeno.[1] For Parmenides, founder of the School of Eleas, our senses deceive us and the real world is apprehensible through logic alone. Everything that is, then, has always been; being is thus unwavering, always complete, and is part of 'the One', so that change is mere illusion. Bergson takes on the most pervasive set of proofs for this position, the Eleatic Paradoxes, in almost every one of his works. In *Matter and Memory*, for instance, he critiques Zeno's 'proof' of the impossibility or the illusion of motion by pointing out that Zeno's famous paradoxes 'consist in making time and movement coincide with the line which underlies them, in attributing to them the same subdivisions as to the line, in short, in treating them like that line' (Bergson 1991: 191). Earlier in the reworking of his second doctoral thesis, *Time and Free Will: An Essay on the Immediate Data of Consciousness*, he focused on the paradox of the racecourse, which, in Zeno's analysis, a runner could not traverse, might not, in fact, even be able to begin the circuit, since the space of the course is infinitely divisible and so the distance from start to finish is subject to infinite divisibility. Bergson counters that 'The mistake of the Eleatics arises from their identification of this series of acts, each of which is *of a definite kind* and *indivisible*, with the homogeneous space which underlies them' (Bergson 2001: 113). That is, what Zeno takes as an inscription coeval with movement, Bergson sees as a metaphor, a representation of that movement.

In some ways, admits Bergson, such reasoning as Zeno posits represents common sense or what Bergson calls 'an element of convention', as Zeno 'carries over to the movement the properties of its trajectories [that is, the divisible line or course]' (1946: 10), but much of Bergson's analysis suspends such common sense whose aim is practical solutions to problems, scientific or philosophical. A decade after *Matter and Memory*, in *Creative Evolution*, his critique of the Eleatics is even more explicit, calling the paradox an 'absurd proposition that movement is made of immobilities' (Bergson 1944: 335), and so the Eleatic paradoxes 'all involve the confusion of movement with the space covered, or at least the conviction that one can treat movement as one treats space, divide it without taking account of its articulations' (Bergson 1946: 170). Bergson's thesis is startlingly simple: 'If movement is not everything, it is nothing' (1946: 171). Denial of motion is thus for Bergson a denial of *durée*, and so of change itself. As he recounts in the autobiographical 'Introduction' to the last of his books, *The Creative Mind*, this insight into the nature of time and its measurement was his initial, his primary, intuition as a student, on which he built an entire career:

Ever since my university days I had been aware that duration [or simply time but not its measurement] is measured by the trajectory of a body in motion and that mathematical time is a line; but I had not yet observed that this operation contrasts radically with all other processes of measurement, for it is not carried out on an aspect or an effect representative of what one wishes to measure, but on something which excludes it. The line one measures is immobile, time is mobility. The line is made, it is complete; time is what is happening, and more than that, it is what causes everything to happen. The measuring of time never deals with duration as duration. (Bergson 1946: 11)

Movement, and hence change, for Bergson, 'is an indisputable reality. We may not be able to say what parts of the whole are in motion; motion there is in the whole nonetheless' (1946: 193), and '[a]ll real change is an indivisible change', he notes in his second lecture on 'The Perception of Change' (172). But Bergson warns us in the same essay that movement is not coeval with kinesis, or movement of natural wholes: 'there is change, but there are no things which change' (177), or again, 'There are changes, but there are underneath the change no things which change [. . .] movement does not imply a mobile' (173). Such might provide some insight into Watt's observations of his time in the Knott house or might be seen as an anticipatory gloss on Beckett's *Endgame*, where even as the characters run out of bicycle wheels, painkillers, and the like, nothing apparently changes. Hamm sits immobile in his chair even as he is moved about the shelter. Is he thus still or in motion?

At the opening of his long Cartesian poem, *Whoroscope* (1961), Beckett works through such qualitative and quantitative motion with the call of a boatswain: 'We're moving he said we're off' (l. 8), the boatswain apparently stationary on the ship. The reference to Galileo and music in the poem (Descartes' confusion of *père et fils* is acknowledged by Beckett in his notes to the poem), the play of harmony and dissonance, is, then, less an issue than the motion of the Earth, which Descartes discounts as 'expedient sophistry' since we appear to be stationary. But even on Earth, Galileo tells us, we are moving while at rest: 'That's not moving, that's *moving*', as the line in *Whoroscope* suggests. But the ship's passenger has a certain degree of freedom to walk against the movement of the ship, at least for a time, and is thus apparently stationary as he walks. Beckett at least raises such contradictions to motion as he thinks through Descartes, or Descartes' errors, and time, through, apparently, Bergson. Murphy may sit out of the sun, at the opening to that eponymous novel 'as though he were free', but he is tied to a chair and lives in a 'mew', a 'medium sized cage', and rocks himself into stasis (*Murphy* 1).

While such a critique of motion is consonant with that of Bergson, Beckett's most immediate source for images of time and motion comes most directly from A. A. Luce's *Bergson's Doctrine of Intuition* (1922)[2] and from J. P. Mahaffy, a Fellow of Trinity College, Dublin, and his monograph *Descartes* (1880), a book Beckett knew thoroughly enough to use freely its ideas, words and phrases for his poem. It is Mahaffy who details Descartes' confusion about the Galileos, father and son, and whether or not major thirds were concords or discords. And it is Mahaffy who foregrounds Descartes' views on motion: 'In his *Principles* [. . .] he formally denies that the earth moves [. . .] The earth indeed did not move, but it was like a passenger in a vessel, who, though he were stationary, and properly said to be at rest, is nevertheless carried along in the motion of the larger system which surrounds him' (Mahaffy 1901: 61). Beckett appropriates the image almost exactly for his long poem. The image returns in *Molloy*, where it is associated with freedom as well: 'I who had loved the image of the old Geulincx, dead young, who left me free, on the black boat of Ulysses, to crawl toward the East, along the deck' (*Three Novels* 51). One might suspect that the allusion to Geulincx may be a red herring, grown out of the connection of Descartes and motion cited in Mahaffy. That is, the allusion is inessential to the image and may deflect attention from the more pertinent possibilities of the sentence which are decidedly Bergsonian, if not Bergso-Deleuzian.

Zeno's argument is further betrayed, Bergson tells us, 'by language, which always translates movement and duration in terms of space' (1991: 191). Bergson's position on language may be something akin to anti-nominalism, or close to that 'nominalist irony' that Beckett calls for in his German letter of 1937, or as Mrs Williams notes in the theatrical fragment 'Human Wishes', 'Words fail us'. Bergson's lifelong critique of Zeno also engages issues of the relativity of motion, as he moves from mathematics to physics in ways that suggest (or even anticipate) Einstein's 'Theory of Special Relativity' of 1905, or perhaps the intersection of Einstein's formulations with Zeno's paradoxes. His clarification of *Matter and Memory* in *An Introduction to Metaphysics* (1903) asserts early on that 'My perception of motion will vary with the point of view, moving or stationary, from which I observe it' (Bergson 1999: 21). Of the Eleatic paradox called the 'Stadium', furthermore, Bergson describes the terms thus, given: 'a moving body which is displaced with a certain velocity, and which passes simultaneously before two bodies, one at rest and the other moving toward it with the same velocity as its own. During the same time that it passes a certain length of the first body, it naturally passes double the length of the other.' Zeno's conclusion that '"a dura-tion [that is, movement, or time, or change] is the double of itself", [is finally in Bergson's retort] a childish argument'. Zeno's error 'in all his reasoning is [. . .] that he leaves real duration on one side and considers only its objective track in space' (1944: 258, n. 2). For Bergson, Zeno's sophistry is a profound attack on change, the consequence of motion. Such a critique brings us up against the Bergsonian first principle: 'a very brief analysis of the idea of dura-tion will show us both why we attribute instants to duration and why it cannot have any' (190).

For Bergson then, representation is of a piece with Zeno's trajec-tory and so a falsification of motion, becoming, or life's flow. Both matter and its representations are then severally, in themselves, false issues without perception, which relies on what Bergson calls a picturing in consciousness (1991: 13), and which finally is also action, or at least, 'my perception displays . . . the eventual or possible actions of my body' (22). Matter and so the universe, for Bergson, 'is an aggregate of images. And by image we mean a certain existence which is more than that which the idealists call a *representation*, but less than that which the realists call a *thing* – an existence placed halfway between the "thing" and the "rep-resentation"' (9). Images are 'perceived when my senses are open to them, unperceived when they are closed' (17). That centre for perception, consciousness, differs from the material organ of the brain, but, 'the brain is an image like others, enveloped in a mass of other images' (41) and so is already 'the theater of very varied molecular movements' (22), which molecular movement is percep-tion, which in turn defines consciousness; that is, perception is the birth of consciousness. The body, brain included, of course, is thus within this 'aggregate of images', itself alert to perceptions in its own theatre of consciousness.

Anthony Uhlmann reframes the issue in *Samuel Beckett and the Philosophical Image* to suggest that Bergson 'is proposing understanding "the image" as a bridge between those objectively existing things and our thoughts. It is a bridge because the image exists *both in the thing*, which has or projects an image consistent with the nature of its own being, *and in our minds*, which receive the projected images in the manner of a screen' (2006: 8, emphasis added). The image is then both matter, that is, material, and a representation; representation is thus outside of neither matter nor the image but complicitous in both. In speaking of Beckett's essay 'Recent Irish Poetry' in particular, Uhlmann draws a theory of art from Bergson's bridging analysis:

> The image, then, offers one way of examining the breakdown of the object/subject relation, one way of *avoiding the rational interference of pre-digested interpretation*. Rather than interpreting its object for us (representing it by cutting it from everything not considered useful to the conscious perception of that object), art presents us with material that we must struggle to understand. (2006: 28, emphasis added)

Bergson himself put the matter directly in *The Creative Mind*:

> What is the aim of art if not to show us, in nature and in the mind, outside of us and within us, things which did not explicitly strike our senses and our consciousness? The poet and the novelist who express a mood certainly do not create it out of nothing; they would not be understood by us if we did not observe within ourselves, up to a certain point, what they say about others. (1946: 159)

A bit later in the same collection he asks his audience 'to put aside some of the artificial schema we interpose unknowingly between reality and us. What is required is that we should break with certain habits of thinking and perceiving that have become natural to us. We must return to the direct perception of change and mobility' (167). While Bergson's definition of art itself teeters on the brink of the conventional, the 'struggle to understand' art is focused on breaking what he calls 'habits of mind' through intuition, and one such habit is the antinomy of mind and body, the dualism detailed by Descartes offering challenges both to Bergson and to Beckett. Bergson's originality is located in his own breaking through those 'habits of mind'. For Bergson, 'Matter [. . .] is composed of images: *we perceive images*. Bergson defines matter in this curious way', suggests film critic Temenuga Trifonova, in order to refute the idea that what we perceive is not the real world, that perception is merely subjective. Perception, Bergson argues instead, is 'outside', in matter, insofar as our body is just an image among other images: perception is material just as matter is already perception, although an unconscious one. [. . .] perception (and therefore consciousness [. . .]) is indistinguishable from the world, perception differing from matter in degree only. (Trifonova 2003: 80–1)

Beyond or outside of the image, there is nought, but Beckett reminds us in *Murphy* of that '*Nothing than which . . . naught is more real*' (*Murphy* 246), or more straightforwardly 'nothing is more real than nothing'. Bergson's dicta are, in many respects, moreover, consonant with the Aristotelian empiricism of Aquinas summarized in the principle, *nihil in intellectu*, 'nothing in the mind', which, as the phrase continues, *nisi prius fuerit in sensu*, 'was not in the senses first'. The phrase is literally parroted in *Malone Dies* as the bird has mastered '*nihil in intellectu*' but is unable to complete the insight: 'These first three words the bird managed well enough, but the celebrated restriction was too much for it, all you heard was a series of squawks' (*Three Novels* 218). The parroted fragment retains its own insight, however; 'nothing in the mind' may be enough to gloss at least Murphy's monadic, if not solipsistic, mind, the narrator's description of which 'was not an impoverishment, for it [Murphy's mind] excluded nothing that it did not itself contain. Nothing ever had been, was or would be in the universe outside it but was already present as virtual, or actual, or virtual rising into actual, or actual falling into virtual, in the universe inside it' (*Murphy* 107). That 'virtual' in Bergson's world seems to fulfil the role of imagination, so that one might imagine Murphy's mind with the universe already contained, that is perceived, or his imagining it in various states. Murphy thus, the narrator suggests, privileges a single, absolute image, his consciousness, on which the arrangement of all other images and image clusters depends, the latter of which only represent duration. That is, besides the system that Bergson describes as that of the 'realist', or scientist, where 'an aggregate of images [is] governed, as to their mutual relations, by fixed laws, in which effects are in strict proportion to their causes, and of which the character is an absence of center . . .' (1991: 26), what the narrator of *Dream of Fair to Middling Women* called Balzac's chloroformed world of 'clockwork cabbages'.

That critique of Balzac and his world is not just literary criticism but an attack on a way of knowing, a system of epistemology. Murphy, and perhaps the Unnamable and Hamm, on the other hand, partake of an alternate system focused on perceptions, 'that is to say in which these same images [the 'aggregate of images' above] seem to depend on a single one among them, around which they range themselves on different planes, so as to be wholly transformed by the slightest modifications of this central image' (1991: 26); consciousness, and its molecular interplay through perception, is the central image to which all other images relate (1999: 26). The Unnamable's doubts about his relationship to his planetary avatars, Malone in this case, centres on such an issue of epistemology, on whether he knows them (or him) from the inside or the outside, on who is, in Hamm's phrase, 'Bang in the Center!' (*Endgame* 27): 'Malone is there. Of his mortal liveliness little trace remains. He passes before me at doubtless regular intervals, unless it is I who pass before him. No, once and for all, I do not move. He passes, motionless' (*Three Novels* 292). A slight disturbance or alteration in Hamm's relative position, for example, realigns or throws off the (or his) entire universe: 'Put me right in the center!' (*Endgame* 27). Beckett may have focused on geometry and called Hamm's preoccupation 'Pythagorean' in his 1967 staging of the play, but Hamm's preoccupation suggests a Bergsonian epistemology as well.

> Hamm: Back to my place. [. . .] Is that my place?
> Clov: Yes, that's your place.
> Hamm: Am I right in the center?
> Clov: I'll measure it.
> Hamm: More or less! More or less!
> Clov: (*Moving the chair slightly*) There.
> Hamm: I'm more or less in the center?
> Clov: I'd say so.
> Hamm: You'd say so! Put me right in the center.
> (*Endgame* 26–7)

Or again with regard to Murphy's interest in astrology:

> Between him and his stars no doubt there was correspondence, but not in Suk's sense. They were *his* stars, he was the prior system. He had been projected, larval and dark, on the sky of that regrettable hour as

on a screen, magnified and clarified into his own meaning. But it was *his* meaning. The moon in the Serpent was no more than an image, a fragment of a vitagraph [that is, a movie projector]. (*Murphy* 183)

What Bergson might take issue with in Aquinas's dictum, '*nihil in intellectu*', however, is the priority, 'prius'; as he sets up his argument about *nihil*: 'I say to myself that there might be, that indeed there ought to be, nothing, and I then wonder that there is something. I represent all reality extended on nothing, and being has come by superaddition to it. Or yet again, if something has always existed, nothing must have served as its substratum or receptacle, and is therefore eternally prior. [. . .] being may have always been there, but the nought which is filled, and, as it were, stopped by it, pre-exists for it none the less . . . ' (Bergson 1944: 300). Bergson thus critiques the monadic model of at least Leibniz, if not that of Murphy's mind, as he demonstrates the insufficiency of this model to derive the material world from consciousness. Such a view, that 'the full is an embroidery on the canvas of the void, and that in the idea of "nothing" there is *less* than in the idea of "something"' (300) is a 'pseudo-idea' and so 'the problems that are raised around it [. . .] become pseudo-problems' (302). Bergson's analysis suggests an inviting gloss on *The Unnamable* or the work of short fiction which asks us to imagine the *nihil* directly, 'Imagination Dead Imagine':

At the very instant that my consciousness is extinguished, another consciousness lights up – or rather, it was already alight: it had arisen the instant before, in order to witness the extinction of the first; for the first could disappear only for another and in the presence of another. I see myself annihilated only if I have already resuscitated myself by an act which is positive, however involuntary and unconscious. So, do what I will, I am always perceiving something either from without or within [. . .] The image, then, so called, of a suppression of everything is never formed by thought. (Bergson 1944: 303–4)

Or again, he notes, a few pages later:

I may suppose that I sleep without dreaming or that I have ceased to exist; but at the very instant when I make this supposition, I conceive myself, I imagine myself watching over my slumber or surviving my annihilation, and I give up perceiving myself from within only by taking refuge in the perception of myself from the without. (307)

If such an argument raises the paradox of apperception, the impossibility of the self perceiving itself, its resolution lies in the Bergsonian method: intuition. His conclusion is thus a bridge between being and nothingness, or matter and memory:

> there is more, and not less, in the idea of an object conceived as 'not existing' than in the idea of this same object conceived as 'existing'; for the idea of the object 'not existing' is necessarily the idea of the object 'existing' with, in addition, a representation of an exclusion of this object by the actual reality taken in block. (311)

For Bergson, much of this argument about the opposition of nought to something – which reaches back at least to the Atomists and Sophists (see the oft cited Democritus's τίποτα δεν είναι πραγματικότερο από τίποτα ['Nothing is more real than Nothing'] [cited in Weller 2005: 41]), which Murphy parrots and which Beckett encountered at least from his reading of Windelband – is thus a 'pseudo problem' (302), since 'The act by which we declare an object unreal therefore posits the existence of the real in general' (310).

There is then a multiplicity and simultaneity of images, perceptions, ideas, and representations within and without, the within part of the without (1991: 25). Murphy's mind is thus a potential site of becoming. Language represented for the young Beckett in 1937 (and we could end the sentence there) a 'veil that must be torn apart to get at the things (or the Nothingness) behind it' (Beckett 1984: 171). Call it music if one will, as Beckett does at this point, but it is the Nothingness (or music) that subsumes matter and being, 'that final music or that silence [or absence, we might add] that underlies All' (172), or what Bergson might call 'the continuous melody of our inner life' (1946: 176). That absence, or music, or silence, beyond or behind the veil of language is the multiplicity that Bergson calls *durée* and the solution not only to Cartesian dualism but to the representative system of language. Beyond the extension produced by language, the representation of knowledge, lies not an absence or an unveiled static truth, but a flux, a multiplicity of images without form, essentially the third zone of Murphy's mind, images within images, Bergson's image complex or the term that Deleuze and Guattari appropriate, multiplicities, accessible only through the metaphysics of intuition, as Krapp may have discovered that stormy night on the Kingstown Pier, and then got it wrong on tape. That is, what Krapp does with his intuited insight is to return to the old habits of analysis, immediately to betray the intuition by 'translating' it into language as he reduces the 'multiple states' of lived and felt experience into something of a chronological line, something akin to the path of the Zeno's arrow in flight. Bergson's essay on metaphysics not so much glosses *Krapp's Last Tape* in some anachronistic slight of hand as outlines the failures of a method that Krapp happens to practice: 'There is a succession of states, each of which announces that which follows and contains that which precedes it. They can, properly speaking, only be said to form multiple states when I have already passed them and turn back to observe their track' (Bergson 1999: 25), that track perhaps Clov's principle insight in *Endgame*, the 'little trail of dust' he observes behind him. What Krapp fails at is the experience of being that Bergson calls *durée*, because 'Pure duration ... excludes all idea of juxtaposition, reciprocal externality, and extension' (1999: 26). Krapp, finally, in his attempt to understand, to know being or its most immediate example, remains fettered by what Bergson calls 'habits of mind' (1999: 26, 27). The tapes do not offer the convergence of images that would access pure *durée* but a quantity of moments. The fallacy is the confusion or conflation of the One and the Multiple; more tapes or more representations on tape do not add up to a life, do not constitute a fuller understanding of what Bergson calls 'an undivided present' (1946: 180), just as additional grains of millet add nothing to the sense or idea of heapness. Insight into the One, or into the 'All' that Beckett references in his 1937 letter and flirts with most of his creative life, would require intuition and the breaking of habit, the impossibility of which is at least represented by Krapp's inability to resist bananas and drink, his continued need to represent in language on tape, and his preoc-cupation with 'concepts'. Krapp's means of knowing is analytic rather than intuitive, the latter of which Bergson also calls meta-physics. At best one of the images that might have formed a mul-tiplicity is singled out and so displaces or excludes others, that of the woman in the punt. Krapp's enterprise, which is at base episte-mological and ontological, collapses as does his material being. It may be little more than coincidence that one of Bergson's images for memory, and so being, in *The Creative Mind*, is reminiscent of or evokes the tape recorder: two spools with a tape running between them, one spool unwinding the tape, the other winding it up (1946: 192–3). But Bergson immediately rejects this image of accumulation, 'To tell the truth, it is neither a winding nor an unwinding, for these two images evoke the representation of lines or surfaces whose parts are homogeneous to and superposable on one another' (193). Krapp seems to have sullied his 'spools' with language, accepted the representation, as the tape captures only a series of moments, still points, and so is itself testimony of his failures. Taping is, or should be, an unnecessary exercise: 'In reality', Bergson tells us in *Creative Evolution*, 'the past is preserved by itself automatically. In its entirety, probably, it follows us at every instant; all that we have felt, thought and willed from our earliest infancy is there, leaning over the present which is about to join it, pressing against the portals of consciousness that would fain leave it outside' (1944: 7), or again in *The Creative Mind*, 'The past preserves itself automatically' (1946: 180). Krapp's taped rendition of the past, its representation, is inauthentic, little more than a series of snapshots. *Endgame* may as well outline such failures of representation, or more generally of language, in Hamm's narrative attempt to remember, even as the play itself sounds very like a meditation on motion, and hence on time and change: to Hamm's 'What time is it?' Clov offers something of a Parmenidian response, 'The same as usual' (*Endgame* 94). Hamm is alarmed, 'But we breathe, we change! We lose our hair, our teeth! Our bloom! Our ideas!' (97); that is we change. Despite what seems like time stopped, 'Something is' indeed 'taking its course'. This Hamm intuits despite evidence to the contrary.

More important, perhaps, is that such a critique of representation suggests something central to Beckett's late work, to his theatre, to Beckett's idea of theatre, particularly the late theatre, and to his late prose, as he abandons narrative and at times intelligibility in favour of perception and the image. Late works like *Company* or *That Time*, to take just two examples, are indeed explorations of memory, but often memory extended into space, memory as external and material, and so often unrecognizable as an image of being to the protagonists. Theatre is by definition spatial, where even images, those mental bridges, occupy space since they are material or partake of the material, and so there is an inherent static quality to theatre, an arresting of *durée*. Even ideas or memories play in theatrical space, as what appears to be something approaching the pure interiority of consciousness or the stream of consciousness is often externalized, especially in Beckett's late theatre, as memory materialized. In Trifonova's analysis of Bergson she notes that

> The image, then, is important since it reveals the origin of consciousness as conscious perception, but insofar as conscious perception differs only in degree from unconscious perception. The image does not reveal the qualitative difference between matter and mind, which consists of the mind's capacity to preserve images, in its capacity for memory. (2003: 81)

In *That Time* externalized voices take on an interrogative function over such an issue, repeatedly asking, 'When was that', or 'Was that the time or was that another time' (*CDW* 388, 390) as they respond to what are essentially snapshots of memory. At best such extension or spatialization of memory into theatrical (or narrative) space, memory observed externally and materially, offers immobile points of memory's mobility, moments of time stopped in a process of continuous motion and change, or, in works like 'A Piece of Monologue' and *Film*, snapshots themselves; they can produce only what Bergson calls 'a counterfeit of real movement' which fails to evoke the 'instability of the real' (1999: 44), hence Beckett's figures are uniformly perplexed at what purports to be memory or the real, even materialized as snapshots, since they are unrecognizable by consciousness as the felt experience of being or self. It is the mind's or memory's participation in matter that seems to perplex the perceivers on stage.

From such a perspective of the image, then, there is no distinction in consciousness between what we might call the corporeal and the incorporeal. The two figures of 'Ohio Impromptu', not named but functionally described as Reader and Listener, are 'as alike as possible' (*CDW* 445) even as one is apparently spirit, one material, but not to consciousness; the image of the one is as the image of the other as we perceive both on the screen of consciousness in images that partake of both the spirit and the material. That is the nature of the image in Bergson's terms. The play's impact lies not in the curious narrative being read aloud, since that is already written and so static, but in the interplay and layering of image and memory, in the flux of such a conjunction, the becoming that defies summary. It is Beckett working on the nerves of his audience. And the issue of *Footfalls* similarly is not to decipher which of the images is corporeal and which not, that is, why the stage remains empty in the brief but essential fourth act, but in the multiplicity of haunting images. The empty stage thus already contains 'it all'.

Such an analysis of Beckett's work as offered here is not designed to suggest that Beckett consciously or necessarily followed Bergsonian models, but that the Bergsonian spirit, his metaphysics, his anti-empirical emphasis on intuition, his critique of language and representation, his emphases on image and the act of perception, and his exteriorization of memory, all of which infused much of Modernism, infused Beckett and his work as well. Writing to his confidant, Thomas McGreevy, on 31 January 1938, Beckett offers some faint praise of McGreevy's essay on Jack Yeats, telling him that he has provided a clue 'to the kind of people who in the phrase of Bergson can't be happy till they have "solidified the flowing"' (*Letters 1* 599). Krapp may be one of those people, one who struggles to arrest the flow of *durée* with concepts or symbols. 'Metaphysics is therefore the science which claims to dispense with symbols', Bergson tells us in *The Creative Mind* (1946: 191), or as the narrator of the seminal, the liminal *Watt* has noted, perhaps reluctantly disclosing something of an aesthetics, 'No symbols where none intended' (*Watt* 254). Watt too, however, may be among those trying to solidify the flowing. In the 'Translator's Preface' to *Time and Free Will: An Essay on the Immediate Data of Consciousness*, F. L. Pogson summarized Bergson's position on concepts thus:

> For him reality is not to be reached by any elaborate construction of thought: it is given in immediate experience as a flux, a continuous process of becoming, to be grasped by intuition, by sympathetic insight. Concepts break up the continuous flow of reality into parts external to one another, they further the interests of language and social life and are useful primarily for practical purposes. But they give us nothing of the life and movement of reality; rather, by substituting for this an artificial reconstruction, a patchwork of dead fragments, they lead to the difficulties which have always beset the intellectualist philosophy, and which on its premises are insoluble. (Bergson 2001: vi)

It is thus not a matter of Beckett's writing through or even against Bergson as such, appropriating Bergson in some unacknowledged way, so much as Beckett writing through consciousness and perception, as Beckett exploring such issues through the only consciousness he *could* know, his own, and that only through what Bergson thought of as the rigorous method of intuition, breaking his own habits of mind in the process, a process at which many of his characters inevitably fail. Bergson was the primary scientist and philosopher of consciousness in France and the English-speaking world in the first half of the twentieth century, and at very least he outlined the central preoccupations of Modernism. He was thus unavoidable. 'There is at least one reality', Bergson tells us, 'which we all seize from within, by intuition and not by simple analysis. It is our own person in its flowing through time, the self which endures' (1946: 191). Beckett may have best described this 'self which endures' to friend and painter Avigdor Arikha in a letter of 11 November 1958. Arikha apparently asked if Beckett was 'working'. 'Not yet', was the reply, 'after Dublin I hope. Try to tell one more time what it is to have been' (Atik 1984: 39). The sentiment was varied in a tribute to the painter, 'For Avigdor Arikha', in 1967, which concludes, 'Truce for a space and the marks of what it is to be and be in face of. Those deep marks to show' (*Arikha* 10).

Notes

1. For further details see *The Routledge Encyclopedia of Philosophy*, Vol. 7 (Craig 1998: 734).
2. We might mention here as well Luce's book connecting Berkeley with the post-Cartesian Occasionalists, *Berkeley and Malebranche: A Study in the Origins of Berkeley's Thought* (London: Oxford University Press; Humphrey Milford, 1934). The 'Introduction' suggests something of a methodology that Beckett will follow for a time as well: 'Reading where Berkeley read [that is in the Trinity College, Dublin Old Library], using sometimes the volumes he used, I studied the authorities he mentions. Malebranche was to me, at the outset, simply one of a large number of such authorities. The extent of Berkeley's debt to *Recherche de la Vérité* came to me as an unanticipated discovery.' As Beckett wrote to Thomas McGreevy on 5 March 1936, two years after Luce's book had been published: 'I have been reading Geulincx in T. C. D., without knowing why exactly. Perhaps

because the text is so hard to come by. But that is rationalization and my instinct is right and the work worth doing, because of its saturation in the conviction that the sub specie aeternitatis [under the aspect of eternity, that is, what is universally and eternally true] vision is the only excuse for remaining alive' (*Letters* I 318–19). Beckett has mentioned to any number of scholars that a central theme of *Murphy* was the *Ubi nihil vales, ibi etiam nihil veils* of Geulincx, 'Where you are worth nothing you will wish for nothing' (Knowlson 1996: 207). See also Arnold Geulincx, *Ethics: With Samuel Beckett's Notes* (Brill's Studies in Intellectual History), ed. Han Van Ruler and Anthony Uhlmann, trans. Martin Ruler, Leiden: Brill Publications, 2006, and David Tucker, *Samuel Beckett and Arnold Geulincx: Tracing 'a literary fantasia'*, London: Bloomsbury Academic, 2012.

References

Atik, Anne (2001) *How It Was: A Memoir of Samuel Beckett*, London: Faber and Faber, 2001.

Beckett, Samuel (1984) *Disjecta: Miscellaneous Writings and A Dramatic Fragment*, ed. Runy Cohn, New York: Grove Press.

Bergson, Henri (1999) *An Introduction to Metaphysics*, trans. T. E. Hulme, Cambridge: Hackett Publishing Co. (1903; first English translation 1912).

Bergson, Henri (1944) *Creative Evolution*, trans. Arthur Mitchell, New York: Modern Library (1907, first English translation 1911).

Bergson, Henri (1946) *The Creative Mind*, trans. Mabelle L. Andison, New York: Philosophical Library.

Bergson, Henri (1991) *Matter and Memory*, trans. Nancy Margaret Paul and W. Scott Palmer, New York: Zone Books (1897, first English translation 1910).

Bergson, Henri (2001) *Time and Free Will: An Essay on the Immediate Data of Consciousness*, Mineola, NY: Dover Publications (1889, first English translation 1913).

Craig, Edward (ed.) (1998) *Routledge Encyclopedia of Philosophy*, Vol. 7, London: Routledge.

Knowlson, James (1996) *Damned to Fame: The Life of Samuel Beckett*, New York: Simon and Schuster.

Luce, A. A. (1922) *Bergson's Doctrine of Intuition: The Donnellan Lectures for 1921*, London: Society for Promoting Christian Knowledge. Available at http://ia351405.us.archive.org/2/items/bergsonsdoctrineoolucerich/bergsonsdoctrineoolucerich.pdf.

Mahaffy, J. P. (1901) *Descartes*, London: William Blackwood.

Trifonova, Temenuga (2003) 'Matter-Image or Image-Consciousness: Bergson contra Sartre', *Janus Head* 6:1 (2003), 80–114. (Much of the essay material was reworked in *The Image in French Philosophy*, Amsterdam: Rodopi, 2007.)

Uhlmann, Anthony (2006) *Samuel Beckett and the Philosophical Image*, Cambridge: Cambridge University Press.

Weller, Shane (2005) *A Taste for the Negative: Beckett and Nihilism*, London: Legenda Press.

7

Beyond the Shadow:
Acts of Unceasing Creation

Now, if some bold novelist, tearing aside the cleverly
woven curtain of our conventional ego, shows us under this
appearance of logic a fundamental absurdity, under this
juxtaposition of simple states an infinite permeation of a
thousand different impressions which have already ceased to
exist the instant they are named, we commend him for having
known us better than we know ourselves. This is not the case,
however, and the very fact that he spreads out our feelings in a
homogeneous time, and expresses its elements by words, shows
that he in his turn is only offering us its shadow. (Bergson,
Time and Free Will, 133–4)

Wearying soon of this he dropped his head on his arms in the
midst of the chessmen, which scattered with a terrible noise. Mr
Endon's finery persisted for a little in an after-image scarcely
inferior to the original. Then this also faded and Murphy
began to see nothing, that colourlessness which is such a rare
postnatal treat, being the absence (to abuse a nice distinction)
not of percipere but of percipi. (*Murphy* 246)

Would you let me add 5 or 6 pages to the last 9 [of *Proust*]?
Or would that make it too long? I would like to develop the
parallel with Dostoievski and separate Proust's intuitivism
from Bergson's. (Beckett, letter to Charles Prentice, 14 October
1930)

In his 1966 study of Henri Bergson, which he calls *Bergsonism*,
Gilles Deleuze focuses on intuition as *the* method in Bergson's
overall philosophical project, a rethinking of metaphysics in terms
of duration (*durée*), that is, time as opposed to space. 'Intuition

is neither a feeling, an inspiration, nor a disorderly sympathy, but a fully developed method', notes Deleuze, 'one of the most fully developed methods in philosophy. It has strict rules, constituting that which Bergson calls "precision" in philosophy', and the method already assumes, and perhaps subsumes, duration (Deleuze 1988: 13). Elizabeth Grosz picks up the analysis in her essay 'Bergson, Deleuze and Becoming', where she notes:

> Intuition is, for Bergson, a relatively rare but ever-productive force in the history of philosophy: it occurs only when old and familiar methods by which intelligence seeks to address the present and the new exhaust themselves and provide only generalizations rather than a concept uniquely suited to its object. [. . .] intuition is an emergent and imprecise movement of simplicity that erupts by negating the old, resisting the temptations of intellect to understand the new in terms of the language and concepts of the old (and thus the durational in terms of the spatial). This eruption of intuition, as rare as it is, marks the history of philosophy, much as Kuhn [in *The Structure of Scientific Revolutions*, 1970] understands that the paradigm shift continually marks and remakes the history of science. (Grosz 2005: 7–8)

In Bergson's restatement of what might be called Cartesian dualism, the brain, especially if conceived as the seat of or reservoir for memory, is part of the spatialization of time since it is connected to the machinery of the body, and perception, as opposed to the perceiver him or herself, the process of connection between the inner and the outer, material world. The interaction of the perceiver and the perceived may have been a central tenet for Beckett's thought, what he often called rapport or relation (see Beckett 1984: 144; 2006: 20), and which he overtly associated with Berkeley's *esse est percipi*, but, thus stated, it is a false question for Bergson, as is the central Cartesian equation 'Cogito ergo sum', since the spatialized 'I' of the conclusion is already posited, *ipse dixit*, as a premise. Thought, on the other hand, is another matter – or rather, something *other* – since it is not matter, or not entirely matter, not a spatialized entity but what Bergson calls pure *durée*, the discussion of which must be segmented and extended in order to be examined and represented. Such representation, that is, all representation, falsifies life's flow, *durée*, as lived experience is segmented and brought into the realm of space, and so representation is always already doomed to failure for Bergson and, finally, for Beckett as well. As Bergson summarizes the issue at the opening of *Time and Free Will*, his 1889 treatise on *The Immediate Data of Consciousness*, as his subtitle proclaims, language itself is a major part of the philosophical confusion:

> language requires us to establish between our ideas the same sharp and precise distinctions, the same discontinuity, as between material objects [. . .]. But it may be asked whether the insurmountable difficulties presented by certain philosophical problems do not arise from our placing side by side phenomena which do not occupy space, and whether, by merely getting rid of the clumsy symbols round which we are fighting, we might not bring the fight to an end. (2001: xix)

Beckett summarizes such an idea in his 1931 lectures on the modern novel as Bergson's 'idea of [the] inadequacy of the *word* to translate impressions registered by instinct' (cited in Burrows 1931: 9); and again, in his analysis of Gide and Dostoyevsky, Beckett notes, 'Bergson denied [the] value of language to translate impression' (17).[1] The issue is thus most often for Bergson, 'a confusion of duration with extensity, of succession with simultaneity, of quality with quantity' (2001: xx). These are the three antinomies or binaries at the heart of the Bergsonian enterprise and the source of most philosophical confusion. Pure *durée* is unrepresentable, ineffable, and constitutes for Bergson (and Beckett) a central metaphysical, ontological, existential, and so literary problem, the attempt to 'eff' the ineffable, to represent, and so segment and spatialize, the flow of being. As Bergson describes it, duration

> is the form which the succession of our conscious states assumes when our ego lets itself *live*, when it refrains from separating its present state from its former states [. . .]. We can thus conceive of succession without distinction, and think of it as a mutual penetration, an interconnection and organization of elements, each one of which represents the whole, and cannot be distinguished or isolated from it except by abstract thought. (2001: 100–1)

Such 'abstract thought' is distortive, by definition, at best a shadow of *durée*. The struggle, or in Beckett's case the imperative, to represent it, to present its flow satisfactorily, wholly, accurately is fore-doomed to failure but is, nonetheless, the driving *élan* of Beckettian men and women (or of the Beckettian narrator), the impossible figures who inhabit Beckett's art, and the unavoidable consequence of being. If duration is accessible at all, it is so through what Bergson, whom Beckett called to his Trinity students 'a philosophical visionary', discovers as his discourse on method, intuition, which he opposed to the scientific, quotidian functioning of mind. Beckett reviewed these issues for his class at Trinity College during Michaelmas 1931, where he distinguished between 'Bergsonian conception of intelligence & intuition'; 'B's [Bergson, but 'B' might equally signify Beckett as well] intuition *is* highest intelligence – *l'intelligence personnelle*'; on the other hand, '*fonctionnement de l'esprit* [that is, function of mind] = lowest form of intelligence, mind doing twice work' (Burrows 1931: 9),[2] Beckett here reiterating Bergson's insistence on the irreconcilability of intelligence and intuition. As part of his definition of postnaturalism, what we might today simply call Modernism, Beckett told his class that 'intuition can obtain a total vision that intelligence can't'. Intelligence can 'apprehend the passage of time but not [the] present moment' (7). In student Rachel Burrows' notes, from which these observations are taken, she is for a time confused about whether Beckett's comments apply to Proust or Bergson, attributing them first in her notebook to 'Bergson', then having doubts and scratching that out to replace it with 'Proust', then again scratching out 'Proust' to reassert 'Bergs' (8). Beckett further related Bergson's 'method' to 'la vision intuitive' of Rimbaud. Against the 'order' of romanticism and naturalism, Beckett posited an 'artistic disorder', its method Bergson's intuition and 'la vision intuitive' of Rimbaud (7). For much of his lecture Beckett cites Julien Benda's 1927 work *La trahison des clercs* (*The Treason of Intellectuals* [or of the man of letters, perhaps]) on Bergson favourably (8); 'B's intuition is heightened intelligence', according to Burrows's notes, what Beckett called 'l'intelligence personnelle', and he reminds his pupils of 'Bergs. contempt for mechanical intelligence' (19–21).

Beckett's preoccupation with time, 'that double-headed monster of damnation and salvation' that he announces at the opening of his anti-academic manifesto on Marcel Proust, is indeed an equation 'never simple', in part because it is as much a critique of Proust's Proust, Henri Bergson (and some Nietzsche), as of Proust himself. The Bergson connection is not often acknowledged by Beckett and so has remained underexplored by his critics; the sole mention in the Knowlson biography, for example, is Beckett's

letter to Thomas McGreevy of 24 February 1931, where he associated the juvenile prank, *Le Kid*, with Corneille and Bergson.
Beckett took pains to separate Bergson from Proust in his class
that same year, noting that the latter was 'detached from the
Bergsonian conception of time but interested in this opposition –
instinct and [or, versus] conscious intelligence. Bergson insists on
absolute time: Proust denies it. For Proust it's a function of too
many things – local but not absolute reality' (Burrows 1931: 9).
But Proustian time, and its corollaries, memory and habit, overlap
Bergsonian time, or duration, and both offer critiques of (or even
solutions to) Cartesian duality. But Beckett seems to misconstrue
here what he calls Bergson's sense of both 'absolute time' and
'absolute reality', or the confusion may have been that of his
seventeen-year-old student. In *Creative Evolution* (1911) Bergson
certainly seems less than absolutist about time, noting that those
who posit what he calls 'radical mechanism' – a problem about
which Beckett, almost quoting Bergson directly, complains as well
in his Proust monograph and in his first novel, *Dream of Fair to
Middling Women* – postulate a time 'complete in eternity, and
in which the apparent duration of things expresses merely the
infirmity of a mind that cannot know everything at once', or in
Beckett's terms, 'We cannot know and cannot be known' (*Proust*
49). 'But duration', Bergson continues, 'is something very different
from this for our consciousness, for that which is most indisputable in our experience. We perceive duration as a stream against
which we cannot go. It is the foundation of our being, and, as
we feel, the very substance of the world in which we live' (1944:
45). And Bergson repeatedly acknowledges 'a cardinal difference
between *concrete* time [. . .] and that *abstract* time which enters
into our speculations on artificial systems' (25).

Admittedly, Beckett could and would find much to resist in
Bergson, or at least to feel ambivalent about, especially Bergson's
mysticism, its corollary the *élan vital*, and his insistence on a
total vision, mystically achieved through intuition, if at all. In his
summary of *Bergsonism*, Deleuze focuses on the idea of the 'certainty' of the whole (or hole?) to which mysticism (or intuition)
offers access, which in some regards is Bergson's resolution to
Cartesian dualism:

> The great souls – to a greater extent than philosophers – are those
> of artists and mystics (at least those of a Christian mysticism that

Bergson describes as being completely superabundant activity, action, creation). At the limit it is the mystic who plays with the whole of creation, who invents an expression of it, whose adequacy increases with its dynamism. Servant of an open and finite God (such are the characteristics of the *Élan Vital*), the mystical soul actively plays the whole of the universe [what Bergson calls 'the real whole' (1944: 36)], and reproduces the opening of a Whole in which there is nothing to see or to contemplate. [. . .] Everything happens as if that which remained indeterminate in philosophical intuition gained a new kind of determination in mystical intuition – as though the properly philosophical 'probability' extended itself into mystical certainty. (Deleuze 1988: 112)

There may be precious little 'mystical certainty' in Beckett, but, as Bergson makes clear in *Creative Evolution*, the *élan vital*, the '"vital principle" may indeed not explain much, but it is at least a sort of label affixed to our ignorance, so as to remind us of this occasionally' (1944: 48). It is decidedly opposed to teleology, or what Bergson calls 'mechanism'. What Deleuze see as certainty, another name for which is evolution, or *durée* itself, moreover, is a process of perpetual becoming. If the whole represents a continuity, it is a 'Continuity of change, preservation of the past in the present, real duration – the living being seems, then, to share these attributes with consciousness. Can we go further and say that life, like conscious activity, is invention, is unceasing creation?' (Deleuze 1988: 27).

Beckett's reading of Proust, and more broadly his critique of music, is, of course, decidedly, avowedly, mystical. As he concludes his monograph on Proust (1931):

Schopenhauer rejects the Leibnitzian view of music as 'occult arithmetic', and in his aesthetics separates it from the other arts, which can only produce the Idea with its other concomitant phenomena [that is, the 'other arts' are decidedly representational], whereas music is the Idea itself [that is, non-referential *durée* at its best], unaware of the world of phenomena, existing ideally outside the universe [of matter, we might add], apprehended not in Space but in Time only, and consequently untouched by the teleological hypothesis [that is, as a constant becoming]. This essential quality of music is distorted by the listener who, being an impure subject, insists on giving a figure [extensity, spatialization] to that which is ideal and invisible [the seamless simultaneity that is *durée*], on incarnating the Idea in what he conceives to be an appropriate paradigm. (*Proust* 70–1)

The passage does indeed summarize Schopenhauer as it also suggests Nietzsche on music, but it is, fundamentally, a gloss on Bergsonian *durée* as well, the art corrupted by the subject's struggles to extend into space that which is pure, seamless, temporal simultaneity. The final apprehension of music, the highest in the hierarchy of the arts, is thus mystical.

Proust, moreover, articulates the distinction between voluntary and involuntary memory; the latter restores the past object and reveals the real. The past is thus contemporaneous with and inextricably part of the present, the smell of the perfume 'new precisely because already experienced' (*Proust* 55). Beckett thus describes Proust's *méthode*, but it is unalloyed Bergsonism as well. As Beckett lays out the argument in *Proust*, voluntary memory is rejected as 'the application of a concordance to the Old Testament of the individual' (19). Linked with Habit as 'attributes of the Time cancer' (7), voluntary memory presents the past in monochrome, like 'turning the leaves of an album of photographs' (19), with no interest in 'the mysterious element of inattention that colours our most commonplace experiences' (19). Murphy's attempt to reconstitute the image of his father (*Murphy* 251), for example, is an allegory of its failings. Involuntary memory, on the other hand, is 'an unruly magician and will not be importuned' (*Proust* 20); Proust's book is a monument to its action. The madeleine episode in particular conjures a childhood world that 'comes out of a teapot' (21); it offers the only possible 'accidental and fugitive salvation' (22). Beckett calls it a 'mystic experience', the factor that resolves the Proustian equation. If *by accident* (Beckett's emphasis), by 'some miracle of analogy' (54), the impression of a past sensation recurs as an immediate stimulus, then the 'total past sensation, not its echo nor its copy [that is, not a metaphor, representation, or simulation] but the sensation itself' (54), rushes in to (re)create the experience, whole and real, apparently, and thus overcoming the gulf between past and present, symbol and substance, perception and remembering, ideal and real. Such moments are real without being actual, ideal without being abstract (Proust 1927: 872), and decidedly of a piece with what we might call Bergsonian material metaphysics.

A summary of Proust's self-consciousness, Beckett's critique serves as a gloss on Bergson as well, who, in *Matter and Memory*, particularly in its justly famous opening chapter, discussed the differences between what he called 'cerebral memory' (that is, 'voluntary memory') and 'pure recollection' (or 'involuntary memory'). Like Proust (but unlike Descartes in this respect), Bergson claimed that all of a human's experience is retained by one or another form of memory. Cerebral or voluntary, memory is tied to the body and is thus the record of habitual actions; pure recollection, on the other hand, cannot be accessed at or by will. It reveals itself through the accidents of living through the method Bergson calls intuition.

For Bergson, memory permits the existence of consciousness, which in turn, supports the idea of self, but in a state of constant becoming. The self is itself memory, and is thus experienced as a spatialized break in the flow of *durée*, which at each moment, at each instant presents a new image of self to consciousness. But even involuntary memory or pure recollection corrupts for Bergson, for it too is an extension, a spatialization of life's flow, time, *durée*. What is perceived thus is a static, spatialized *image* of life's flow, further removed from *durée* by attempts to represent it in language, an agent of habit. At best one can experience, and so represent, not images of *durée* itself, but, because of the temporal delays of consciousness, afterimages of *durée*, the shadow of *durée*, the ghosts of *durée*. As Bergson notes in *Matter and Memory*, 'The moment of which I am speaking is already far from me [. . .]. The physical state, then, that I call my "present", must be both a perception of the immediate past and a determination of the immediate future' (1991: 138). That perception then itself is thus always late, belated, its image always and only an afterimage:

> Every *active* perception truly involves a *reflection* [. . .] that is to say the projection, outside ourselves, of an actively created image, identical with, or similar to, the object on which it comes to mould itself. If, after having gazed at an object, we turn our eyes abruptly away, we obtain an 'afterimage' of it: Must we not suppose that this image existed already while we were looking? [the originary image, if such there were, is thus already an afterimage] [. . .] Any memory-image that is capable of interpreting our perception inserts itself so thoroughly into it that we are no longer able to discern what is memory and what is perception. (Bergson 1991: 102–3)

Cognitive scientists like Antonio Damasio have confirmed Bergson's intuitions as he comments on the neurological belatedness of perception. As Damasio suggests in *Descartes' Error*, 'Present continuously becomes the past and by the time we take stock of it [that is, consciously perceive it] we are in another present, consumed with planning for the future, which we do on stepping stones of the past. The present is never here. We are hopelessly late for consciousness' (1994: 240). As Bergson puts it early in *Matter and Memory*: 'However brief we suppose any perception to be, it always occupies a certain duration, and involves, consequently, an effort of memory, which prolongs, one into another, the plurality of the moment' (1991: 34); and again, 'the process of perception consists in an exteriorization of internal states' (52); and yet again, 'We assert, at the outset, that if there be memory, that is, survival of past images, these images must constantly mingle with our perception of the present and may even take its place' (66). We have to remind ourselves reading Bergson that he is actually not glossing individual works of Beckett, in this case, perhaps, 'The Cliff' ('La Falaise') written for the painter Bram van Velde in 1975.[3]

> Any hint in the sky at a land's end? The yonder ether? Of sea birds no trace. Or too pale to show. And then what proof of a face? None that the eye can find wherever set. It gives up and the bedlam head takes over. At long last first looms the shadow of a ledge. Patience it will be enlivened with mortal remains. A whole skull emerges in the end. One alone from amongst those such residua evince. (*CSP* 357)

Such 'survival of past images [. . . that] must constantly mingle with our perception of the present and may even take its place' is less an appropriation of the perceived, cliff or painting, by Bram van Velde or any other painter, than the fleeting, evanescent bridge between matter and memory, the 'bedlam head', or mind, or consciousness that 'takes over' perception in a moment of intuition to suggest the flow of *durée*.

For a time Beckett accepted this sense of involuntary memory, or pure recollection, as epiphanic. His metaphor of the vase and the paradox of a perfume that is new because already experienced (*Proust* 55) imply a validation of the Proustian and Bergsonian experience (see also the poem 'Rue de Vaugirard'). But the unity of the self with its past implied in the acceptance of involuntary memory is parodied as early as *Dream of Fair to Middling Women*, where the only unity is *involuntary* (*Dream* 132), the hawthorn (1) and verbena (128) irreverently gloss the Proustian moment, and the ending parodies Joyce's 'The Dead'. Beckett's work is marked by an increasing distrust of epiphanic moments, perhaps not the psychological experience but its lasting significance. Arsene tries to define the mystical sense of something that slips; and Watt has residual memories of flowering currant; but the ineffable experience remains fugitive for both. In *Words and Music*, Croak is enthralled by a face in the ashes, while texts as distant as 'Enueg II' and 'Old Earth' share a motif of the sky suddenly turning to faces, underlining the persistence of involuntary memory throughout Beckett's oeuvre. But whatever unity exists between perceived image, memory or past, and imagination is as accidental as the coincidence of dampers, hammers and strings in Mr Knott's piano, the attempted 'chooning' of which is the mission of 'the Galls father and son' (*Watt* 70). This 'incident of note' is one of the defining moments in Watt's stay with Mr Knott and exemplifies Watt's failure of memory, the failure to connect experience with memory, in decidedly Bergsonian terms. In *Matter and Memory*, Bergson details the dialectic between memory and perception: 'these two contrary hypotheses, the first identifying the elements of perception with the elements of memory, the second distinguishing among them, are of such a nature that each sends us back to the other without allowing us to rest in either' (1991: 127). Bergson's analysis here not only serves as an anticipation of Beckett's shortest poem-like prose work, 'neither', but outlines Watt's final demise, his inability to accept 'the simple games that time plays with space', or that memory (time) plays with perception (space). Bergson's metaphor for the machinery of this connection in 'the cerebral centers' is the keyboard, the piano:

> This organ [that is, the brain] is constructed precisely with a view to allowing the plurality of simultaneous excitants to impress it in a certain order and in a certain way [as in a chord, say], by distributing themselves, all at one time, over selected portions of its surface. It is like an immense keyboard, on which the external object executes at once its harmony of a thousand notes, thus calling forth in a definite order, and at a single moment, a great multitude of elementary sensations corresponding to all the points of the sensory center that are concerned. (1991: 128)

Since memories are not stored or deposited in any sort of receptacle for Bergson (or for contemporary philosophers of cognition like Steven Pinker and Antonio Damasio), in the brain or any other material organ, but remain part of a constant process of distribution, electronic and chemical, the machinery, the perpetual correspondence of memory, sensation and stimulus, is paramount to its adequate functioning, and for Watt that machinery has broken down. For Bergson, memories exist as images, and in the example that follows he is discussing 'auditory images', music, perhaps: the 'region of images, if it exists, can only be a keyboard of this nature', he reminds us, 'the auditory image called back by memory must set in motion the same nervous elements as the first perception and that recollection must thus change gradually into perception' (1991: 129). Watt's recitation of the word 'pot' is the novel's central example of the dislocation of that machinery; or as Bergson puts the matter, 'The strings are still there, and to the influence of external sounds they still vibrate; it is the internal keyboard which is lacking' (129), as it is in Mr Knott's establishment. When Bergson changes his metaphor, he moves to the image of a circle: 'Our distinct perception is really comparable to a *closed circle*, in which the perception-image, going toward the mind, and the memory-image, launched into space, careen the one behind the other' (103, emphasis added). Bergson may finally reject the linear implications in 'the one behind the other', but he retains the metaphor-image of the circle for his qualification: 'reflective perception is a circuit, in which all the elements, including the perceived object itself, hold each other in a state of mutual tension as in an electrical circuit, so that no disturbance starting from the object can stop on its way and remain in the depths of the mind: it must always find its way back to the object from where it proceeds' (104). Such circuitry is short-circuited for Watt, the image of pot never returning to 'the object from where it proceeds'; the circuit, like the painting in Erskine's bedroom, remains broken, the hammers (almost) never corresponding to the strings of Watt's (or Knott's) keyboard.

If we examine *Waiting for Godot* as a memory play, or at least as an exploration or taxonomy of the ways that memory systems break down, we are again led to consider the neurological implications of the process. Didi and Gogo cannot re-call, that is, cannot call to mind, the exact details of their appointment with Godot, and Pozzo's sensory systems begin to break down as well; he is blind, after all, apparently a sudden neurological problem, in Act 2, and he cannot remember his previous meeting with Didi and Gogo, which occurred, apparently (if the text can be trusted), the preceding day. Such vagaries or failures of memory, remind us of the imagery used by contemporary analysts of memory (all in the wake of Bergson, whose influences they only scantly acknowledge, unfortunately). Damasio notes that 'whenever we recall a given object, or face, or scene, we do not get an exact reproduction but rather an *interpretation*, a newly constructed version of the original' (1994: 100), and he continues, 'a dispositional representation for the face of Aunt [. . .] contains not her face as such, but rather the firing patterns which trigger the momentary reconstruction of an approximate representation [. . .]' (102). In *Waiting for Godot* (and in much of Beckett's work, for that matter), something seems to have gone awry with the 'firing patterns'. Furthermore, none of the characters seems able to recognize the hopelessness of their situation, which condition may be a form of anosognosia, the 'inability to acknowledge disease in oneself' (for examples see Damasio 1994: 62). One of the play's most enigmatic moments, when all four characters collapse and cannot rise, may be most explicable as another, simultaneous in this case, memory or neurological lapse, a failure to remember the system or the habit of locomotion. As they consciously try to remember how to get up, voluntary or habitual memory fails, their final success a matter of *inattention*, that is, a return to the habit of movement. Bergson describes the link between memory and action: 'Pure memories, as they become actual, tend to bring about, within the body, all corresponding sensations. But these virtual sensations themselves, in order to become real, must tend to urge the body to action and to impress upon it those movements and attitudes of which they are the habitual antecedent' (1991: 130). What may break down for the four principles of *Waiting for Godot* is, at least sporadically, the habit of memory, or, the memory of habit, most dramatically with Didi and Gogo's immobility at the end of both acts: 'They do not move.' Their mobility, their ability to act in general, seems to have been (at least sporadically) short-circuited.

All this is not to suggest that Beckett created his art with Bergson spread on the table before him, but that his study of Bergson, if only in his preparation for teaching his Trinity students, remained with him as a ghost, an afterimage that informed much of his work for the remainder of his career. Bergson's study of memory and his emphasis on what I have earlier called his material metaphysics seem perfectly consonant with Beckett and Proust's 'ideal real', which Beckett considered 'the essential, the extratemporal' (*Proust* 56). One of Hamm's insights, 'I was never there' (*Endgame* 74), moreover, suggests what is perhaps the most fundamental of Bergson's and Beckett's principles, of life and art, that we engage the world solely and indirectly on the level of image, the direct, actual world unknowable and inaccessible. The afterimage comes up in Part 3 of *Footfalls*, as May, who may only be narrated and hence an image, narrates a semblance of what is on stage and calls attention to her apparitional, ghostly state. May's anagrammatic other, the semblance Amy, replies to her mother, Mrs Winter, about attendance at Evensong: 'I observed nothing of any kind, strange or otherwise. I saw nothing, heard nothing, of any kind. I was not there' (*CDW* 243). The short fourth act of *Footfalls*, the final ten seconds with 'No trace of May', is a crucial reminder that May was always already 'not there', or there only as a 'trace', an image or afterimage.

The depth of Beckett's debt to Bergsonism is yet to be fully established, but at very least it appears clear that Beckett seems to have answered Bergson's 1889 call for 'some bold novelist, [to tear] aside the cleverly woven curtain of our conventional ego, [and show] us under this appearance of logic a fundamental absurdity, under this juxtaposition of simple states an infinite permeation of a thousand different impressions which have already ceased to exist the instant they are named' (2001: 133–4).

Notes

1. Rachel (Dobbin) Burrows's notebooks to lectures given by Samuel Beckett at Trinity College in 1931 (held at the archives of Trinity College, Dublin) explicitly indicate Beckett's strong knowledge of Bergson. See also Gontarski et al. 1988.
2. Bergson goes on here to discuss the Külpe School and so the Würzburg School, usually called 'the School of imageless thought' from its contention that 'states of awareness have no sensory content, representation, or image' (Ackerley and Gontarski 2006: 306). For Bergson here, 'The experiments of Münsterberg and of Külpe leave no doubt as to this latter point: any memory-image that is capable of interpreting our actual perception inserts itself so thoroughly into it that we are no longer able to discern what is perception and what is memory'

(Bergson 1991: 103). One of its followers, by the by, was Henry J. Watt (1879–1925). For the Külpe school in Beckett see *Murphy* (80).

3. Translated from the French by Edith Fournier, and first published in *The New Yorker*, 13 May 1996. For an interesting assessment of the piece see Estrin 2013.

References

Ackerley, C. J. and Gontarski, S. E. (2006) *The Faber Companion to Samuel Beckett: A Reader's Guide to His Works, Life, and Thought*, London: Faber.

Beckett, Samuel (1984) 'Three Dialogues with George Duthuit', in *Disjecta: Miscellaneous Writings and a Dramatic Fragment by Samuel Beckett*, ed. Ruby Cohn, New York: Grove.

Beckett, Samuel (2006) Letter to Georges Duthuit, 9–10 March 1949, in S. E. Gontarski and A. Uhlmann (eds), *Beckett After Beckett*, Gainesville: University Press of Florida, 18–21.

Bergson, Henri (1944) *Creative Evolution*, trans. Arthur Mitchell, New York: Modern Library.

Bergson, Henri (1991) *Matter and Memory*, trans. Nancy Margaret Paul and W. Scott Palmer, New York: Zone Books.

Bergson, Henri (2001) *Time and Free Will: An Essay on the Immediate Data of Consciousness*, trans. F. L. Pogson, Mineola, NY: Dover.

Burrows, Rachel (1931) Ms notebook on deposit at Trinity College, Dublin (MIC 60 and Misc photocopy 166).

Damasio, Antonio R. (1994) *Descartes Error: Emotion, Reason and the Human Brain*, New York: Avon.

Deleuze, Gilles (1988) *Bergsonism*, trans. Hugh Tomlinson and Barbara Habberjam, New York: Zone Books.

Estrin, Barbara L. (2013) '"The Invisible Suction of the Past": Paul Muldoon Through Samuel Beckett', *Literary Imagination* 15:3, 327–44.

Gontarski, S. E., McMillan, Dougald and Fehsenfeld, Martha (1988) 'Interview with Rachel Burroughs', *Journal of Beckett Studies* 11–12, 1–15.

Gontarski, S. E. and Uhlmann, Anthony (eds) (2006), *Beckett After Beckett*, Gainesville: University Press of Florida.

Grosz, Elizabeth (2005) 'Bergson, Deleuze and Becoming', Lecture delivered at the University of Queensland, Australia on 16 March 2005. (Similar material appears in her 'Deleuze, Bergson, and the Virtual', in *Time Travels: Feminism, Nature, Power*, Durham, NC: Duke University Press, 2005, 93–112.)

Knowlson, James (1996) *Damned to Fame: The Life of Samuel Beckett*, New York: Simon and Schuster.

Proust, Marcel (1927) *Le Temps retrouvé. À la recherche du temps perdu*, Paris: Editions de la Nouvelle revue française (1919–1927).

8

A Theatre of Deterritorialization and the Questions We Ask

[. . .] a rhizome is not amenable to any structural or generative model. It is a stranger to any idea of genetic axis or deep structure. [. . .] A rhizome has no beginning or end; it is always in the middle, between things, interbeing, intermezzo. (Gilles Deleuze and Félix Guattari, *A Thousand Plateaus* (12, 25))

'There's No Key'

One particularly telling, oft cited but rarely unpacked exchange is the (now) famous London meeting between Samuel Beckett and the eminent actor Ralph Richardson, the incident recounted by Beckett in a letter of 18 October 1954 to his American publisher, Barney Rosset, who would soon take on the additional responsibility of being Beckett's American theatrical producer as well:

had a highly unsatisfactory interview with SIR Ralph Richardson who wanted the low-down on Pozzo, his home address and curriculum vitae, and made the forthcoming of this and similar information the condition of his condescending to illustrate the part of Vladimir. Too tired to give satisfaction I told him that all I knew of Pozzo was in the text, that if I had known more I would have put it in the text, and that this was true also of the other characters. (*Letters 2* 507)

Beckett's citing the exchange so forcefully to Rosset may have constituted something of a pre-emptive warning as the American publication of *Godot* had just appeared (two years ahead of the British edition) and its American theatrical premiere was imminent, if delayed; the play would finally open in try out, ill advisedly, as it turned out, in Miami Beach, Florida on 3 January 1956. Beckett had rehearsed the Richardson vignette a few days earlier, on 14 October, in almost identical phrasing to confidant Mary Manning Howe, telling her that Richardson 'Wanted the low-down on Pozzo, his home address, family background and *curriculum vitae*'. He repeated the incident to Howe yet again on the same day he wrote Rosset, this time with an even stronger admonition: 'He asked a lot of stupid questions I was too tired to answer. There are no answers to such questions but less tired I could have found some. [. . .] he is not the man for the play, and I do not think that the W. E. [West End] is the place for it either' (*Letters* 2 508, n. 1).[1]

Richardson's questions seem on the surface reasonable enough, an actor's search for some grounding for this very new play, but how new Richardson apparently failed to appreciate. For many an actor (audience members as well, we might add) such foundation lies in the correspondence between the dramatic world – the world on stage, the represented world, art, as generally understood, as some sort of simulacrum of the world that we know, the familiar or actual world off stage – and the psychological complexities of recognizable, coherent, knowable characters. Much of contemporary acting theory accepts such assumptions, especially those principles laid down and codified in 1936 with the publication of Konstantin Stanislavski's *An Actor Prepares*, the first volume of the director's acting trilogy. In Chapter IV on the 'Imagination', he lays out the six critical questions an actor must ask while creating a part. They begin to sound like the opening of *The Unnamable*: Who am I? Where am I? When am I here? Why am I here (that is, backward looking to the causality of how one got here)? Perhaps the most important of the six questions are the final two: for what reason am I here (that is, forward looking, what do I want to do next), and how shall I go about it? Answers to these questions should be rooted then in personal experience, personal memory, and imagination. Richardson, thus, was behaving like a contemporary professional actor. For Beckett, however, these were the 'stupid questions' to which he objected, 'There are no answers to such questions', Beckett not accepting the assumptions with which Richardson was working. What Richardson failed to comprehend was the degree of difference that *Waiting for Godot* represented, how 'foreign' a play it was. In Beckett's art, reference outside the text, or what he called 'relation' in his aesthetic comments to Georges Duthuit in 1949,[2] is not at issue. In Beckett's own exploration of imagination, *Lessness* and *Imagination Dead Imagine*, say, he will call the space of not only his stories but of his art 'issueless'. Beckett's, we might say, is not a world of resemblances (or analogies, or representations, or simulations) but a world of differences, not a world of metaphors (or similes or other analogical tropes) which suggest likenesses but a world, an art of images, the value, thus, opposed to the 'neatness of identifications' that Richardson (presumably, among others) requested.

Not that Beckett's art is wholly divorced from or unrecognizable as our world. Art has what Deleuze calls a functional quality as well as an expressive quality, the former something of a reterritorialization. But such function, such connection or relation to the familiar, a representation of our world, is at best tenuous or fabricated if not accidental or forced in Beckett's art; at its best functional features of Beckett's art become expressive features. And yet some of the most memorable and discussed productions of *Waiting for Godot*, for one, have been site specific, rooted, functional, and so have had just such a relation, those beginning with the Herbert Blau and his San Francisco Actors' Workshop production within the maximum security confines of San Quentin Prison in 1956 with which Martin Esslin opened his groundbreaking *The Theatre of the Absurd* of 1969. Set within the prison, the work instantly and inevitably took on the character of prison life, and it was comprehended by its incarcerated audience as something of a commentary on their existence. Such function as I am suggesting, the play defined by if not driven by its context, furthermore, is powerfully evident in the all African-American cast of the Classical Theatre of Harlem's 2007 production of *Waiting for Godot*, directed by Christopher McElroen, featuring New Orleans native Wendell Pierce and J. Kyle Manzay, first on a simulated New Orleans rooftop in their Harlem theatre in 2006 and then in November 2007 directly on the streets of the Lower 9th Ward of New Orleans, the area most devastated by hurricane Katrina. Free admission to the outdoor production was offered on successive weekends, November 2–3 and 9–10, although the 'free' production reportedly cost some $200,000 to stage. Writing for the *Times-Picayune* on 9 November 2007, David Cuthbert noted that 'The time has long since passed when *Godot* was regarded as "a mystery wrapped in an enigma," as Brooks Atkinson famously described it in his 1956 *New York Times* review of its Broadway debut.' Cuthbert went on to note, in lines reminiscent of the San Quentin *Godot* of 1957, 'Christopher McElroen's staging is the most accessible, the funniest, the most moving and meaningful *Godot* we are ever likely to see. It is ours, it speaks directly to us, in lines and situations that have always been there, but which now take on a new resonance.' Writing in *The New Yorker* in December of 2013, Hilton Als was still rhapsodic about the Classical Theatre of Harlem's production in that part of New Orleans still devastated:

> Like Susan Sontag, who staged the play in war-weary Sarajevo, the collaborators presumably *found some truth* in the bleak, science-fiction-like devastation that surrounded them, *a real life metaphor* for Vladimir's observation, near the end of the play, that 'in an instant all will vanish and we'll be alone once more, in the midst of nothingness'. In the midst of our 'nothingness', I could smell the stench of the nearby Mississippi. I saw how the white overhead lights lit the stage and the actors' black skin and the black night sky. I heard grass rustling, and sometimes a dog howling. And, in the pauses between Beckett's lines about the continuum of hope or the comedy of death (I couldn't settle on which), I heard something else: a silence as heavy as a solid. The show was staged in a residential neighborhood that no longer had its residents. There was no sound of daily life: no one to turn a television on or off, no one to clink ice in a glass or to curse the weather. All that was left in the damaged, desolate space was evidence that the world could disappear in a moment, leaving you God knows where. (Als 2013: 94, emphasis added)

Productions like those of the San Francisco Actors' Workshop or the Classical Theatre of Harlem offer one approach to making the play 'accessible', specifying a work itself fighting against such specification. And yet such productions punctuate the fact that Beckett's is a flexible, living art. The alternative may be that Beckett's work is simply presented as what it may indeed have already become, a curio in a box of curiosities, a museum piece preserved within the Museum of Modernism, performances without deviation (except perhaps for deterioration), exactly as written (at least in some hypothesized version). As Fintan O'Toole argues, discussing the issue of fidelity to Beckett's texts: 'The merely efficient translations of what are thought to be the great man's intentions will fade into dull obscurity. The productions that allow their audiences to feel the spirit of suffering and survival in our times will enter the afterlife of endless re-imaginings'

(O'Toole 2000: 45). Most easily productions could be re-imagined and altered radically in alternate, site-specific environments. Like the symbolic 1993 production of *Waiting for Godot* directed by Susan Sontag in a Sarajevo under siege (see Sontag 1993), a Japanese theatre group filmed its take on *Godot* on a country road, with the stacks of the Fukushima Daiichi nuclear plant in the background, just over 20 kilometres away. As *Wall Street Journal* critic Kenneth Maxwell reported on 16 August 2011, 'The version [of *Godot*] filmed by the Kamome Machine theater group begins with 30 seconds' footage of the barrier to the evacuation zone around the ravaged plant, as well as roads crumpled by the force of the March 11 earthquake and tsunami.'[3]

Other productions have attempted repetitions of or minor variations on the San Quentin experience, some indeed with unexpected consequences. In Stockholm in April of 1986, Jan Jonsson directed *Godot* with 'five inmates of the country's top maximum security jail. [. . .] Four out of five, all drug offenders, absconded through an open dressing room window just before the first night at the City Theatre in Göteborg.'[4] For all we know that audience is still waiting. Such site-specific productions create a foundation for the play, which the play itself either does not have or even resists, by foregrounding one of its narratological possibilities – at the expense of others, we might add. Such productions associate themselves with locations or situations already pregnant with affect that they borrow or of which they become part. This is the sort of reterritorialization parodied by Clov in *Endgame*: 'Here's the place, stop, raise your head and look at all that beauty. That order! They said to me. Come now, you're not a brute beast, think upon these things and you'll see how all becomes clear. And simple!' (*CDW* 132).

In his very favourable review of *Waiting for Godot* in the *New York Times* on 20 April 1956 (contrary, say, to Walter Kerr's[5]), noted critic Brooks Atkinson expressed assumptions about the nature of art suggesting a strong correspondence between theatre (or art) and a world we know, one that we are already familiar with, the world of common sense and the everyday that we often call real or actual. He calls *Godot*, 'Mr. Beckett's acrid cartoon of the story of mankind', and further refers to it as an 'allegory written in a heartless modern tone, a theatre-goer naturally rummages through the performance in search of a meaning', that is, for some connection or grounding to the familiar or actual. Atkinson and his rhetorical ploy, the fabricated theatre-goer, thus seem to share Richardson's assumptions about art (here theatre) and life, assumptions Beckett himself not only did not share but resisted. And yet near the end of his review, almost as a throw-away, Atkinson offers his most prescient insight: '*Waiting for Godot* is all feeling. Perhaps that is why it is puzzling and convincing at the same time. Theatregoers can rail at it, but they cannot ignore it. For Mr. Beckett is a valid writer' (cited by Levy 1956: 96). Beckett would, purportedly, offer Gabriel D'Aubarède just such an analysis in 1961, as the two discussed 'modern' philosophy:

> 'Have contemporary philosophers had any influence on your thought?'
> 'I never read philosophers.'
> 'Why not?'
> 'I never understand anything they write.'
> 'All the same, people have wondered if the existentialists' problem of being may afford a key to your works.'
> 'There's no key or problem. I wouldn't have had any reason to write my novels if I could have expressed their subject in philosophic terms.'
> 'What was your reason then?'
> 'I haven't the slightest idea. I'm no intellectual. All I am is feeling. Molloy and the others came to me the day I became aware of my own folly. Only then did I being to write the things I feel.' (D'Aubarède cited in Graver and Federman 1997: 219)

After *Godot*'s Miami fiasco and the subsequent cancellation of other 'out of town' previews, the New York premiere finally occurred at the John Golden Theater on 19 April 1956 with director Herbert Berghof replacing Alan Schneider, who was at least reportedly unavailable as recorded by Alan Levy: 'Five days after the first *Godot* folded, he was busy casting a new comedy' (Levy 1956: 35). Berghof, founder in 1945, with his wife Uta Hagen, of the Herbert Berghof Studio, essentially workshopped the play extensively in his New York studio before opening it on Broadway.

At this early stage of his relationship with Beckett, Schneider's take on the play is fairly elementary and seemingly dualistic. To Levy's question, 'What is Godot?' Schneider replies, 'Godot means certainty. Night means death. It shows the nullity of life and it means nothing. In awareness that there is no meaning to life, there is meaning' (cited in Levy 1956: 35). Schneider's restating the conclusion of Camus' 'Myth of Sisyphus' aside, his casual comment

that 'Godot means certainty' gets at the heart of at least one iteration of what will not be forthcoming for characters and audience.

Despite the Miami failure (perhaps because of it to some
extent), the Grove Press edition was selling well: 'The publishing house had sold out its original $4.75 edition of the play. In
February 1956 *Waiting for Godot* appeared as a $1 paperback
[with which Beckett was delighted], and its first printing of 5,000
copies sold out before publication' (Levy 1956: 35).[6] In April
of 1956, producer Michael Myerberg took out advertisements
in New York newspapers to announce that *Godot* was coming
to New York for a limited engagement. A signed postscript by
Myerberg warned: 'I respectfully suggest that those who come
to the theatre for casual entertainment do not buy a ticket for
this attraction' (Levy 1956: 96). Subsequently, in an interview
with Michael Gelb for the Sunday *New York Times* the weekend
before the play opened, Myerberg appealed for '70,000 bona fide
intellectuals in New York' to support the play. The headline for
the interview announced, 'Wanted: Intellectuals' and followed
with 'Producer Seeks 70,000 of Them to Support New Play' (for
details see Harrington 1997: 132–4). The 'new play' ran its ten-
week 'limited engagement' but without extension. It did, however,
generate interest from Columbia Records, probably because of its
headliner, and was recorded with the latest recording technology,
High Fidelity (02L-238),[7] and so we have a good auditory record
of that New York production, and Beckett was pleased with the
results, 'as a record, especially', despite its addition of music,
which Beckett called 'hardly disturbing'.[8]

The liner notes to the album were written by American author
William Saroyan, the commission offered by Goddard Liberson,
President of Columbia Recordings, who wired Saroyan on 13
June, 'Did you see *Waiting for Godot* and did you like it? I have
recorded the whole thing and would like liner notes by you two or
three thousand words. Not much dough probably hundred bucks
but need soon. Wire me collect and don't keep me waiting for
Saroyan.' In his return wire Saroyan admits, 'Didn't see the play
but read it. Of course liked it very much and of course will write
what you want. Meantime send the recording as soon as possible'
(cited in Bryden 2008: 262).

Although Saroyan's 'Introduction' is something less than unalloyed praise, he does speak of the artist's role as 'making-over of
the "real" by one man (not God) by means of drawing, painting,

sculpture, or writing', and he does conclude that 'It is an important play because it reveals what else can be done in the theater, on the stage [. . .]' (liner notes for the recording). For the *New York Times*, 'Saroyan [. . .] all but weeps with emotion when he speaks of *Godot*' and believes 'It will make it easier for me and everyone else to write freely in the theatre' (cited in Harrington 1997: 133). That is, even amid what read like unrevised ramblings and despite his suggestion that now 'cleverer and more skillful playwrights' have a new world opened to them, Saroyan too is strangely insightful. For Saroyan, *Godot* is not a play for Myerberg's 70,000 'intellectuals', but a play of elegant simplicity. To Tom Driver in a 1961 interview, Beckett too would reject the sort of intellectualism that Myerberg was flogging, rejecting any intellectualism, philosophical system or transcendental truth to his play, invoking, as it turns out, the philosophers he denied reading:

> What is more true than anything else? To swim is true, and to sink is true. One is not more true than the other. One cannot speak anymore of being, one must speak only of the mess. When Heidegger and Sartre speak of a contrast between being and existence, they may be right, I don't know, but their language is too philosophical for me. I am not a philosopher. One can only speak of what is in front of him, and that now is simply the mess.[9] (Beckett to Driver cited in Graver and Federman 1997: 217)

What characterizes many of these legendary and oft cited exchanges is the persistence among interrogators of asking the wrong questions and thereby under-appreciating the play's newness. The apposite question may be less how Beckett was rendering our recognizable world than how he was creating new and unfamiliar worlds, decreating worlds we thought we knew.

'Skeleton Simple'

As *Godot* marks more than sixty years in the repertory of world drama and as Beckett criticism itself likewise marks some sixty plus years of existence, we might ask ourselves, readers and spectators of Beckett's *oeuvre*, whether or not we have been mis-asking questions about Beckett's art. Especially suspect are questions that suggest occasion, relation, or correspondence, questions that take us outside the text, or in the theatre outside of performance, that is, outside the image, finally. That is, what do we expect from literary works, in this case Beckett's in particular? If we seek some sort of transcendental truth, some grand comments about humanity or the human condition, say, what Michel Foucault has called an 'ethics of knowledge', we doom ourselves inevitably to disappointment. After all is this not what Didi (whom Beckett characterized as being of the air) and Gogo (whom Beckett described as being of the earth) yearn for, something like solid ground, while both being, apparently, doomed to disappointment? 'Nothing to be done' launches our linguistic encounter with this experience of persistent hope and as persistent disappointment. But what is the alternative to such an ethics, a reach for transcendence, transcendental truths, or, conversely, a grounding of and in experience? One alternative is that posed by Beckett in his critique of Proust's romanticism (and offered to D'Aubarède as well), 'his substitution of affect for intelligence' (*Proust* 61).

Beckett seems consistently to have urged us to take his characters and their situations at face value, and he seemed perplexed by what he considered perpetual misunderstanding. In a letter to Pamela Mitchell of 18 August 1955 (*Letters* 2 540), Beckett notes: 'I am really very tired of *Godot* and the endless misunderstanding it seems to provoke. How anything so skeleton simple can be complicated as it has been is beyond me' (540). Beckett liked the remark well enough to repeat it to Mary Manning Howe that same day, on 18 August, which letter does not appear in the collected *Letters* in toto but is doubly cited: as a note to the Pamela Mitchell letter (541, n. 5), and in note 1 to the letter to Barney Rosset cited above (508).

Since Beckett's physical demise in 1989, and amid the post-biographical critical era as his notebooks and letters emerge in print (the latter not only slowly but incompletely, only 2,500 of an estimated 17,000 known letters in possession of the editors), we have learned as critics that the context of Beckett's art, its intellectual milieu, or the generation and production of the published works is invaluable. As Anthony Uhlmann acknowledges, such material, what I have elsewhere called the 'grey canon', 'allow[s] us to more fully understand the contexts from which Beckett's ideas emerge' (2014: 146). Beckett's direct denial of philosophical interest, 'I never read philosophers', may have been designed to deflect questions about his own philosophical reading and so his philosophical leanings, even as it is belied by textual evidence.

Ever the autodidact, he was fully if not aggressively engaged in philosophical inquiry for much of his life, particularly, as John Pilling notes, in his 1935 'Whoroscope Notebook':

> Nothing better illustrates Beckett's catholicity of interests in the *Whoroscope* notebook than the pages in which he moves from Céline's *Bagatelles* (on this evidence trifles indeed) through Mauthner's *Beiträge* (a much more substantial obstacle), and then on to Sartre and at about the same time the philosophy of Immanuel Kant (arguably an even more demanding figure than Mauthner). The trajectory reflects a Beckettian tendency throughout the *Whoroscope* notebook to treat ideas – especially ideas developed in an elaborate and systematic manner – as of more potential importance than mere literary snippets [. . .]. (Pilling 2012: 83)

The Ideal-Real

Beckett may have fudged a bit on his reading of the *Complete Works* of Kant in eleven volumes since most of his notes in the *Whoroscope* notebook refer to the *Life and Work* critical biography by Ernst Cassirer, the eleventh volume in that *Complete Works*, according to Pilling. Beckett's subsequent denial of reading philosophy may have, strictly speaking, referred principally to postwar philosophy, to the period he characterized as 'the day I became aware of my own folly', although he had read Sartre in considerable detail. He had read Henri Bergson, closely, as well, since he was teaching him at Trinity College, Dublin (1930–1), where he drew a distinction for his class between Proust's sense of time and that of Bergson, Proust's more dualist and relative, Bergson's an absolute time, at least according to notes recorded by one of his students in that class, Rachel Burrows.[10] Beckett seems to have relied on Julian Benda's distinction of epistemologies between these writers for some of his understanding, or at least Burrows records Beckett's saying to his class that 'Julien Benda tries to clarify Bergsonian conception of intelligence and intuition – says that B's [presumably Bergson through Benda through Beckett, then] intuition is the highest intelligence – l'intelligence personelle'; and further that 'Proust [was] detached from Bergson's conception of time but interested in this opposition – instinct [or 'instinctive perception' or, finally, intuition, since Beckett seems to have used all three terms interchangeably]. We might, however, usefully turn to Gilles Deleuze for further elucidation on these issues, even as we can affirm that Beckett probably did not read philosophers like Deleuze, or at least not directly. On the other hand, he was, rather both were, independently reading a set of parallel and formative philosophers and artists: Hume, Spinoza, Kant, Bergson and Proust, all of whom became threads both in Deleuze's and in Beckett's thinking. In *Time and Free Will*, Bergson asks himself the central question, '"Can time be adequately represented by space?" To which we answer: "Yes, if you are dealing with time flown; No, if you speak of time flowing"' (2001: 221). Beckett's summary in *Proust* gives as follows: 'At the best, all that is realized in Time (all Time produce), whether art or life, can only be *possessed* successively, by a series of partial annexations – and never integrally and at once' (*Proust* 7, emphasis added). It's the 'integrally and at once' here that suggests something like Bergson's apparent monism. On a basic, theoretical or philosophical level, then, this ontological and epistemological issue is why all art must inevitably and perpetually fail. It can never capture anything but 'a series of partial annexations', fragments, say. At best then, what art can offer is a still snapshot of time, the problem exacerbated in the literary arts by language, which spatializes the flow of time. Unity of space and time, as Watt will discover to his detriment, is likewise impossible. Like Kant and Bergson, Deleuze considers the unity of space and time as imposed by a subject, itself unstable and fragmented.[11] Deleuze concludes, therefore, that pure difference is non-spatial; it is an idea, what Beckett valorized in *Proust* as 'the Idea' (*passim*) and what Deleuze calls 'the virtual'.

Such coinage in Deleuze refers to or even relies on Proust's definition of what is constant in both past and present, that is, in that intersection of past, present and the imagination, a conjunction of the material and immaterial (or the ethereal), of matter and memory, accessed through what Beckett in *Proust* calls 'involuntary memory' and Bergson calls intuition. As Beckett notes, 'Proust is positive only in so far as he affirms the value of intuition' (*Proust* 66). Further, Beckett, quoting Proust directly, put the matter thus: involuntary memory (or instinctive perception, or intuition [63]) is 'at once imaginative and empirical, at once an evocation and a direct perception, real without being merely actual, ideal without being merely abstract, the ideal real, the essential, the extra-temporal' (56). The phrasing further suggests Bergson's analysis of the image at the opening of *Matter and Memory*. That is, what appears to be an almost mystical experience described by Proust and cited by Beckett comes close to Bergson's intuition of *durée* which, in Beckett's words, 'communicates an extratemporal essence, it follows that the communicant is momentarily an extratemporal being' (56), time, thus, less recovered than obliterated. Beckett's essay on Proust finally considers Proust as artist not as philosopher, for whom the Idea or the virtual is embodied not in allegory but in the concrete, in the sensory, in, we might add, the image, through which the material is dematerialized as the immaterial, the spirit, while the absent is materialized. Beckett thus acknowledges a Romantic strain in Proust: unable, like the classical artist (Joyce), to seek omniscience and omnipotence (61), transcendence, we might say, he affirms, like Bergson, the primacy of intuition (63) or instinct not vitiated by habit, that is, the 'non-logical statement of phenomena' before they have been distorted into intelligibility (66). Musing on the prospect of his death, Marcel offers us an extended summary of such extra-temporality in the final volume, volume 8, of *À la recherche du temps perdu*, *Le Temps retrouvé* of 1927 (*Time Regained* in one English translation[12]), in the third chapter, 'An afternoon party at the house of the Princesse de Guermantes'. Beckett cites snippets in his *Proust*, but the climactic fullness of the experience warrants an extended quotation since it is one on which Beckett and Deleuze draw, if not where they converge:

> this cause I began to divine as I compared these diverse happy impressions, diverse yet with this in common, that I experienced them at the present moment and at the same time in the context of a distant moment, [Blossom cites the three sensory triggers here], so that the past was made to encroach upon the present and I was made to doubt whether I was in the one or the other. The truth surely was that the being within me which had enjoyed these impressions had enjoyed them because they had something in common to a day long past and to the present, because in some way they were extra-temporal, and this being made its appearance only when [. . .] it was likely to find itself in the one and only medium in which it could exist and enjoy the essence of things, that is to say: outside of time.
>
> [. . .] a marvellous expedient of nature which had caused a sensation – the noise ['sound' in the Blossom translation] made both by the spoon and by the hammer,[13] for instance – to be mirrored at one and the same time in the past, so that my imagination was permitted to savor

it, and in the present where the actual shock to my senses by the noise, the touch of the linen napkin, or whatever it might be, had added to the dreams of the imagination the concept of existence which they usually lack, and through this subterfuge had made it possible for my being to secure, to isolate, to immobilize – for a moment brief as a flash of lightning – what normally it never apprehends: a fragment of time in the pure state. The being which had been reborn in me when with a sudden shudder of happiness I heard the noise [i.e., sound] that was common to the spoon touching the plate and the hammer striking the wheel, or had felt, beneath my feet, the unevenness that was common to the paving-stones of the Guermantes courtyard and to those of the Baptistry of St. Mark's, this being was nourished only by the essence of things, in these alone does it find sustenance and delight. In the observation of the present, where the senses cannot feed it with this food, it languishes, as it does in the consideration of a past made arid by the intellect or in the anticipation of the future which the will constructs with fragments of the present and the past, fragments whose reality it still further reduces by preserving of them only what is suitable for the utilitarian [cf. Bergson], narrowly human purpose for which it intends them. But let a noise [i.e., sound] or a scent, once heard or once smelt, be heard or smelt again in the present and at the same time in the past, *real without being actual, ideal without being abstract*, and immediately the permanent and habitually concealed essence of things is liberated and our true self [. . .] is awakened [. . .]. (Proust 1981: Vol. 3, 904–6, emphasis added)

Despite his denials, much of Proust here reads like a paraphrase of Bergsonism, especially on habit and the quotidian usefulness of voluntary memory, and further suggests something of a common ground for Beckett and Deleuze, with, of course, Proust's essentialism, 'the essence of things', excepted, what Beckett calls 'the *key* to his life and works' (*Proust* 25, emphasis added). (Evidently, despite Beckett's disclaimer, some literary works do have 'keys'.) Deleuze would then call such an experience virtual and one achieved through intuition that breaks the habits of the everyday. Such ideas may superficially resemble Plato's forms or Kant's ideas of pure reason, but they are not originals or models, not a grounding of thought or being. They transcend possible experience without being transcendental and are actual experience, the internal difference in itself. 'The concept they [the conditions] form is identical to its object' (Deleuze 2004: 36). The Idea or concept of difference for Deleuze and Beckett is not an abstraction of a perception or the experienced thing, but is a real system of differential relations that creates actual spaces, times and sensations.

In Betweenness

In his assessment of French cineaste Jean-Luc Godard, Deleuze stresses the in betweenness of Godard's work, between sound and vision, between television and cinema, between image and text. This is Deleuze's critique of postwar cinema as a 'time image', which offers the perspective of a disinterested, bodiless perceiver and which at its best presents the pure flow of time, becoming. Such in betweenness admittedly owes much to Bergson's *durée*, and whose formulation of the image, which Deleuze essentially follows, is something between matter and memory, presence and absence, as much material as immanence, the material spiritualized; the spirit materialized, the image both and wholly neither. As Deleuze reminds us in his essay on Beckett's teleplays, 'The Exhausted', the image is neither representation nor thing, but a process, a constant becoming, which, as it creates affect is the ultimate impact of art, not only in cinema, that is, but in other arts as well (Deleuze 1995: 19). Such process, an emphasis on flow and becoming, a perpetual in betweenness – between text and image, between past and present, between sensation and matter – suggests an incipient theory of theatre as well. Certainly such is the case in Beckett's work, particularly his late work for theatre and media in which we find a preponderance of spectral figures, ghosts, absences, what Deleuze calls the 'ghostly dimension' (14). What appears on stage as a something, a material object, a body, perhaps, or body part, is not always fully present, something not quite wholly material, nor quite simply immaterial or ethereal either, something in between presence and absence, sound and image, or matter and image, between the real and surreal, Beckett himself an artist in between, neither wholly of his time nor wholly of ours, say, fully neither, even as he is always, if partly, both. The pacing May of *Footfalls* is a case in point: apparently a physical entity on stage, or at least we perceive an image in motion, she may not be there at all, or not fully there as the final short scene of the stage without her figure suggests. Spirit thus becomes light, perhaps a beam of light as the final image of the play suggests and as the assailing voice of *Eh, Joe* would have it. Beckett's theatre is thus not about something, not a representation, the image or images of the artistic creation not images of something outside the work; they are 'that something itself', as he famously quipped in 1929 in reference to James Joyce's then-titled 'Work in Progress'. 'The identification of the immediate with the past experience, the recurrence of past action or reaction in the present, amounts to a participation between the ideal and the real, imagination and direct apprehension, symbol and substance' (*Proust* 55).

In 'Ohio Impromptu' two figures seated at a table are 'As alike in appearance as possible' (*CDW* 445), as the text reminds us. At very least they look to be materially equal entities, two physically present bodies. And yet the narrative or memoir read by the figure functionally called Reader suggests otherwise, one a spiritual representative of an absent one, a former lover. If we assume some continuity, some congruence between the visual image and the narrated images, a self reflexivity to the performance, say, or an embodiment of the narrative, that is, theatre as illustrative of a text, then one of the perceived figures on the stage, and perhaps the one apparently controlling the reading, the one called Listener, is a material presence, one an emissary, a shade, a spirit sent by the absent lover for something like consolation, 'my shade will comfort you', may not be. Our perception then may be faulty, the stage image 'ill seen' since at least one of the figures may not be there – at least not as a material presence. Something of a dream may be suggested here as indicated in the narrative by the third person, 'in his dreams . . . ', but reading the work as dream does not necessarily solve the issues of presence and absence, the material and the immaterial. Moreover, the narrative suggests something of the fluidity of being as the image of the Seine divided by the Isle of Swans is reunited on the far side of the Isle, and so finally, 'grew to be as one'. Is this merging, this reunion, that of the lovers of the narrative, or of the two figures we believe we perceive on stage, one apparently material, one not, or the merger of dream and reality? But each of these possibilities is complicated, made problematic, say, as the narrative is both materialized and deterritorialized. We might add that a third active entity is present in performance, the text itself, at least some forty pages long, on stage, taking on a life, shaping our response to the performance and so to the central, thematic, philosophical issues. Text itself, we might say, our third player in the performance, is a link, a bridge, between the lovers, between Reader and Listener, between the real and the unreal, or the real and the virtual, between materiality and imagination, or memory, thus linking past with present, giving spirit or shade a material form and simultaneously questioning materiality itself since both figures may be dream images, or versions of the same figure as 'they grew to be as one', at which point, 'nothing is left to tell'. But such a phrase, the 'nothing' left 'to tell', is already written, already in the text at the telling, and thus a repetition. Text, as text, has presumably been thought and read before, and will doubtless be read again, the imaginative image or memory (and they amount to the same) that we as audience perceive will be repeated, with difference, over and over again, the 'Impromptu' not a telos, but a loop, a repetition, always with difference, and a bridge between the material and the immaterial, between presence and absence, the engagement not between figure and figure but between figure(s) and text, text already written.

Beckett's move into television re-emphasized the imagistic nature of performance with bodiless narrators' voices near or contrary to those images we see on the screen, the process offering further narrative dislocations. In Beckett's 1985 television version of the play *What Where*, a disembodied narrator tells us, for instance, that 'This is Bam' (Beckett 1999: 409); Bam as character is thus already an object other than the narrating voice, who apparently is himself plural already, a multiplicity. 'We are the last five' (*CDW* 470), Voice continues, the grammar sliding from singular, Bam, to the multiple, a voice that is a 'We'. At best, however, images of four characters appear, Bam, Bim, Bom and Bem, the mysterious fifth, apparently 'Bum' if we follow the vowel sequence, only incipient or already dispatched. 'In the present as were we still', the voice continues, the subjunctive tense alerting us to the fact that this statement is contrary to fact. These are characters not there, the pattern of images coming and going, moving to and fro, to an off stage fraught with possibility, to receive 'the works', Beckett already anticipating such in betweenness in his *Proust*: 'But he is not there because she does not know he is there. He is present at his own absence' (15).

Such images with their narrative and visual disjunctions disrupt expected continuity and are part of or offer insight into the pure flow of time, what Deleuze calls the Plane of Immanence, perceptions always on the verge of becoming, that is, becoming other, something else, unsettling the received, that which we expect; they are thus a material bridge that generates affect, an emotional response not always specified or describable. The classical artist assumes an omnipotence and 'raises himself artificially out of Time in order to give relief to his chronology and causality to his development', as Beckett notes in his *Proust* treatise (62). On the other hand, great art, minoritarian art, Deleuze would say, is the pure expression of pure feeling, or as Beckett noted in *Proust*, a 'non-logical statement of phenomena in the order and exactitude of their perception, before they have been distorted into intelligibility in order to be forced into a chain of cause and effect' (66). Such a non-logical statement of phenomena is difficult to achieve through language, and Beckett recognized that fact: 'At that level you break up words to diminish shame. Painting and music have so much better a chance', he admitted to Lawrence Harvey (1970: 249). Billie Whitelaw describes her performance in *Footfalls* thus: 'Sometimes I felt as if he were a sculptor and I a piece of clay [. . .]. Sometimes I felt as though I were modeling for a painter or working with a musician. The movements started to feel like dance' (Whitelaw 1996: 144). Beckett's language thus is always a foreign tongue, Hiberno-English in his native land; an outsider's French in his adopted, language at times almost a non-language, sound, music, even pauses. Speaking of his direction of *Fin de partie*, Beckett's French director Roger Blin noted:

> he had ideas about the play that made it a little difficult to act. At first, he looked on his play as a kind of musical score. When a word occurred or was repeated, when Hamm called Clov, Clov should always come in the same way every time, like a musical phrase coming from the same instrument with the same volume. I thought that this idea was very much a product of the intellect and would result in an extraordinary rigor. He didn't see any drama or suspense in Clov's imminent departure. He would either leave or he wouldn't. (Blin in Gontarski 2012: 172)

Beckett is thus, like Kafka, as Deleuze characterizes him, always a foreign and so a minoritarian writer.

Neural Theatre

Such worlds as Beckett creates are thus virtual worlds that include past and present, material figures, imagination, and memory; off stage or what appears to be empty space is thus a virtual whole, a nothing full of possibilities, including all possible actions and movements. In this regard Beckett's theatre runs contrary to that described by Peter Brook in his famous theatrical treatise, *The Empty Space*; for Beckett the stage is never empty but full of the potentially possible. For Deleuze, 'Space enjoys potentialities as long as it makes the realization of events possible: it precedes realization, then, and potentiality itself belongs to the possible. But wasn't this equally the case for the image, which already proposed a specific means of exhausting the possible?' (1995: 11). That is, space too is an image and so as material as it is ethereal. The fourth scene of *Footfalls* with its apparently empty stage remains full of interpretive possibilities, for instance, opens those possibilities even further. It is always replete, full of potential meanings and worlds, of all the possibilities that theatre has to offer since it includes the whole of the past as well as the full potential to create new worlds. The space then is always already full; in short, it contains the process of the virtual, part of what Deleuze will call the Plane of Immanence. Beckett's plays then do not represent or realize a world of actuality, worlds outside themselves, do not represent at all, but offer images that make us feel in their affect the movement of existence, its flow, becoming, *durée*. Possibilities are not closed off by separating inside from outside, matter from spirit, present from past.

What too often frustrates readers or theatre-goers is precisely this resistance to representation that characterizes Beckett's art, since most of us operate on the Plane of Transcendence that produces or alludes to an exterior to the artwork, the world we know and try to represent in art. This is the world of what Beckett calls the classical artist, a world from which he separated himself. For Deleuze the perceiving mind of a doubting Cartesian subject is a piece of ribbon that separates inside from outside. The ribbon itself or a piece of paper, or as Beckett dubs it in *The Unnamable* a membrane or a tympanum vibrating, is in between, neither inside nor out but both in relation to the other, the vibration evading the Plane of Transcendence or a grounding of any sort, ultimate truths, say, that we are driven to obey. The series of plateaus, perhaps 1,000, that Deleuze critiques in the book of that title, is an assault against such groundings, the stability of language included, as is Beckett's art. Transcendence is a human disease that Deleuze calls 'interpretosis', or what the director of *Catastrophe* in the process of creating an image calls 'This craze for explicitation. Every I dotted to death. Little gag. For God's sake!' 'We're not beginning to . . . to . . . mean something', asks Hamm. 'Mean something!' responds Clov, 'You and I mean something? Ah, that's a good one' (*CDW* 108), and they share a communal laugh over the false promise of Transcendence, that they might be part of a greater system, or a greater truth beyond images of themselves in process. The alternative to transcendence is to accept, even to love, simply what is; Deleuze's term like Foucault's is also an ethics, but, after Nietzsche in *The Gay Science*, an 'ethics of the *amor fati*', the love of not exactly fate but of what is. One anecdote that Hamm tells has often been cited but less than satisfactorily discussed. The 'madman' that Hamm visits in the asylum is shown the beauty of the exterior, the corn, the herring fleet, from which the madman turns away appalled (*CDW* 113–14). Hamm's conclusion is that 'He alone had been spared'. Critics may point out the likely reference here to the visionary poet William Blake, but what or how the 'madman' has been spared is seldom parsed. One possibility is that he has been spared preoccupation with a transcendent world, what Deleuze will call the illusion of transcendence, that will close and explain experience. Hamm's 'madman' is thinking 'other', possible, alternative worlds. It may indeed be just those alternative worlds that Hamm keeps asking Clov to find beyond the shelter, but they are within as well. In Act II of *Waiting for Godot* the issue is put thus: '[*Aphoristic for once.*] We all are born mad.[14] Some remain so' (*CDW* 75). Perhaps those are the saved, the parallel to the one thief on the cross. Hamm's position is evidently to pull the madman back from the end of the world, a position that would resist or stop the flow of alternatives, becoming, *durée*. Later Hamm concludes the prayer scene with an overt statement about such transcendence, such 'ethics of knowledge'. Of a transcendental reality, God, he says, 'The bastard. He doesn't exist' (*CDW* 119). Perhaps Hamm too has been spared, saved. As a seated figure Hamm is at a decided disadvantage, however. 'It is the most horrible position in which to await death', Deleuze tells us, 'sitting without the force either to rise or to lie down, watching for the signal [*coup*] that will make us draw ourselves up one last time and lie down forever. Seated, you can't recover, you can no longer stir even a memory' (1995: 6).

In his dramaticule of 1968 that Beckett designates as images of motion, *Come and Go*, we are denied access to information that would, if disclosed, shut down the process of thinking. Without

that knowledge, the process of thinking, the generation of possibilities, alternatives, parallels the flow of movement on stage.
Language is not so much devalued among the 128 (or so) words
in this playlet since much of it is elegant and poetic, language
as part of (and not apart from) an image of flow. Or at the end
of Beckett's late masterwork, *Rockaby*, as the 'recorded voice'
reveals another narrative thread, 'and rocked / rocked / saying to
herself / no / done with that [. . .]', we might ask, 'Done with what'
or 'saying [what] to herself' (*CDW* 442)? What is resisted in such
interruption is knowledge that would still such movement and
freeze it, and end a process that Deleuze calls philosophy. When
the American actress Jessica Tandy complained, first to director Alan Schneider and then, bypassing him, directly to Samuel
Beckett, that *Not I*'s suggested running time of twenty-three
minutes rendered the work unintelligible to audiences,[15] Beckett
telegraphed back his now famous but oft misconstrued injunction,
'I'm not unduly concerned with intelligibility. I hope the piece may
work on the nerves of the audience, not its intellect' (Brater 1974:
200). If we take Beckett at his word and don't simply treat this
comment as a one off, as a dismissal of the actress or an admonition that she listen to her director, through whom, he told her,
he would hence communicate, then he is suggesting a theoretical
position, a theory of theatre. Evidence for the latter may be found
in his attitude about *Play*, which similarly should be staged at
incomprehensible speed, language become sound, music even, a
pace which, admittedly, many a director, Alan Schneider among
them, has resisted. Beckett's instructions to Schneider were that
'*Play* was to be played through twice without interruption and at
a very fast pace, each time taking no longer than nine minutes',
that is, eighteen minutes overall. The producers of the New
York premiere, Richard Barr, Clinton Wilder, and, of all people,
Edward Albee, threatened to drop the play from the programme
if Schneider heeded Beckett's pacing. Schneider capitulated, and
wrote to Beckett for permission to slow the pace and eliminate
the *da capo*: 'For the first and last time in my long relationship
with Sam, I did something I despised myself for doing. I wrote to
him, asking if we could try having his text spoken only once, more
slowly. Instead of telling me to blast off, Sam offered us his reluc-
tant permission' (Schneider 1986: 341).

What then are we to make of so neural a theatre, one that seems
to put the emphasis on what Deleuze, writing *after* Beckett, will call

'pure affect'? We can resist Beckett here, as Schneider's producers and, finally, Schneider himself did, or take him at his word; that is, this is how theatre works, not by creating simulacra, not by dealing with overall truths, but by demonstrating process and change, life as immanence, even as it is materially rooted. 'Make sense who may', as Beckett concluded his valedictory work for the theatre, *What Where*. In these shorter plays, then, Beckett's most radical artistic vision, his most revolutionary theories of theatre, emerge. This brings us, moreover, to one of the most vexing and contentious questions in Beckett studies, the degree to which Beckett's work is representational at all, or, on the contrary, whether its persistent preoccupation is with resisting representation, or rather to focus on how slippery and artificial representations are as they are played amid the Plane of Immanence, the perpetual flow of being. That is, Beckett's art on stage or page is not a stand-in for another reality; it is that reality and more often than not 'virtual' in the Deleuzian sense of that term. Beckett's theatre is always a theatre of becoming, of deterritorialization, a decomposition moving towards re-composition, itself decomposing. It is a theatre of perpetual movement or flow, all comings and goings, a pulse that creates affect. Even as it often appears stationary or static, even amid the Beckettian pauses, images move, flow, become other, not representing a world that we know, but perpetually creating new worlds. Bergson would call this *durée*, Deleuze 'becoming', Beckett simply art. It is a theatre struggling to resist the world we know, struggling to resist conceptualizing our world and the condition of being since those are mere snapshots and not the process, the flowing, becoming.

Notes

1. Inexplicably, this letter is not included in full in the second volume of Beckett's *Letters*, but teasingly offered as snippets, fragments, excerpts.
2. See *Letters* 2, 134–43, but better, since the translation is more accurate, see Beckett 2006: 15–21.
3. See   http://blogs.wsj.com/japanrealtime/2011/08/16/waiting-for-godot-%E2%80%94-in-fukushima/   and   the   film: http://www.youtube.com/watch?v=GeEPEUIRp14.
4. 'Audience Wait and Wait for Prison Godots', *The Times*, 31 April 1986.

5. Eric Bently opens his *New Republic* (16 May 1956) critique thus: 'The minute the statement was released to the press that Beckett's "Waiting for Godot" was not for casual theater goers but for intellectuals, I could have written Walter Kerr's review for him' (20, cited in Graver and Federman 1997: 104).

6. The play itself appeared in full on pp. 36–61.

7. The original cast album of 1956 was reissued by Pickwick in CD format on 14 March 2011 and so is now readily available. The following year, 1957, Beckett's second New York production, *Endgame*, at Off-Broadway's Cherry Lane Theater, was also recorded, but this time by Rosset and Grove Press and released as Evergreen Records EVR 003 MON – 33 1/3 RPM – High Fidelity Recording, the second edition packaged with a copy of the Grove text in a pocket of the album.

8. Writing to Barney Rosset, on 30 August 1956, Beckett notes: 'I saw Lieberson of Columbia Rdgs [Recordings] who gave me the *Godot* record. I find it quite good, as a record, especially Act 1 where Pozzo is remarkable. The sound element (finger on cords of grand piano blown up through micro) is hardly disturbing, except perhaps at end of 1st act. Some changes and interpolations annoyed me mildly, especially at beginning of Act II. I thought Vladimir very wooden and did not at all agree with Epstein's remarkable technical performance in the tirade. The boy I thought very good' (*Letters* 2, 645–9).

9. Compare to William Burroughs's comment in *Naked Lunch*: 'There is only one thing a writer can write about: what is in front of his senses at the moment of writing . . . I am a recording instrument . . . I do not presume to impose "story" "plot" "continuity" . . . Insofar as I succeed in Direct recording of certain areas of psychic process I may have limited function . . . I am not an entertainer' (Burroughs 1959: 221). Cf. Beckett's 'I do not feel like spending the rest of my life writing books that no one will read. It is not as though I wanted to write them' (*Letters* 1: 362).

10. As discussed above in Chapter 7. See the Rachel Burrows notebook archived at Trinity College, Dublin (TCD MIC 60); see also Gontarski et al. 1988, and Juez 2008, *passim*.

11. The Wikipedia webpage on Deleuze is very useful as an overview on these issues: http://en.wikipedia.org/wiki/Gilles_Deleuze.

12. *The Past Recaptured* in the Blossom translation.

13. See Beckett's outline of these triggers in *Proust* (23).

14. 'All' and 'are' are reversed in the American edition.

15. Of late, performances of *Not I* have taken on as much the character

of athletic competitions as theatre events, actresses performing not only for a personal best but for a world record as well. In May 2013, forty years after the landmark 1973 Billie Whitelaw world premiere under Samuel Beckett's direction, *Not I* returned to the Royal Court Theatre with a performance by anointed Billie Whitelaw successor, Lisa Dwan, who was 'tutored in the role by Billie Whitelaw', as the Royal Court's press release and the post production video interview with Whitelaw (from 2009) inform us. Dwan's iteration was first performed at BAC in 2005, at the Southbank Centre in 2009, and the inaugural International Festival of Beckett in Enniskillen in 2012. The running time for Dwan's performance is an astonishing nine minutes, but still at a £20 ticket price, we might add, although on the night I saw the performance, 25 May, critic Michael Coveney proudly announced in the post production chat-up, the talk back to fill out the scant programme, that the nine-minute barrier had been broken. The evening's first question from the audience was whether or not Ms Dwan had a back story for the monologue. She admitted that she had as an *aide-mémoire*, but, mercifully, for the integrity of the performance, that is, she did not disclose it.

References

Als, Hilton (2013) 'Two for the Road: Samuel Beckett's Metaphysical Slapstick', *The New Yorker*, 9 December, 94–5.

Beckett, Samuel (1999) *The Theatrical Notebooks of Samuel Beckett: The Shorter Plays*, ed. S. E. Gontarski, New York: Grove Press.

Beckett, Samuel (2006) Letter to Georges Duthuit, 9–10 March 1949 (trans. Walter Redfern) in *Beckett After Beckett*, ed. S. E. Gontarski and Anthony Uhlmann, Gainesville: University Press of Florida, 15–21.

Bergson, Henri (2001) *Time and Free Will: An Essay on the Immediate Data of Consciousness*, trans. F. L. Pogson, Mineola, NY: Dover.

Brater, Enoch (1974) 'The "I" in Beckett's *Not I*', *Twentieth-Century Literature* XX.

Bryden, Mary (2008) 'The Midcentury *Godot*: Beckett and Saroyan', *Beckett at 100*, ed. Linda Ben-Zvi and Angela Moorjani, Oxford: Oxford University Press.

Burroughs, William (1959) *Naked Lunch*, New York: Grove Press.

Burrows, Rachel (1931) Ms notebook on deposit at Trinity College, Dublin (MIC 60 and Misc photocopy 166).

Deleuze, Gilles (1995) 'The Exhausted', trans. Anthony Uhlmann, *SubStance* 24:3, 3–28.

Deleuze, Gilles (2004) *Desert Islands and Other Texts, 1953–1974*, trans. Michael Taormina, New York: Semiotext(e).

Graver, Lawrence and Federman, Raymond (eds) (1997) *Samuel Beckett: The Critical Heritage*, London: Routledge and Kegan Ltd.

Gontarski, S. E., McMillan, Dougald and Fehsenfeld, Martha (1988) 'Interview with Rachel Burrows', *Journal of Beckett Studies* 11–12, 1–15.

Gontarski, S. E. (ed.) (2012) *On Beckett: Essays and Criticism*, London: Anthem Press, second edition.

Harrington, John P. (1997) '*Waiting for Godot* in New York', in *The Irish Play on the New York Stage: 1874–1966*, Lexington: University of Kentucky Press, 1997.

Harvey, Lawrence (1970) *Samuel Beckett: Poet and Critic*, Princeton: Princeton University Press.

Juez, Brigitte le (2008) *Beckett Before Beckett: Samuel Beckett's Lectures on French Literature*, trans. Rose Schwartz, London: Souvenir Press.

Levy, Alan (1956) 'The Long Wait for Godot', *Theatre Arts* XL:8 (August), 33–5, 96.

O'Toole, Fintan (2000) 'Game Without End', *The New York Review of Books*, 20 January, 43–5.

Pilling, John (2012) 'Dates and Difficulties in Beckett's "*Whoroscope* Notebook"', in *The Beckett Critical Reader: Archives, Theories, and Translations*, ed. and with an Introduction by S. E. Gontarski, Edinburgh: Edinburgh University Press.

Proust, Marcel (1981) *Remembrance of Things Past*, trans. C. K. Scott Moncrieff et al. New York: Random House.

Schneider, Alan (1986) *Entrances: An American Director's Journey*, New York: Viking Press.

Sontag, Susan (1993) 'Godot Comes to Sarajevo', *The New York Review of Books*, 21 October, http://www.nybooks.com/articles/archives/1993/oct/21/godot-comes-to-sarajevo.

Uhlmann, Anthony (2014) 'Beckett, Duthuit and Ongoing Dialogue', *The Edinburgh Companion to Samuel Beckett and the Arts*, ed. S. E. Gontarski, Edinburgh: Edinburgh University Press, 146–52.

Whitelaw, Billie (1996) *Billie Whitelaw ... Who He?*, New York: St. Martin's Press.

Posteriors

9

Becoming Degree Zero:
Authors Vanishing into the Zone
of Imperceptibility

> The fact is, it seems, that the most you can hope is to be a little
> less, in the end, the creature you were in the beginning, and the
> middle. (*Molloy* 28)

> Don't wait to be hunted to hide, that was always my motto.
> (*Molloy* 109)

> Becoming imperceptible is Life. (Deleuze, *Essays Critical and
> Clinical*, 26)

In many respects American writer William Burroughs was an
apostle of invisibility, assiduously pursuing versions of physical vanishing and advocating, above all, authorial disappearance. He has on occasion declared himself simply an ethereal
medium through which his texts pass into the visible world,
as he does in his most celebrated work *Naked Lunch*: 'I am a
recording instrument . . . Insofar as I succeed in Direct recording
of certain areas of psychic process I may have limited function . . .'
(Burroughs 1959: 221). On 24 November 1960, not long after
the novel's publication by Olympia Press in Paris, the nomadic
Burroughs delivered a talk to the Heretics Society at Cambridge
University entitled 'The Cut up Method of Brion Gysin', focusing
on the method's extra-authorial mystical and magical qualities. By
then it had become 'The Cut up Method of William Burroughs' as
well, although Burroughs has suggested that the process of cutting
up texts was already implicit in *Naked Lunch*. Through such aesthetics Burroughs was becoming what Alexander Trocchi called
himself (in response to an attack by fellow Scots writer Hugh
MacDairmid), 'a cosmonaut of inner space' and a technician of
consciousness. The cut up method was for the visionary Burroughs

'The Future of the Novel', as he notes in an essay that credits Trocchi with the phrase he adopts: 'In my writing I am acting as a mapmaker, an explorer of psychic areas, to use the phrase of Mr. Alexander Trocchi, a cosmonaut of inner space, and I see no point in exploring areas that have already been thoroughly surveyed' (Burroughs 1998: 272). Burroughs will explore, he informs us, not only inner space but time, especially inner time, as well, and so he becomes what we might call an involutionary explorer, as well.

The Cambridge talk had come about after Burroughs had relocated once again, from London to Cambridge, and Cambridge engineering student Ian Sommerville had arranged the talk with his student group that had adopted the name of the original Heretics Society, which was active between 1909 and 1932 and had a distinguished history with a profound impact on Modernist thought. T. E. Hulme delivered his formative lecture 'Anti-Romanticism and Original Sin' to the group in 1912, and he also introduced the Heretics to the work of Henri Bergson, whose *Introduction to Metaphysics* he was then translating. Subsequently, the eminent philosopher Bertrand Russell would launch the first of his attacks on Bergson to the same group when he delivered 'The Philosophy of Bergson', also in 1912, and the follow up 'Mysticism and Logic' in 1914 – Russell's charge in both lectures: too much of the former not enough of the latter in Bergson. A decade later, on 18 May 1924, Virginia Woolf would deliver her talk 'Character in Fiction' after some two years of festering over a 1922 revue of *Jacob's Room* by Arnold Bennett, who accused Woolf of failing to develop characters in her work, the mainstay, as Bennett saw it, of contemporary fiction: 'The foundation of good fiction is character-creating and nothing else' (cited in Woolf 1924: 3). It was in her Cambridge talk that Woolf debuted her observation that 'on or about December 1910 human character changed', an event, apparently, that went unobserved by Mr Bennett. Woolf would further develop her talk and move Bennett to the headline of the essay in 'Mr Bennett and Mrs Brown', which she published as a monograph with her own Hogarth Press that same year. Woolf was undoubtedly introduced to the work of Henri Bergson at such Heretics lectures, which she attended only irregularly.[1] Burroughs would have been an unlikely lecturer to the original Heretics, although it had its share of controversy, but it was to a like named, resurrected group of student Heretics that he explained his new aesthetics in 1960 in a talk that might have been called 'On or about November 1960 the writing of novels changed – yet again', since the method that Burroughs described to the students was that being used to develop *The Soft Machine* from the 'word hoard' left over from *Naked Lunch*. *The Soft Machine* would be the first novel of a cut up 'Nova Trilogy', and its process of composition or arrangement invoked the magic and mysticism that the likes of Russell abhorred since it involved something of a disappearing act as Burroughs would cede through that process a considerable degree of authorial function to something of an eternal, cosmic force.

Not long after his talk, in December 1960, Burroughs left Cambridge to return to Paris and to the familiarity of the Beat Hotel, the famous beat digs – from, roughly, 1958–1963 – at 9, rue Git-le-Coeur, where he and Brion Gysin had developed the 'cut up' method in 1959 that would become central to Burroughs's work thereafter. Their first publication was *Minutes to Go* (1960), which Burroughs called 'unedited unchanged cut ups emerging as quite coherent and meaningful prose' (1963: 346).[2] A further collection of incidental pieces, interviews, fiction and essays exploring their 'cut up' techniques was collected as *The Third Mind* (1979), Burroughs's term for the results of such interactions and collaborations. Soon after his return to Paris Burroughs was joined by his Cambridge contact and companion, Ian Sommerville, and the two began to develop a series of performance pieces, the most startling of which was that of the vanishing author, as Sommerville dematerialized Burroughs, who had often referred to himself as *l'homme invisible*, or *el hombre invisible*, as the title of an early Barry Miles biography has it, before an invited audience. The trick or performance was the brainchild of Sommerville, who invited the guests of the Beat Hotel to room 15 where Burroughs sat on a chair before a white wall. Miles describes the event thus in his 2014 biography, *Call Me Burroughs*:

Ian projected a color slide of his [Burroughs's] face, actual size, onto him, then moved it out of focus. The projection moved slowly in and out of focus for a while, then a black wooden frame crossed by like a venetian blind was lowered in front of Burroughs. The projection now focused on the strings, then on Burroughs, then on the strings, slowly back and forth. At one point, when the image was focused on the strings, Bill lowered himself to the ground so the projection focused instead on the white wall behind him. Bill slid along the floor and behind the curtain while the audience continued to stare first at the string frame, then at the wall, thinking it was still him. Then the lights went up and Bill vanished. Photographer Harold Chapman, who was in the audience, said, 'It was absolutely brilliant, and well rehearsed. Burroughs is a brilliant performer.' (Miles 2014: 381–2)

The Beat Hotel was the focus of any number of such collaborative experiments, as Matthew Levi Stevens details in 'The Lost Boys: William S. Burroughs, Ian Sommerville and Alan Portman', a chapter from *The Magical Universe of William Burroughs*:

> Curses, mirror-gazing, spells and trances, and the non-chemical expansion of awareness made possible through Cut ups, Flicker, and Playback – all would be diligently explored with Bill's new acolytes and lovers: the Cambridge mathematician, Ian Sommerville ('the Technical Sergeant'), who would facilitate the Dreamachine and tape-recorder experiments, and spoilt rich-kid jailbait, Mikey Portman ('the Medium') – who, despite his bad habits, good looks, money and youth (or, perhaps, even because of them) would eventually drive Burroughs to distraction. These two Lost Boys were each, in their way, vital to the collaborations being undertaken by Burroughs and Gysin in the 1960s, and how they sought to extend their 'Third Mind' to others. Indeed, the Acknowledgment for Burroughs' 1962 novel, *The Ticket That Exploded*, gives notice of the importance of this new spirit of collaboration:
>> The sections entitled *in a strange bed* and *the black fruit* were written in collaboration with Mr. Michael Portman of London. Mr. Ian Sommerville of London pointed out the use and significance of spliced tape and all the other tape recorder experiments suggested in this book. The film experiments I owe to Mr. Antony Balch of Balch Films, London. The closing message is by Brion Gysin.
>
> (Levi Stevens, 'Lost Boys', Reality Studios)

Among the more interesting experiments with shifting, slipping, or unstable identity is Burroughs's 1971 film collaboration with Balch entitled *Bill and Tony*, which involved superimposition of alternate faces on the filmed body of the other so that identity drifts, becomes at least untethered. The idea that identity and so being were lifelong shifting performances constituting a degree zero of being would become more commonplace late in the twentieth and into the twenty-first centuries, but in the 1960s and '70s Burroughs was among its few experimenters, that is, with the exception of the parallel, independent work in literature, film and television of Samuel Beckett, the last of which has been singled out as exceptional by Gilles Deleuze. Beckett, however, deplored Burroughs's descriptions of his 'cut up' method at their first meeting in 1959. Victor Bockris, editor of *With William Burroughs: A Report from the Bunker*, interviewed Burroughs about his Berlin visit with Beckett in 1980, but Burroughs also talked with Bockris about his famous initial 1959 meeting with Beckett in publisher Maurice Girodias's Brazilian nightclub in Paris (and so soon after Girodias had published with his Olympia Press what in his version, and in the subsequent British editions from publisher John Calder, was called *The Naked Lunch*). Burroughs describes there being 'quite a bit of antagonism between us'. The issue was in part Burroughs's cut up aesthetics: 'I'd evolved the cut ups, which Beckett didn't approve of at all' (Bockris 1981: 211).

We might note here that despite his opprobrium, Beckett – whose basic unit of composition may also be said to be the inconclusive or incomplete entity, the fragment, say – himself conducted at least one overt cut up experiment in 1971 (that is, a work produced with what might be deemed the Burroughs method of 'cut ups', which, Burroughs acknowledges, might equally be called the Tzara method) with his narrative piece 'Lessness', mixing fragments of his imagistic, poetic prose, sixty sentences, in a container and drawing out the fragments blindly for the final sequence, then repeating the process to create a prose work of 120 sentences, a narrative in two-acts, say (see Gontarski 1985: 13–14). The Beckett cut up was of his own text, however, and was designed to remain invariant, fixed after the random or aleatory ordering; the Burroughs's texts integrated magazine and newspaper pieces into his narrative like cubist collage, and the result was to remain open, fluid and subject to additional cuttings by Burroughs or by other potential and perhaps future collaborators. As late as 1981, Beckett was asked about the connections with or influence of Burroughs's work on his, and he replied quite cordially to John Pages on 17 March, 'Thank you for yrs. of March 4. I had not the example of William Burroughs before me when concocting *Lessness*.'

Beckett's initial rejection on first meeting Burroughs in 1959 was not solely or particularly to the aleatory nature of the process but to the fact that the cut up method involved using the writing of other authors. Burroughs's reply to such charges generally suggested what we today might call intertextuality, that all writing was cut up or collage in one way or another and that his was different from those only by degree. In something of a refinement of the Gysin method, Burroughs subsequently called the alternative strategy the '"fold in" method'. In the opening of the revised and edited version of his Cambridge talk, in an introductory section to a 'Note on Vaudeville Voices', an appended response to his piece in the body of Jones' anthology called 'Vaudeville Voices', Burroughs acknowledges something of an authorial function:

> In writing this chapter I have used what I call 'the fold in' method that is I place a page of one text folded down the middle on a page of another text (my own or someone else's) – The composite text is read across half from one text and half from the other – The resulting material is edited, re-arranged, and deleted as in any other form of composition. This chapter contains fold ins with the work of Rimbaud, T. S. Eliot, Paul Bowles, James Joyce, Michael Portman, Peter Weber, Fabrizio Mondadori, Jacques Stern, Evgeny Yevtushenko, some newspaper articles and of course my own work. (Jones 1963: 345–8)

Burroughs ends his 'Note' with an example, a cut up version of the final, now apparently penultimate paragraph of his 'Note'. Despite Beckett's resistance, both writers seem to share, that is, at least to accept, some form or degree of extra- or limited authorial process, something of a relinquishing of volition, of a selfless creative and composition process through which the author begins to disappear.

Burroughs' commitment to the aleatory, to chance, while a commitment to randomness, is also a commitment to the inevitability or the necessity of the result, as the roll of the dice is arbitrary but the result is inevitable, as Deleuze argues in his critique of Nietzsche. Moreover, the cut up fragment is already the whole of the work, the segment or part already the whole for both Burroughs and Beckett. Deleuze and Guattari analyze the relationship between a whole and its fragments, or alternately between the One and the many, in the second chapter of *What is Philosophy?*, as the authors explore the Plane of Immanence and its relationship to other Planes of Immanence and to concept formation, concepts that are 'fragmentary wholes that are not aligned with one another [. . .] but are outcomes of throws of the dice' (Deleuze and Guattari

1994: 35), that is, the result of chance, but chance as necessity, or what Nietzsche calls destiny. Deleuze analyses the 'throw of the dice' as well in *Nietzsche and Philosophy* in terms of the One and the many, so that the single throw of the dice is already necessity, destiny: 'The dice which are thrown once are the affirmation of *chance*, the combination which they form on falling is the affirmation of *necessity*. [. . .] For just as unity does not suppress or deny multiplicity, necessity does not suppress or deny chance' (Deleuze 1983: 26). The acceptance of such necessity, the destiny of chance, is the *amor fati* of both Deleuze and Nietzsche, the love or acceptance of fate or of that which simply is. And so the One and the many become a One-All, an 'Omnitudo', in *What is Philosophy?*

The issue of the One and the many remained central to the thinking of Deleuze and Guattari as it suggested something of a permanent betweenness, as it was to Pythagoras, a between the limited and the non-limited, say, or between odd and even, between light and darkness, good and bad, rest and motion, straight and crooked. In his philosophical self-study, Beckett copied out precisely such notes as he worked his way through the Pre-Socratic philosophers in the 1930s and was as preoccupied with the distinction between the One and the many, unity and multiplicity, between being and becoming, as Deleuze would be, and essentially through the same genealogy, in Beckett's case on a Beckettian Plane of Immanence that intersects with or overlaps in places those of, at least, Deleuze, Spinoza, Nietzsche and Bergson, as well as others like Burroughs. In his philosophical notebooks Beckett wrote (for future reference), 'In this ceaseless transformation of all things nothing individual persists, but only the order, in which the exchange between the contrary movements is effected – the law of change, which constitutes the meaning and worth of the whole . . . The Becoming of Heraclitus produces no Being, as the Being of Parmenides no Becoming.'[3] Beckett thinks through such paradoxes throughout his career, 'the law of change, which constitutes the meaning and worth of the whole', particularly the paradox of the One and the many foregrounded in *Endgame*, which opens with Clov's comments, 'Grain upon grain' (*CDW* 93). Hamm later refers to 'that old Greek' (*CDW* 126). Most have assumed the allusion was to Zeno the Eleatic, and in rehearsals for his direction of the play in Berlin, Beckett spoke to his cast of 'Zeno's grains, a logical jest' (1992: 47). The jest is the paradox of the part and the whole; that is, at what point do one grain and other separate grains make up a unit called a heap? That is, if a single grain is not a heap and a second grain is not a heap, how does one non-heap added to another non-heap constitute a heap. Heapness is apparently either impossible or already at least implicit in the single grain, the part already the whole. Hamm restates the paradox in human terms: at what point do separate moments of existence make up a whole, a life: 'all life long you wait for that to mount up to a life' (*CDW* 126). Beckett told Dubliner Eoin O'Brien that the allusion was not to Zeno but to a philosopher he no longer recalled; Windelband (1938: 89), a major source for much of Beckett's Greek philosophy, indicates Eubulides of Miletus, dialectician of Megaria, to whom is attributed a series of 'little catches', retraceable to Zeno: 'Which kernel of grain by being added makes the heap? Which hair falling out makes the bald head?' The exact philosopher then is less important here (and for Beckett) than the line of flight. Directing the play in London, Beckett recorded in his *Riverside* Notebook: 'C [Clov] perplexed. All seemingly in order, yet a change. Fatal grain added to form impossible heap. Ratio ruentis acetvi'. The Latin alludes to Horace who in the *Epistle* to Augustus (II.i, 47) uses the logical puzzle called *sorites* or 'heap' (*acervus*) to consider how long it takes for a poet to be considered an 'ancient' and hence great: '*dum cadat elusus ratione ruentis acervi*' ['till after the fashion of the falling heap he is baffled and thrown down'] (Beckett 1992: 47). Clov senses the almost imperceptible change, the single grain 'needed to make the heap – the last straw', according to Beckett (1992: 47). Such a line of thought situates Beckett directly in a philosophical genealogy, a line of flight that includes even philosophers he doubtless never read, like Deleuze and Guattari. For Deleuze (as for Beckett, we might add) multiplicity will finally replace substance, as the event will replace essence (the novel *Watt* its most dramatic example, perhaps), and virtuality possibility.

Beckett's interest in such paradoxical philosophical issues, in the psychology and ontology of being and consciousness, in the vagaries of memory and perception, in immaterialism or dematerialization, dates at least from his introduction to the work of Henri Bergson and George Berkeley, Bishop of Cloyne, by his original Trinity College tutor, A. A. Luce, whose name and reputation Beckett invoked as late as July 1937 as a reference in application for a position of Lecturer in Italian at the University of Cape Town shortly after his resignation from a similar position in French at Trinity College, Dublin. Luce had published his monograph on Bergson, *Bergson's Doctrine of Intuition*, in 1922, just before Beckett matriculated at Trinity College, and his *Berkeley's Immaterialism* in 1945, as Beckett was returning from his Rousillon exile. In his one and only film, commissioned by his American publisher, Barney Rosset of Grove Press, and called simply, generically, *Film* (originally *The Eye*), Beckett acknowledgedly explored Berkeley's Immaterialist or Idealist dictum, principal #3, *esse est percipi*, as something of a disappearing act, a pursuit of immaterialism if not a performance of dematerialization, but Beckett kept part of Berkeley's dictum under erasure. Tellingly, Berkeley's full phrase includes the parenthetical extension '(*aut percipere*)', so that '*esse est percipi*', that 'being is being perceived', has the added tenet of '(or perceiving)'. Certainly, Beckett was not interested in merely illustrating any principle of philosophy, or even exploring its artistic implications. As in much of Beckett's use of philosophy, such tenets are adapted, transformed, critiqued and even distorted. *Film*'s nameless protagonist, called simply O (for 'Object' and thus a character) is in flight from but is pursued by E, or Eye, O's own, presumably. O's object, so to speak, is to avoid E, or avoid being perceived generally, and hence, perhaps, to achieve something of a dematerialization, a vanishing, immaterialism, or some form of non-being, a being degree zero, say, by avoiding perception by others in the street, and, in what is apparently his mother's room which O is tending, by animal eyes and even the metaphorical eyes of the rocking chair. But, of course, O is being perceived even when he does not perceive his being so, and he himself is perceiving throughout, to one extent or another. O is pursued by E and flees or hides from its or his own perception, unaware, perhaps, that is, not conscious of being constantly pursued and so being constantly perceived even as he attempts to blend with a wall of the street. O is conscious of being perceived in the gaze of others, who also recoil from his perception, or when he perceives himself perceiving himself, as when he notices that E has violated the 45 degree 'angle of immunity', arbitrarily established by Beckett but a convention having something to do, no doubt, with peripheral vision. E's being within the 'angle of immunity' produces little anxiety in O, until E's direct confrontation of the denouement. The issue then seems less that of being perceived than O's consciousness of being perceived and so of O's own perception generally, faulty as that is.

Berkeley might suggest that we are always within the perception of the deity, who or which ensures or validates our existence. O destroys the photographic image of one such anthropological deity hanging on the wall of the flat to eliminate that potential, but E, of course, perceives all such activity, as it does the destruction of other photographic images of O's static past. In fact, E never looses sight of O, except for a momentary escape on the street. The issue then seems less perception and being perceived than consciousness of both, hence the horror of the double image of the ending as O simultaneously perceives and is perceived, at which point O, presumably, is forced to confront the inescapability of consciousness, which is memory, finally, and self-consciousness, and so confronts the inescapability of being, except perhaps through death, which the film may suggest – after which O indeed disappears, dematerializes. One reading of this film work, then, is as a vaudeville trick by a vaudeville entertainer (Buster Keaton), an act of vanishing, a dematerializing, a disappearing character, then a disappearing observer, E, the result then a cinematic trick that finally ends in a blank screen, like the blank wall in room 15 of the Beat Hotel, both authors, and/or their characters, having vanished, Burroughs performing the trick in 1960, Beckett in 1964. Buster Keaton, as it turns out, would himself not live long after the completion of the film. Shortly thereafter Beckett would more fully offer dematerialized character in a work that some critics consider a theatrical joke, but is rather another trick of vanishing, 'Breath', a twenty-three second theoretical if not dramatic masterwork.

Even as Burroughs was becoming an entertainer as well as a writer, a performer or performance artist, at least, he saw himself primarily as a writer. Noting in *Naked Lunch* that 'I am not an entertainer' (1959: 221), Burroughs's proclamation comes at almost the exact moment that he was, in fact, becoming an entertainer, that is, what Burroughs was was his performances, and his argument since 1959 was that he apparently had very little control of his output, very little authorial function, that he was a direct recording instrument of the flow of perception, memory and immediate affective experience, or, finally, that the author has very little relationship to the emerging text, which is foregrounded in the process, the author losing his or her identity and disappearing, in this case, into the text rather than behind a curtain at the Beat Hotel. In such a process then, the result, the fragment of text, is already complete, inevitable.

Deleuze and Guattari take on the issue of authorial identity at the onset of their second major collaborative effort, in their 'Introduction: Rhizome' to *A Thousand Plateaus*. In this case the slippery issue is that of individual identity in a co-authored book, although the implications reach far beyond into single-authored monographs as well: 'The two of us wrote *Anti-Oedipus* together. Since each of us was several, there was already quite a crowd.' They use their real names, 'Out of habit, purely out of habit'; this crowd, this pack, this multiplicity *we* call Gilles Deleuze and Félix Guattari out of habit, and Foucault calls an 'excessive sign'. They go on to describe the goal of their collaboration: 'To reach not the point where one no longer says I, but the point where it is no longer of any importance whether one says I. We are no longer ourselves. Each will know his own. We have been aided, inspired, multiplied' (Deleuze and Guattari 1987: 3). The authors seem to be arguing for a 'Third Mind' here, Burroughs' image of multiplicity. Such multiplication, such denial of individuation, the replacement of the individual author by multiplicity, by external forces, is a dispersal, another disappearing act. As Foucault noted of Beckett in 'What is an Author?', quoting *Stories and Texts for Nothing*, 'what matter who's speaking someone said what matter who's speaking?' (2001: 1477; see also *CSP* 109). Foucault may see the author outside and preceding the text; for Deleuze and Guattari, however, he or she is inside or has become the text. When they turn their attention to literature and the arts in 'Percept, Affect, and Concept', Chapter 7 of *What is Philosophy?*, they focus on the preservation of the artwork and the disappearance of the author: 'Art preserves, and it is the only thing in the world that is preserved' (1994: 163), a dictum that Beckett not only well understood but advocated – art preserved in itself, however, not necessarily in a material form or in an industrial way, from which material and 'various personae' the artwork establishes an independence as a 'bloc of sensations' (164), so that percepts are not particular perceptions and affects are not particular feelings or affections *per se*; that is, such 'Sensations, percepts, and affects are *beings* whose validity lies in themselves and exceeds any lived' (164, emphasis in the original). The work of art, then, 'is a being of sensations and nothing else: it exists in itself' (164), its action is not memory but fabulation: 'what great writer has not been able to create these beings of sensation [. . .]. The percept of the landscape before man, in the absence of man' (169), and so Mrs Dalloway 'perceives the town [. . .] passed into the town [. . .] and becomes imperceptible herself. *Affects are precisely these nonhuman becomings of man*, just as percepts – including the town – are *nonhuman landscapes of nature*. [. . .] Everything is vision, becoming. We become universes. Becoming animal, plant, molecular, becoming zero' (169, emphasis in the original). The percepts and affects of art are not the perceptions or the emotional responses of any particular individuals but are created on a Plane of Composition, itself a corollary to the Plane of Immanence. That is, the work of art creates impact and affect as a being. It is itself a line of force, a process of abstraction, rich, according to Deleuze, in animal force:

> the abstract line of force is rich in animal motifs. Animal, plant, and molecular becomings correspond to cosmic or cosmogenetic forces: to the point that the body disappears into the plain color or becomes part of the wall, or conversely, the plain color buckles and whirls around in the body's zone of indiscernibility. In short the being of sensation is not the flesh [that is, not the author or even the character] but the compound of nonhuman forces of the cosmos, of man's nonhuman becomings, and of the ambiguous house that exchanges and adjusts them, makes them whirl around like winds. Flesh [or the author] is only the developer which disappears in what it develops: the compound of sensations [which is the artwork]. (Deleuze and Guattari 1987: 183)

Burroughs became 'part of the wall' in the Beat Hotel in 1960, but Beckett too was a 'developer', as his flesh 'disappears in what it develops', that is, into his words, into his artwork, into and becoming new worlds. Most simply, this is what Beckett has been telling us all along, asking his readers, too, to disappear into his texts, into his 'compound of sensations'.

Notes

1. For more background on Bergson, Russell, Woolf and the Heretics Society see Chapter 3.
2. See Oliver Harris's excellent commentary on this text, '"Burroughs is a Poet Too, Really": The Poetics of *Minutes to Go*', http://reality-studio.org/scholarship/burroughs-is-a-poet-too-really-the-poetics-of-minutes-to-go.
3. Samuel Beckett, Notebooks, Trinity College Dublin MS 10967/26.

References

Beckett, Samuel (1968) 'Film', in *Cascando and other Short Dramatic Pieces*, New York: Grove Press.

Beckett, Samuel (1992) *The Theatrical Notebooks of Samuel Beckett*, Vol. II, *Endgame*, ed. S. E. Gontarski, New York: Grove Press.

Bockris, Victor (1981) *With William Burroughs: A Report from the Bunker*, New York: Seaver Books.

Burroughs, William (1959) *Naked Lunch*, New York: Grove Press.

Burroughs, William (1960) *Minutes to Go*, Paris: Two Cities Editions.

Burroughs, William (1963) 'The Cut Up Method', in *The Moderns: An Anthology of New Writing in America*, ed. Leroi Jones, New York: Corinth Books.

Burroughs, William (1979) *The Third Mind*, London: John Calder.

Burroughs, William (1998) *Word Virus: The William Burroughs Reader*, ed. James Grauerholz and Ira Silverberg, New York: Grove Press.

Deleuze, Gilles (1983) *Nietzsche and Philosophy*, trans. Hugh Tomlinson, London: Athlone.

Deleuze, Gilles (1997) *Essays Critical and Clinical*, trans. Daniel W. Smith and Michael Greco, Minneapolis: University of Minnesota Press.

Deleuze, Gilles and Guattari, Félix (1987) *A Thousand Plateaus*, trans. Brian Massumi, Minneapolis: University of Minnesota Press.

Deleuze, Gilles and Guattari, Félix (1994) *What is Philosophy?* trans. Graham Burchell and Hugh Tomlinson, New York: Columbia University Press.

Foucault, Michel (2001) 'What Is An Author', in *The Norton Anthology of Theory and Criticism*, Second Edition, ed. Vincent B. Leitch et al., New York: W. W. Norton & Co.

Gontarski, S.E. (1985) *Intent of Undoing in Samuel Beckett's Dramatic Texts*, Bloomington: University of Indiana Press.

Jones, Leroi (1963) *The Moderns: New Writing in America*, New York: Corinth Books.

Levi Stevens, Matthew (n.d.) 'The Lost Boys', Reality Studio, http://realitystudio.org/biography/the-lost-boys. Revised in *The Magical Universe of William Burroughs*, Oxford: Mandrake of Oxford, 2014.

Miles, Barry (1993) *William Burroughs: El Hombre Invisible*, London: Virgin Publishing.

Miles, Barry (2014) *Call Me Burroughs: A Life*, New York: Twelve (Hachette Book Group).

Windelband, W. (1938) *A History of Philosophy: The Formation and*

Development of Its Problems and Conceptions, trans. James H. Tufts, New York: Macmillan.

Woolf, Virginia (1924) *Mr Bennett and Mrs Brown*, London: Hogarth Press.

Index

Page numbers for illustrations are in *italics*.